This work is an attempt by the authors to give as full and detailed a history as possible of the confrontation between Soviet fighters and the principal strike force of the United States Far East Air Force – the B-29 'Superfortress' bombers – during the course of the Korean War between 1950–53.

Military documents, which the authors have studied over many years of work in the Central Archive of the Ministry of Defence of the Russian Federation in Podolsk – as well as published Western sources – form the basis of this book. The recollections of pilots who served in the 64th Fighter Air Corps, and who participated personally in the events described, are also widely used.

Almost all of the battles that took place between Soviet fighters and the Superfortresses are analysed in detail. The authors have, on the basis of a comparison of Soviet archive documents and data from published Western sources, attempted to clarify the actual losses on both sides in these battles. Particular attention has been paid to key events in the history of the confrontation between the MiG-15 and B-29, such as the air battles of April and October 1951, which had a significant impact on the course of the Korean War and influenced the development of military aviation in both the USSR and the USA.

Following the encounters on the approaches to the bridges at Andung on 12 April 1951, Strategic Air Command decided against using Superfortresses close to the area around the MiG bases. The outcome of a series of air battles from 22-27 October 1951 – the most famous of which was the battle between MiGs and B-29s in the area close to the airfield at Namsi on 23 October ('Black Tuesday') – was a ban by Strategic Air Command on daylight operations by Superfortresses in the Soviet fighter's zone of operation; these battles also influenced the technical policy of the United States Air Force in relation to strategic bombers.

Extensive losses in combat with the MiGs served as one of the most influential arguments for curtailing the piston engine B-36 and B-50 bomber programmes, and boosting development of one of the most famous aircraft in the history of global aviation: the B-52 'Stratofortress'. Night operations – to which the B-29s and, subsequently, Soviet fighters were transferred – are also analysed in detail in this book; these nocturnal operations culminated in the air battles of December 1952 and January 1953. After sustaining losses in these battles that were comparable to those of October 1951, the Superfortresses would subsequently only carry out nocturnal sorties to the MiGs' zone of operation in poor weather conditions.

In this work, the authors have analysed the advantages and the disadvantages of the La-11 and the MiG-15bis – the principal fighters of the 64th Fighter Air Corps – from the point of view of their ability to intercept the B-29s. Attention has been paid to the tactics of the opposing sides, and to how these changed over the course of the war. The technical aspects of the confrontation between Soviet fighters and Superfortresses have been examined, as well as identifying the reasons behind the different periods of success or failure in terms of performance in combat.

A great deal of statistical material has been provided in this book, which characterises combat operations carried out by the B-29s and the fighters of the 64th Fighter Air Corps, both within the text itself and in the form of easy-to-use tables. The book is illustrated with photographs obtained both from the personal archives of veterans of the 64th Fighter Air Corps; from the Central Archive of the Ministry of Defence of the Russian Federation; and the US National Archives. Colour profiles showing camouflage and markings are also included.

Leonid Krylov and Yuriy Tepsurkayev are, by profession, aviation engineers. They began examining the role of Soviet aviation units in the Korean War back in 1989 during their studies at the Moscow Aviation Institute. In the course of more than a quarter of a century of research, the authors have corresponded extensively with veterans of the Korean War – meeting with them on their journeys around Soviet cities and capturing the recollections of more than a hundred veterans of the 64th Fighter Air Corps.

Since 1992, Krylov and Tepsurkayev have worked at the Central Archive of the Ministry of Defence of the Russian Federation in Podolsk – starting with post-flight briefings provided by pilots and ending with the affairs of the secretariat of the commander-in-chief of the Soviet Air Force. On the basis of the materials they had collected, they have, since the mid-1990s in the last century, published articles on different aspects of the Soviet Air Force's role in the Korean War in both Russian and foreign aviation journals such as *Mir Aviatsii*, *Aviatsiya*, *Aviamaster*, *Combat Aircraft*, *Avions*, *Military Aircraft Monthly International* and *Model Aircraft*. Several books have been printed on this topic by the publishing houses Armada, Yauza and Osprey Publishing.

Aside from his research into the Korean topic, Yuriy Tepsurkayev is one of Russia's leading aviation artists. He regularly provides illustrations for Russian and Western aviation publications – both those in which the author's work has been published, and those linked to the Korean topic. He specialises in providing 'side-on views' of Soviet and Russian military aircraft, as well as in designing covers and 'two-page spreads'. Aside from periodicals, Tepsurkayev has illustrated a series of monographs such as *The Su-25 Ground Attack Aircraft and its Modifications*, *The MiG-29*, *The Su-27 Fighter. Part 1. The Beginning of the Story*, *The Su-27 Fighter. Part 2. The Birth of a Legend* and *The Su-25 Ground Attack Aircraft. Thirty Years in Service* amongst others.

About the Translator

Kevin Bridge BA MCIL is a Russian to English translator/editor specialising in aviation and aeronautics and Russian translation for the publishing sector. He has been working as a translator since October 2007 and his professional endeavours have encompassed technical articles which have been published in an historical aviation journal, as well as manuscripts for publication and news and current affairs articles. He has also acted as an interpreter for Russian and Western aircrew at aviation events such as the Farnborough Airshow.

Kevin gained a BA degree in Russian and Soviet Studies from the University of Portsmouth in 1998 and has travelled extensively in Russia. He also worked for a period of five years as a Russian linguist before embarking on a career in translation. He joined the Chartered Institute of Linguists in March 2012 as a full Member (MCIL) and was elected to the Board of Trustees of the Russian Aviation Research Trust (RART) in view of his translation work and Russian-language skills in September 2013. Further details about his work can be found via www.bridge-translation.com

THE LAST WAR OF THE SUPERFORTRESSES

MiG-15 vs B-29 Over Korea

Leonid Krylov & Yuriy Tepsurkaev

Translated by Kevin Bridge BA MCIL

Helion & Company

Helion & Company Limited
26 Willow Road
Solihull
West Midlands
B91 1UE
England
Tel. 0121 705 3393
Fax 0121 711 4075
Email: info@helion.co.uk
Website: www.helion.co.uk
Twitter: @helionbooks
Visit our blog http://blog.helion.co.uk/

Published by Helion & Company 2016
Designed and typeset by Farr out Publications, Wokingham, Berkshire
Cover designed by Paul Hewitt, Battlefield Design (www.battlefield-design.co.uk)
Printed by Hobbs The Printers, Totton, Hampshire

Text © Leonid Krylov & Yuriy Tepsurkaev 2016
Photographs © Leonid Krylov & Yuriy Tepsurkaev unless noted otherwise
Maps © Helion & Company 2016. Redrawn by George Anderson and transliterated by Kevin Bridge

Front cover: A B-29 Superfortress with an unusual name (and an unusual war record) is the 'Fujigmo' of the 20th US Air Force's 19th Bomb Group. The 'Fujigmo' – a veteran of 98 combat missions – took part in the first medium bomber attack against the enemy by the 19th Bomb Group on 28 June 1950. (Courtesy of the US National Archives). Colour profile on front cover: MiG-15 No. 034 serial No.110034, flown by Captain I.A. Suchkov of the 176th Guards Fighter Air Regiment, 324th Fighter Air Division. He participated in battles with B-29s on 7 and 12 April 1951 and scored two B-29 kills.
Rear cover image: B-29s of the US Far East Air Force speed to dump tonnes of bombs on the military targets, January 1951. (Courtesy of the US National Archives).

ISBN 978-1-910777-85-5

British Library Cataloguing-in-Publication Data.
A catalogue record for this book is available from the British Library.

All rights reserved. No part of this publication may be reproduced, stored in a retrieval system, or transmitted, in any form, or by any means, electronic, mechanical, photocopying, recording or otherwise, without the express written consent of Helion & Company Limited.

For details of other military history titles published by Helion & Company
Limited contact the above address, or visit our website: http://www.helion.co.uk

We always welcome receiving book proposals from prospective authors.

Contents

Acknowledgements	vi
1 War from Dawn to Dusk	9
2 War from Sunset to Sunrise	63

Appendices

I Deployment of formations and units from United States Air Force Bomber Command in the Far Eastern Zone	97
II Deployment of formations and units from the 64th Fighter Air Corps of the Soviet Air Force engaged in active combat with the B-29	100
III Results of air combat	102
IV Contemporary geographical names for sites mentioned in quotes from 64th Fighter Air Corps documents	109
Bibliography	110

Acknowledgements

This book is based upon the 64th Fighter Air Corps' archive documents, as well as Western open-source material. Naturally, we understand that every fact we mention should be accompanied by a footnote referencing the corresponding document, book and so on. We would only stand to gain from this, in that the book would be transformed into a fundamentally academic work of some kind, which would serve the self-interests of the authors. How does it feel, however, to read a text and come across a numerical reference to a footnote after every word?! Therefore, we considered it necessary to only record references to the sources if we are quoting a text word for word. We are sure that in allowing ourselves to express our personal opinions and suggestions, we have not substituted the text of a document, and that we have not allowed any of 'our own words' to enter the mechanism of the historical narrative. A full list of all the materials used in this work is provided in the Bibliography.

The authors would like to express our sincerest thanks to Aleksandr Pavlovich Smorchkov for his consultation, and for providing a number of valuable comments which we received during the course of the work on this topic. We are eternally grateful to the pilots and technicians of the 64th Fighter Air Corps who shared their recollections: Viktor Georgievich Monakhov, Dmitriy Pavlovich Oskin, Viktor Pavlovich Popov, Dmitriy Akelsandrovich Samoylov, Nikolai Mikhaylovich Chepelev, Nikolai Ivanovich Skodin and many others, as well as Mr Harold E. Fischer, who provided a manuscript of his memoirs. We also would like to express our thanks to Smithsonian Museum specialist Carl J. Bobrow for his assistance in obtaining photos from the US Archives.

We hope that thanks to the personal accounts provided by veterans, we have succeeded in some small way in making this material – burdened generously as it is with names, figures, dates and so on – easier on the reader.

We burned nearly every city in North and South Korea, we killed more than a million civilians and several million more were left homeless.

General Curtis E. LeMay, Head of Strategic Air Command in the United States.

More than anything I remember the encounters with the 'heavies'...

Captain D.A. Samoylov, 523rd Fighter Air Regiment, 303rd Fighter Air Division.

Part 1

War from Dawn to Dusk

On Sunday, 25 June 1950, South Korean Army units fired on Korean People's Army security units around Ongjin. This, in turn, gave rise to a border skirmish – of which there had been many over the previous year. South Korean Army soldiers however, who were the first to fire at the northern side of the border that night, had made a tragic mistake ... This border incident, which to one of the antagonists was nothing out of the ordinary, turned out to be a long-awaited *casus belli* for the other. At 0400 the roar of gunfire and the clatter of tank tracks shattered the pre-dawn silence. In a matter of minutes, Korean People's Army tanks had overcome South Korean Army resistance – the latter's units entering into a disorganised retreat. Korean People's Army tanks pressed forward to Kaesong and Chuncheon – capturing the South Korean capital in a huge pincer movement – and North Korean airborne forces landed on the eastern seaboard close to Gangneung. Frontline units of the Korean People's Army arrived at Kaesong at 0900; war had come to the 'land of the morning calm'.

The Korean People's Army held an absolute advantage. Soviet T-34/85 tanks – the Second World War's finest – cleared the way for infantry units, whilst Il-10 aircraft floated overhead, escorted by Yak-9s. The South Koreans, who were only equipped to counter partisans, were powerless; assistance came to them from beyond their borders.

'A Policing Operation'

The decisive push by Kim Il Sung's army to the south put the possibility of using South Korean airfields as bases for United States Air Force aircraft in doubt from the very first day of the war. Any response from United States aviation would be confined to long-distance bombing raids. On 25 June 1950, the United States Far East Air Force had just one detachment of medium bombers at their disposal. There were B-29s from the 19th Bomb Wing, based at the Anderson air force base on the island of Guam, which was made up of the 28th, 30th and 93rd Squadrons. The Commander of the United States Far East Air Force, General George E. Stratemeyer, took these 'Fortresses' to war. A few hours after the start of the North Korean offensive, the Superfortresses were ordered to deploy closer to the conflict zone: to Kadena air base on Okinawa; nobody could have imagined the true scale of the conflict on the Korean Peninsula. Crews were told that ' ... It will take about a week to mop this up, so don't pack all your gear. Take

B-29 Superfortresses are shown at Yokota air base, Japan. In their role of the 'big stick' in the Korean War, high-flying 'Superforts' make nightly attacks against key military targets in North Korea and along the enemy's front lines. (Courtesy of the US National Archives)

A B-29 Superfortress with an unusual name (and an unusual war record) is the 'Fujigmo' of the 20th US Air Force's 19th Bomb Group. The 'Fujigmo' – a veteran of 98 combat missions – took part in the first medium bomber attack against the enemy by the 19th Bomb Group on 28 June 1950. (Courtesy of the US National Archives)

A formation of B-29s flying over enemy territory in Korea. (Courtesy of the US National Archives)

one flight suit and some extra skivvies'.[1] None of the crews in the wing would have guessed that a lightning 'policing operation' would turn into a 37-month-long war – one of the bloodiest in human history.

The first priority for any branch of aviation was to support the infantry that were surrounded by the North Koreans. With this in mind, the United States Far East Air Force had prepared and embarked upon a programme of bombing enemy infantry on the front line – even before President Truman had announced that America was at war. The B-29s arrived over Korea for the first time on the afternoon of 27 June. A quartet of bombers from the 19th Bomb Wing bombed Seoul's railway station, as well as the bridges over the Han River. On 28 June, the United States launched an operation under the United Nations (UN) flag to 'offer all necessary assistance to South Korea in restoring peace and stability to the region'. The air force programme became a full-scale operation. The following day (29 June), the 'Fortresses' found themselves in fighter gun sights for the first time since the war with Japan. During the night, the North Koreans captured the airfield at Gimpo (near Seoul). Since it had only been slightly damaged, it could be used by the Korean People's Army for its intended purpose. At 0800 [here and further on in the text, Korean Standard Time is used] on the orders of the Commander of United States Armed Forces Far East, General Douglas MacArthur, nine B-29s dropped dozens of 227 kg bombs from an altitude of a 1,000 metres on the airfield and on the city of Gimpo. The North Koreans attempted to disperse this bombardment using Yak-9s, but were not able to intercept the bombers. Western publications state that one of the Yaks was shot down by the gunners on board the Superfortresses, while another was damaged. On the other hand, the victories scored on that day were not recorded in the official tally of United States Air Force victories in Korea.

On 29 June 1950, the North Koreans broadcast a message via the Central Korean News Agency from the Korean People's Army Central Command stating that their air force had 'Shot down one four-engine aircraft, and two four-engine bombers, and three light bombers had been destroyed on the ground' on that day.[2] In reality, the only loss the Far East Air Force had incurred was a C-54 transport aircraft, which was destroyed by a North Korean Il-10 on Suwon airfield. Summing up the previous day's losses, Korean People's Army Central Command announced on the morning of the 1 July that ' ... Aircraft from the People's Army destroyed two B-29s at Suwon and seven fighters on 30 June. Two B-29s were shot down in air combat'. That evening, news came through of the loss of another Superfortress.

In general – judging by the messages transmitted by the Central Korean News Agency – the air battle with the B-29s had been exceptionally successful: Kim Il Sung's fighters and anti-aircraft artillery had shot the Superfortresses that had appeared in the air over Korea, along with other very exotic aircraft, down with impunity – thus on 7 July, fighters shot down a pair of B-29s. The following day, a further two Superfortresses were shot down by fighters and anti-aircraft artillery. These were followed by ' ... Three B-29s and three B-38s' on 11 July. On 12 July, two B-17s fell victim to the fighters – and on 16 July, another pair of 'four-engine bombers' and so on. We could go on and on with this glorious list; it is, however, time to return to reality.

On 3 July the Commander of the United States Air Force, General Hoyt S. Vandenberg, deployed Strategic Air Command's 92nd and the 22nd Bomb Wings to Korea on

---

1 Davis, L., *Air War over Korea*, (Carrollton: Squadron/Signal Publ.Inc., 1982) p.25.

2 The authors obtained the texts of the messages from the Korean State News Agency and the Korean People's Army Central Command from Colonel V.A. Bukhtoyarov of the Lenin Military-Political Academy.

his own initiative. On 8 July, Far East Bomber Command was formed of these groups, along with the 19th Bomb Wing and the 31st Strategic Squadron operating the RB-29. General Emmet O'Donnell Jr took up command – and on taking responsibility for the most powerful aviation force in the region, he spectacularly belied the notion that it was difficult for generals to formulate phrases consisting of more than three words. He expressed the hope that:

> We will arrive there [in Korea] with a psychological advantage knowing that we were so quick to get to this region and enter into a war, which began with such heavy bombardment of the North Korean forces, and possibly with advanced warning of how far the North Koreans have come in their military activity, which we consider to be an act of aggression. Then we can start to burn the five principal cities in North Korea to the ground and to completely destroy each one of the 18 principal strategic targets.[3]

From the first days of the war, the Far East Air Force, which had a qualitative (as well as a numerical) advantage over the Korean People's Army Air Force, established an unrivalled superiority in the skies over Korea. The Superfortresses were able to fly over almost the entire territory of North Korea without the threat of encountering enemy interceptors. The only loss to North Korean fighters was a B-29 from the 19th Bombardment Group, which was shot down close to Seoul on 12 July by three Yak-9s.

The B-29s from the 22nd and 92nd Groups flew their first sortie on 13 July; the targets were a marshalling yard and an oil refinery in Wonsan. During the course of this sortie, the 92nd Bombardment Group suffered its first casualty. Flying over the Sea of Japan on their way to the Korean Peninsula, the crew of one of the aircraft from the 325th Squadron urgently began to jettison their bomb load close to the Oki Islands due to a technical problem on board – and the aircraft exploded.

The Wonsan raid was the first bombing raid that formed part of the plan for the strategic bombing of North Korea. This plan was, however, cancelled shortly afterwards – and all Bomber Command's efforts were diverted to provide close support for ground forces. The Superfortresses acted as tactical bombers operating over the battlefield – and achieved significant results. The 227 kg high-explosive bombs were commonly used to strike concentrations of ground forces, together with 1,800 kg high-explosive shells in a light casing that served as 'psychological' warfare.

During one of the sorties on 28 July, gunners on board Superfortresses serving with the 22nd Bomb Wing spotted North Korean Yak-9s at some distance that were preparing to go on the attack. After opening fire furiously, they shot down one fighter aircraft. It turned out that this was a 'Seafire' of 800 Naval Air Squadron, which had taken off from the aircraft

This formation of B-29s is shown flying over enemy territory in Korea. Over 24 million lbs of bombs have been dropped from B-29 bomb bays during the months of July and August 1950 (Courtesy of the US National Archives)

carrier *Triumph* in support of UN forces. Fortunately, the pilot was able to bail out of the aircraft by parachute and was picked up a short time later by the rescue service. Incidentally, to begin with, English pilots flying 'Seafires', 'Fireflys' and 'Sea Furys' often came under fire from Allied forces due to the unusual outline of their aircraft. The 'Seafires', which bore some resemblance to Yaks, very often found themselves on the receiving end.

By the end of July, MacArthur (who by that time had been named Commander of the UN contingent of forces in Korea) thought it possible – having kept some B-29s in reserve to meet the needs of the army – to use the rest against strategic targets. After Wonsan, the second strategic target chosen was Hungnam, with its many suburban industrial sites. At 0930 on 30 July, following extensive reconnaissance of the target by RB-29s from the 31st Strategic Reconnaissance Squadron, 47 B-29s from the 22nd and 92nd Bombardment Groups 'emptied' their bomb load over a munitions factory in Changjin in heavy cloud – destroying or damaging around 70 percent of its buildings. The following day, bombers from these same groups dropped 227 kg bombs on Chandzhin's nitrus fertiliser plant in clear weather from an altitude of 5,000 m. This time, crews reported seeing powerful explosions and thick smoke emanating from the factory site. The last target on the east coast (close to Hungnam) was the Bogun chemical plant; 39 of O'Donnell's bombers visited this site on 3 August.

By the end of the first half of August, Pyongyang – with its huge marshalling yards, railway works, and munitions and aircraft factories – had also been hit, as had the steelworks and marshalling yards at Chongjin and a military base, oil storage depot and a railway complex at Rasin. This latter city was an especially difficult target, as it lay on the Soviet-Korean border just 100 km from Vladivostok. On 12 August, crews from Bomber Command bombed it with the help of radar sights. However, the majority of the bomber's 'payload' fell on the surrounding area and did not inflict any damage on the

---

3   Jackson, R., *Air War over Korea* (London: Ian Allan, 1973), p.57.

With wartime precision, B-29s have been conducting operations against the North Korean forces. The B-29 pictured here has just landed after a mission, and the crew have not yet left the aircraft. Already, the ground crews are gassing up and a bus waits to take the crew to the interrogation room. (Courtesy of the US National Archives)

industrial and military targets.

Meanwhile, the North Koreans pressed the advance – drawing the UN forces south. From mid-August, the bombers had once again been transferred to providing support for ground troops; the largest concentration of Korean People's Army forces was around Daegu. By 15 August, the city was semi-encircled by five North Korean divisions – and the front line was just 30 km from the city. The situation became so dangerous that the government of the Republic of Korea was forced to move temporarily from Daegu to Pusan; the majority of the North Korean forces were concentrated outside Waegwan. On 15 August, MacArthur discussed with Stratemeyer the possibility of launching a bombing raid using Superfortresses on the city. The next morning, 98 B-29s took to the skies – every aircraft that General O'Donnell had at his disposal. Their designated target was a district to the north-west of Waegwan, where according to intelligence up to 40,000 Korean People's Army soldiers were concentrated in an area 12 km long and 5.5 km wide. The bomb bays of the B-29s were crammed full with 227 kg high-explosive bombs.

In the space of 26 minutes, almost 100 Superfortresses laid waste a strip of land on the banks of the Nakdong River. When the smoke from the massacre had cleared, an RF-80 photographed the area – and the largest operation in support of ground troops since the Normandy landings had turned into an enormous military blunder. Not one North Korean soldier had suffered as a result of the raid, in which more than 1,000 tonnes of bombs had been dropped, as they were never in that location. The intelligence, which spoke of hordes of enemy soldiers, had proved incorrect.

Strategic bombing resumed at the end of August/

More than 24 million tonnes of bombs have been dropped on North Korean industrial and rail centres, and on bridges by US Air Force B-29 Superfortresses, such as the one pictured in this photograph in Okinawa. (Courtesy of the US National Archives)

beginning of September. On 27 August, Bomber Command again attempted to bomb Rasin, but this was not successful. Dense cloud over the target forced the Superfortresses to divert to reserve targets at Chongjin. Subsequently, Rasin was removed from the list of targets (owing to its proximity to the Soviet Union). On 28 August, 47 B-29s bombed the radar equipment at Kimchaek – destroying up to 95 percent of its structures. On 22 September, Superfortresses of the 19th Bomb Wing struck the marshalling yard at Antung, despite UN warnings over its proximity to China. The official target had been Sinuiju, but the pilots had strayed inadvertently off course. Bomber Command flew up to 36 sorties a day in support of ground troops – and in spite of this diversion of forces, by 25 September the 18 strategic targets that had been designated a priority had been destroyed. Having flown around 4,000 combat sorties, the Superfortresses dropped 30,000 tonnes of bombs in around 4,000 sorties – and lost four aircraft.

The March Northwards

In the meantime, the ground forces were undergoing significant changes. UN forces went on the offensive after running the North Korean Army into the ground on a defensive line close to Busan. On 15 September, the 5th Battalion, US Marines landed behind Korean People's Army lines at Incheon Bay – clearing the way for the arrival of the 10th US Army Corps. While the corps was stepping up its attacks to the east and south-east, the Marine Battalion broke through to the airfield at Gimpo – taking it on 18 September. The 8th Army broke through the 'Pusan Perimeter' on 22 September – and four days later, they met advance units from the 10th Corps close to Osan (and in doing so, surrounded the North Korean forces). On 28 September, UN forces captured Seoul; there was no longer any doubt that South Korea would be liberated successfully.

Another issue came to the fore: since the North Koreans had been forced back to the pre-war border, the UN Security Council resolution could be considered resolved. However, since some of the Korean People's Army forces will have to return to their own territory, would it therefore not make sense to pursue them north of the 38th parallel? MacArthur insisted on the complete destruction of Kim Il Sung's army, regardless of its location; these intentions evidently went beyond the framework set out by the UN Security Council. Following a deliberation, the White House decided to give MacArthur a *carte blanche*. On 27 September, the Committee of the Joint Chiefs of Staff ordered General MacArthur to chase the Korean People's Army forces out of North Korea and to establish a single state across the whole country under President Syngman Rhee. There was a subtlety to this order, however, that didn't suit MacArthur – namely that only South Korean forces were allowed to fight in the Chinese and Soviet border regions, and the borders themselves must be left untouched come what may. The General wanted complete autonomy for US forces, and felt that any offensive against the Korean People's Army and its eventual routing could not be restricted by any territorial borders. He immediately sent Kim Il Sung an offer of complete and unconditional surrender.

On 1 October, the South Korean Army, advancing in the vanguard of UN forces, crossed the 38th parallel and entered North Korean territory. Such a sudden change in the situation on the Korean Peninsula, which took place within the space of just two weeks, could not fail to unnerve the North Korean Government; a defeat of Kim Il Sung would result in a large-scale compulsory alignment of American forces along the Chinese border. Under the state of 'China' in the United Nations, Chiang Kai-shek, who had settled in Taiwan, was perceived with obstinance – and as such, Mao Zedong did not have any diplomatic or economic levers with which to prevent the defeat of the regime in Pyongyang, even though it was an ally. On the other hand, he did have military levers: on 2 October, the Chinese Prime Minister, Zhou Enlai, handed the UN a warning via Pannikar, the Indian ambassador in Peking, stating that China would support North Korea should the 38th parallel be crossed.

It is appropriate at this point to make an interesting comparison with events not so long ago in the Persian Gulf:[4] then UN forces, under the leadership of General Schwarzkopf, supported an occupied Kuwait – and in a similar way to MacArthur's forces, they chased Iraqi forces out of the country. The UN then held round-table negotiations with Iraq – rejecting a wholesale destruction of Saddam's forces on his own territory. It was possible that Schwarzkopf was wiser and more civilised than MacArthur; the main reason, however, is that the political climate had changed. In the 1950s, the political climate was not so easy-going – and it is probable that in Korea, the United Nations (along with the United States of America as the undisputed leader of the organisation) were not simply driven by a desire to assist the Republic of Korea, but also by a willingness to put the 'Reds' in their place once and for all.[5] Therefore, the Korean and Kuwaiti scenarios could not be more different.

During heated debates, the USSR's representative at the UN, Yakov Malik, insisted on a ceasefire and the immediate withdrawal of all overseas forces from the peninsular; nobody, however, would listen to the communists. In the meantime, Kim Il Sung turned down MacArthur's ultimatum. In response, on 7 October the General Assembly of the UN – ignoring the Chinese warning, and under pressure from Washington – allowed UN forces to pursue the enemy north of the 38th parallel. The assembly also formed an anticipatory committee for the reunification and post-war reconstruction of Korea. That day, frontline 8th US Army units entered the Democratic People's Republic of Korea – and that same day, the civilised 'policing operation' became a bloody, primeval war, although the 'police' themselves were, as yet, unaware of this.

On 9 October, the US 8th Army began a general offensive to the north via Kaeson towards Sariwon and Pyongyang. On 11 October, the 3rd Division South Korean Army, which was fighting on the Eastern Front, took the key port of Wonsan. The following day, the committee for the reunification and reconstruction of Korea suggested to General MacArthur that he take responsibility for the administrative management of the Korean territory occupied by UN forces. On 19 October, the 8th Army captured Pyongyang – and less than a week later (on 24 October), MacArthur lifted all restrictions on an offensive by non-Korean forces.

---

4 The article was written in 1996.
5 Moreover, 'Desert Storm' was only aimed at restoring democracy to Kuwait on paper. When has there ever been democracy in Kuwait? It does, however, have oil, which is something America needs.

During October, the Superfortresses had transferred to carrying out tactical missions over the battlefield – providing support for the advance of UN troops. General MacArthur said later:

> In the absence of strategic targets the versatility of the operations performed by bomber crews and their weaponry in providing close support for ground troops made a great impression on me. These missions were not typical of those flown by medium bombers, but their successful completion slowed the North Korean advance and made it possible for our troops to advance during intense enemy resistance.[6]

The skies over the front line, however, become congested for the almost 100 'Fortresses'. At that time (and in the absence of worthy targets), one crew of an enormous Superfortress chased a motorcyclist down the streets of a ruined city, throwing 227 kg bombs down at him, while another hunted a train at low level – trying to stop it by firing at it from its machine gun turrets. The bomber crews were languishing for want of something to do. The 22nd and 92nd Bomb Wings returned to the US, and Bomber Command Headquarters prepared to disband, since it was no longer required; it seemed like the war was almost at an end. On 26 October, the Committee of the Joint Chiefs of Staff informed MacArthur that further attacks on targets that may (in the relatively distant future) hold militarily significance, should cease. The military industrial potential of North Korea, as it was, had already been severely undermined well into the post-war years. MacArthur's slogan: 'We will be home by Christmas!' however, remained just a slogan.

On 14 October, China began to deploy nine field armies to Korea – totalling up to 300,000 men. Forces 'pushed' their way across the border by night – for the most part across two bridges close to the cities of Sinuiju and Manpo, as well as in small groups on rafts and boats along the entire length of the Yalu River. It has to be said that this border crossing by the Chinese 'volunteers' was exceptionally successful. In the space of just two weeks – and unnoticed by the UN forces – advanced groups of soldiers from 18 infantry divisions (forming a defensive line from Pakchon to Hungnam) had crossed into North Korea.

On 27 October, UN units suddenly encountered fierce resistance as they advanced towards the Yalu River. Close to Hungnam, the 3rd Division, South Korean Army halted its advance northwards under enemy fire and requested back-up. On 1 November, the 7th Battalion, US Marines came to their aid. However, even they became bogged down mounting a fierce defence, and they sustained heavy losses over the next four days during continuous fighting for control of the main roads close to Sui-Dong. On the Western Front, the situation had become just as severe. The US 8th Cavalry Regiment; the 1st Division, South Korean Army, as well as units from a British brigade, encountered the fiercest resistance near the river crossings at Pakchon. On 2 November (near Unsan), a powerful attack by the enemy forced US 8th Army units to draw back south of Ch'ongch'on – forming a dangerous pocket in the front line. Apart from that, advanced army detachments had become separated from logistics units during their push northwards, and only had provisions and ammunition to last them for two to three days. Army Commander General Walton Walker could not continue fighting in these conditions – and on 3 November, the army was ordered to draw back to a defensive line along the Ch'ongch'on River to regroup and resupply.

To the surprise of UN infantry commanders, on 5 November the enemy suddenly stopped fighting whilst staging a show of strength, and withdrew along the entire front. Several captured soldiers ended up in Allied hands dressed in a strange olive-green uniform. Their interrogations proved that the Allies' worst fears had come true: China had joined the war.

By the end of October, UN pilots had agreed that the situation in the air appeared 'somewhat unrealistic'. They flew over Korea without encountering even a single enemy aircraft – completely destroying any target that either was used, or could be used, for military purposes. Some of the higher-ranking military officers at that time regarded aviation as little more than airborne artillery, or as some sort of adjunct to ground forces which did not have a specific role to play in warfare. The more far-sighted officers, however, understood that a trouble-free spell such as this could not last long – and they were correct. On 1 November, pilots in a flight of Mustangs from the 18th Air Wing were attacked by swept wing jet fighters they had never seen before. A new player had entered the fray: the Soviet MiG-15 ...

The Story Behind the 'Korean Mystery'

North Korea's powerful neighbour, the People's Republic of China, was highly displeased with the course of events on the front line in the Korean War. Instead of the easy and rapid reunification of Korea they had hoped for (as a result of which, the power of the regime allied to Peking would have spread across the entire peninsular), the conflagration of war had reached China's own borders – and sparks from this fire were straying into Chinese territory. For American aircraft, the concept of a 'border' was a completely notional one. On 27 August, a pair of US Air Force Mustangs bombed Antung airfield on the Chinese border.

On 22 September, despite the UN warning about not touching Chinese territory, Superfortresses from the 19th Bombardment Group bombed the marshalling yard at Andung (the original target had been Sinuiju), but the crews

---

6 Stewart, James T., *Air Power the Decisive Force in Korea* (Toronto, London, New York: Van Nostrand, 1957), p.100.

B-29 Superfortresses are shown at Yokota air base, Japan. (Courtesy of the US National Archives)

had, by chance, strayed off course. Apart from the violation of its borders and the bombing of her own territory, China was unhappy with the presence of American forces so close to home.

After China's warning that she would act in support of North Korea if non-South Korean forces crossed the 38th parallel was ignored, it was inevitable that China would join the war immediately.

As China was preparing to launch its offensive, UN fighter-bomber forces flew over Korean territory as if they were over a practice range – reducing any ground target they came across to rubble – so the Chinese were forced to solve the critically important issue of air cover: first and foremost, an 'anti-aircraft umbrella' had to be set up above the bridges over the Yalu River and the principal communication links in North Korea, as the Chinese forces needed to use these same links for their deployment (and also to supply their troops with everything they needed during the course of the fighting). Apart from that, if the People's Republic of China were to join the war, it may result in US Air Force bombing raids on the principal targets in South-Eastern China – and fighter aircraft would be needed to defend them.

Aviation units that were earmarked for combat with the US Far East Air Force, which was a more than ambitious adversary, had to fulfil two very important requirements: firstly, they needed to be equipped with the latest jet fighter technology, which would not concede to any of the UN aircraft in Korea in terms of their flight-performance characteristics; secondly, their pilots had to be at least on a par with American pilots both in terms of their knowledge and in their willingness to fight for air supremacy.

The remnants of the North Korean Air Force did not fulfil these requirements in any way; heavy losses had long since knocked them out of the game. A great deal of effort and, most importantly, time would be needed to make up for the losses, train aircrew and for them to undergo conversion onto new technology; the North Koreans did not have time for this.

The People's Liberation Army Air Force (PLAAF), which had only been in existence for a year by that time, was not in any condition to counter American aircraft either. In accordance with the Sino-Soviet Friendship and Mutual Assistance Agreement dated 13 February 1950, Soviet aviation units and formations were to provide assistance to the Chinese Air Force in training and converting crews to modern aircraft technology. The latter units were equipped with what were, for that time, the most modern jet fighters in the Soviet Air Force – the MiG-15 – and were staffed by highly competent and experienced pilots. It was they who met all the requirements for countering the US Air Force in the Korean theatre of operations – therefore the decision to make use of Soviet Air Force units in Korea was a logical one; and it would seem to have been the only option.

In the first four months of the war, the assistance that the Soviet Union provided to North Korea comprised (in the main) of deliveries of armament, ammunition, fuel and so on … in other words, military-technical assistance. Apart from that, there were a large number of Soviet instructors and military advisors serving within the Korean People's Army, but who were not directly involved in the fighting. As it turned out, the Armed Forces of the USSR were never directly engaged in the conflict. However, the war – which was raging on the Soviet borders – did make its presence felt. On 4 September 1950, a Soviet A-20G – which had taken off from Port Arthur naval base – was attacked and shot down by 11 American fighters. The burning Boston crashed into the sea close to the island of Hayon-tao, situated more than 180 km to the west of the Korean Peninsula. On 8 October, the Soviet Union was hit directly when in clear weather, which ruled out the possibility of a navigational error; a pair of Shooting Stars attacked the airfield at Sukhaya Rechka just outside Vladivostok – destroying several Kingcobras on the ground. It is doubtful that this was an accident. On an official level, American commanders imposed strict controls – and the F-80 pilots attended a tribunal; their commander was removed from his post. It would appear that the formalities had been observed … however, the tribunal declared the pilots not guilty – and their commander, who had been sacked, became the Director of Flight Planning for the 5th Air Army! Years later, American pilots were convinced that this intentional demonstration of military might deterred the Soviet Union from direct involvement in the war. Contemporary American historians see this incident from completely the opposite perspective: 'In fact, the mistake infuriated the latter [Russia], and heavily influenced their decision to move an anti-aircraft corps, including two MiG-15 air defence divisions, into Manchuria'.[7] In reality, this strike on the airfield did not influence the Soviet Union at all – not in terms of the decision over direct involvement in the war, or the decision to support North Korea covertly with aircraft. Both these decisions had, by that

---

7   Dorr, Robert. F.; Lake, Jon; Thompson, Warren, *Korean War Aces* (London etc.: Osprey Publishing, 1995), p.14.

time, already been taken 'at the very top'.

From mid-October onwards, Soviet pilots began to provide air cover for the deployment and build-up of Korean People's Army and People's Liberation Army troops on USSR and Chinese territory as a precursor to their offensive; this did not go all the way to direct confrontation with the enemy. One of the units engaged in training pilots to fly jet aircraft and, at the same time ensuring the air defence of South-Eastern China, was the 151st (formerly the 5th) Guards Fighter Air Division. This unit met the most exacting requirements: flight crews within this division had begun to assimilate jet technology back in the summer of 1947 – flying first the Yak-15; then the MiG-9 and finally, from October 1949, the MiG-15. During the course of the Great Patriotic War, pilots in the three regiments – which in October 1950 became part of the 151st Guards Fighter Air Division – shot down more than 1,000 enemy aircraft. This division, which was part of the air defence system for the Moscow district – and which was based in the Kalinin region at Migalovo, Khotilovo and Borki airfields – were sent on a government assignment in July 1950. On 1 August, troop trains carrying personnel and equipment crossed the Manchurian border. The bases for the 151st Guards Fighter Air Division were designated as the two Mukden airfield complex bases at Anshan and Liaoyang. Having gathered their aircraft together, the three regiments – the 28th Guards Fighter Air Regiment, the 72nd Guards Fighter Air Regiment and the 139th Guards Fighter Air Regiment – began to perform their allotted tasks.

From the very beginning of the government assignment, the division's pilots were convinced that sooner or later, they would have to engage American pilots in combat (when the division was sent to China, the war had been raging full blast in Korea for a month). Although the mission and role put before the 151st Guards Fighter Air Division made no mention of their involvement in combat activity, the deployment of regiments to airbases close to the Chinese border provided much food for speculation and supposition. An event that occurred in the first half of October also put the crews on alert: the 67th Fighter Air Regiment was formed from the personnel allocated to the 151st Fighter Air Division units – and which along with the 139th Guards Fighter Air Regiment, formed the new 28th Fighter Air Division. The head of this formation was one of the most famous Soviet aces and twice Hero of the Soviet Union, A.V. Alelyukhin. Apart from that, the divisional regiments went to state 15/39 – in accordance with which the number of squadrons within a regiment was reduced from four to three, and the number of aircraft was also reduced to 30. If one considers that the Soviet Air Force only ever resorted to reducing its numbers when it was on a war footing, the pilots of the 28th and 151st Fighter Air Divisions could expect the situation to turn very serious. However, this was not followed up by any decrees, military orders or explanations that would have amended or changed the mission and role for our forces in North-Eastern China.

In November 1950, all the supposition, doubts and

Test Pilot S.A. Mikoyan standing next to a MiG-15 with an RD-45F engine, serial No. 120077 (the 77th aircraft in the 20th production series at Factory No. 1 in Kuibyshev). These MiG aircraft, which bore only Chinese markings, were in service with the 28th Fighter Air Division and the 151st Guards Fighter Air Division in November 1950.

A MiG-15 with an RD-45F engine, serial No. 0615316 (the 16th aircraft in the 6th production series at Factory No. 153 in Novosibirsk) at the State Air Force Scientific-Research Centre of the Order of the Red Banner. These MiG aircraft, which bore only Chinese markings, were in service with the 28th Fighter Air Division and the 151st Guards Fighter Air Division in November 1950.

arguments came to an end, when at around 1330 the telephone rang at the 1st Squadron, 72nd Guards Fighter Air Regiment dispersal ... an order came through: put six MiG-15s on the first state of readiness. It took the tugs a few minutes to draw the MiG-15s out to the 'holding area', and the pilots – the Commander of the 1st Squadron and Hero of the Soviet Union Major Stroykov, Senior Lieutenants Guts and Kaznacheyev and Lieutenants Monakhov, Chizh and Sanin – sat in their aircraft. Twenty minutes later, a loud bang rang out across the airfield and a flare jumped up from the Command Post. The background noise of the airfield was drowned out by the strained, high-pitched whistle of aircraft starting equipment – eventually giving way to the heavy rumble of jet engines spooling up, which reverberated into the ground. Less than two minutes later, the aircraft from this duty flight had vanished into the bluish haze on the horizon. Major Stroykov's group had set off on the first combat sortie flown by Soviet pilots in the Korean War.

On the very first day, regiments from the 151st Division

flew three sorties into Korea. The pilots were engaged in two dogfights, and recorded one Mustang and one Shooting Star each in their tally. Subsequently, the area leading up to the Yalu River was dubbed 'MiG Alley' by UN pilots.

The First Encounters in 'MiG Alley'
Repeated requests by the Commander of the 5th Air Army United States Far East Air Force – General Earl E. Partridge – to allow his pilots to pursue enemy aircraft over Manchuria and to destroy them on the ground met with so many rejections from Washington. However, the fierce resistance from Chinese units that had joined the war at the end of October pushed General MacArthur towards the idea of a bombing raid behind enemy lines close to the Chinese border. General Stratemeyer allowed the fighter-bombers to attack targets across the whole of North Korea, right up to the Yalu River. At the same time, General O'Donnell set new challenges for his Superfortresses ... this time, however, the illusion of waging a 'humanitarian war' – with highly accurate bombing of military targets without wishing to inflict losses on the civilian population – was abandoned. The B-29s' designated targets were the cities of North Korea – and O'Donnell ordered his crews to bomb them from end to end using incendiary bombs. On 1 November, B-29 bombers struck the cities of Nanam, Chongjin and Kanggje; then came raids on Sonchon, Bukchang, Maeng-san and Changjin. Worst hit was Hoeryong, as O'Donnell's bombers had dropped 32,000 'incendiaries' on the city. On 5 November, MacArthur gave the order to start a two-week-long operation to inflict maximum damage on the enemy. By issuing this order, he had ratified the directives issued by Stratemeyer and O'Donnell – and despite the bans put in place by Washington, he in fact had unleashed Bomber Command; the 5th Air Army; the 77th Operational Fleet Detachment and US Marine aviation for the unprecedented and unrestricted bombing of the entire territory of North Korea. The portfolio of targets included those that could be used by the enemy in any way; the kilometre-long bridge over the Yalu River linking Andung and Sinuiju, along which the mass deployment of troops which had crossed from China into Korea, were designated a priority target.

In the middle of the day on 5 November (in accordance with the plan for two weeks of bombing) Superfortresses from the 19th Bomb Wing dropped 170 tonnes of bombs on Kanggje – destroying more than half of the city's buildings. Word of this raid reached Washington that evening, along with a copy of MacArthur's order. The news of the raid caused a storm in government – and the decision to bomb the bridges over the Yalu River was a cause of particular concern. Close to midnight – and on the personal orders of President Truman – the Committee of the Joint Chiefs of Staff ordered MacArthur to abandon any plans to use UN aircraft any closer than five miles from the Sino–Korean border. MacArthur himself immediately responded by telegram – stating that he was unable to carry out this order, since all the supplies to the Chinese forces at the front come across these bridges. This unforeseen concern, which was sent by telegram, persuaded the Committee of the Joint Chiefs of Staff to approve MacArthur's order, but that the raids on the bridges be carried out without violating Chinese airspace. Apart from that, the Joint Chiefs of Staff categorically ruled out any combat activity on the eastern side of the Korean Peninsula (close to the border with the USSR), no matter how enticing the targets in that region might be.

The first sortie under this newly-approved plan was set for 7 November – and the target was Sinuiju; a total of 70 Superfortresses were due to take part in the raid. The crews took their positions in the bombers at dawn, but the operation was cancelled at the last minute due to adverse weather conditions; the sortie took place the following day. That morning, Mustangs from the 8th Group and Shooting Stars from the 18th and 49th Groups rained down rockets on anti-aircraft artillery positions on the southern bank of the Yalu River close to Sinuiju – clearing the way for the bombers. Above them (at an altitude of 6,000 m) two flights of F-80s provided fighter cover for the raid. Half an hour later, 70 Superfortresses appeared one kilometre above Sinuiju and dropped 580 tonnes of incendiary bombs on the city. After the main bombing force had left, a further nine Superfortresses flew over the city and bombed the bridge over the Yalu River. This time, the crews of the 19th Bomb Wing, who were 'bridge specialists', missed the target ... the 454 kg high-explosive bombs damaged the approaches to the bridge, but the structure itself was undamaged.

On 9 November, the task was transferred to naval aviation. At 1000 Skyraiders and Corsairs, with 'Panthers' providing cover, descended on the bridge – and 20 minutes later, an RB-29 appeared overhead to monitor the results of the raid ...

The eighth day of combat activity for the 28th and 151st Fighter Air Divisions in Korea – 8 November – began at 0941 with a sortie by two flights of MiG-15s from the 72nd Guards Fighter Air Regiment. Over the course of the next hour, dogfights took place in the air over Sinuiju between MiGs from the 72nd and 139th Guards Regiments and Mustangs and Shooting Stars that were attacking anti-aircraft artillery positions. During these dogfights, one MiG sustained a bullet hole to an external drop tank, and two pilots recorded one Mustang kill each. This series of morning dogfights, however, were but a precursor to the main event of the day: the mass raid by B-29s on Sinuiju and the bridge over the Yalu River.

There was a delay in scrambling the MiGs to intercept the bombers ... as V.G. Monakhov, a veteran of the 28th and 72nd Guards Fighter Air Regiments recalled, this delay was not a significant one (a little more than five minutes), but it was enough to decide their fate. The MiGs were still some 50 km from the Yalu River when the pilots noticed aerial bombs exploding ahead of them. On finally reaching Sinuiju, the fighters just caught the last of the departing bombers by surprise, and there was no longer any sense in pursuing them.

It is hard to define categorically why the intercept failed. It is possible that our fighter commanders had not anticipated a mass raid on targets located in such close proximity to the Chinese border; it is likely that a scenario such as this had been considered, and they could not fail to examine this possibility, being so close to the front line! When this perceived threat became a reality, however, they were not ready. An extra five minutes were wasted on evaluating the situation, making a decision and seeking approval from those further up the chain. Another reason could be that there were not enough aircraft on red alert to counter such a massive bomber raid. An examination of the statistics for combat sorties flown by 28th and 151st Division aircraft in the first few days of the war reveals that they rarely launched more than eight MiGs at a time. Two flights is nowhere near the number required to counter 70 Superfortresses, with their 840 large-calibre machine guns. It would have taken the same amount of time (five minutes) to bring the required number of fighters up to the first state of readiness, and for them to take off. Either way, for one reason or another, the fighters were delayed.

The following morning, American naval aircraft appeared over the bridge and MiGs from the 28th, 72nd and 139th Guards Fighter Air Regiments were scrambled to intercept them. At 1000 – when the battle had only just begun – the radar at the Antung Auxiliary Command Post (ACP) detected a large group of up to 40 Superfortresses; their heading would have brought them straight to the Antung Bridge and Sinuiju. Eight minutes after the first indication of the bombers, six MiG-15s were scrambled from the 72nd Guards Fighter Air Regiment, led by Major Bordun. According to calculations, our fighters were to approach Sinuiju, along with the 'Fortresses'. However, the bombers were soon turning back. One possible reason for this was that they had been informed that MiGs were active in the area, although it cannot be ruled out that Sinuiju was not their intended target. Bordun's group continued to fly south – and at the same time, the radar station at Antung detected a new target. At 1020 an RB-29 strategic reconnaissance aircraft – flanked by two flights of F-80s – appeared over Sinuiju to monitor the results of the raid by naval forces.

Meanwhile, fighters from the 72nd Guards Regiment were approaching Sinuiju from the south-west; they were given a heading to intercept the reconnaissance aircraft from the radar station. Apart from that, anti-aircraft artillery made it easier to locate this aircraft by following the explosions of the anti-aircraft shells. At 1025 Major Bordun's wingman, Senior Lieutenant Dymchenko, spotted a Superfortress heading south at an altitude of 4,000 m and escorted by eight Shooting Stars ...

The following is from *An Overview and Analysis of 151st Fighter Air Division Air Battles* [Here – and further on – the style of the document has been retained. The document uses Peking Time, but we have provided the equivalent in Central Korean Time in square brackets]:

At 0929 [1029] Major Bordun gave the order: "I'm going to attack the enemy aircraft with two fighters, using the rest for cover!" and began to close on the B-29s in a climb. As he closed on the enemy to a distance of 1,000 m to 600 m the bomber's gunners started to rake him with machine gun fire from their lower gun turrets.

At an altitude of 3,500 m his wingman Snr Lieutenant Dymchenko opened fire with a short burst from a distance of 1,000–1,200 m, while Major Bordun's wingman opened fire from a distance of 800–1,000 m. The first long burst was aimed at the tail gunner, while the second short burst from a distance of 600 m was aimed at the engines on the port flank of the B-29, the third burst was aimed again at that part of the B-29 from a distance of 400–350 m. As a result of the three bursts licks of flame were observed around the engines on the aircraft's port side.

It was Snr Lieutenant Dymchenko who made the second attack, from a distance of 600 m and an aspect angle of 0/4 and noticed flames coming from the aircraft's port side, it then departed back to Korean territory descending sharply and banking to port.[8]

The B-29 did not return fire when Snr Lieutenant Dymchenko gave it a second burst.

At the end of the attack Snr Lieutenant Dymchenko was given an order: "Enemy fighters attacking from above and to your left". As they broke off the attack with a half wing over to starboard, the enemy fighters attempted to attack the leader of the group but they were late in their attack, since they had broken away from the bomber following anti-aircraft fire. The B-29 had entered dense cloud cover at an altitude of 4,000 m just before the attack and the escorting enemy fighters became separated by anti-aircraft fire and were behind and to the left of the bomber out of the cloud. Seizing this opportunity Major Bordun attacked the B-29 successfully and the enemy fighters were not able to head off Major Bordun's group in time.

After this attack Major Bordun's group broke away and returned to base. The enemy did not attempt to pursue them or force them into a dogfight.[9]

On the basis of the outcome of this battle, Major Bordun and Senior Lieutenant Dymchenko were credited with one joint kill. Western sources confirm that the RB-29 they attacked was destroyed during an emergency landing at Gimpo (just outside Seoul) and that five crewmembers were killed, while

---

8   Here, aspect angle is understood to mean the ratio of the visible length of an object at an angle to its actual length. The aspect angle is approximately equal to the sine angle between the line of sight (the aiming line) and the fuselage axis of the aircraft under attack. An aspect angle of 1/4 corresponds approximately to 15 degrees, 2/4 30 degrees and so on.
9   Fund of the 151st GvIAD, inventory 152691s, file. 8, pp.99-100.

A view of an RB-29 of the 31st Reconnaissance Squadron; somewhere over Korea, 1951. (Courtesy of the US National Archives)

The Squadron Commander of the 139th Guards Fighter Air Regiment, Grigoriy Ilyich Kharkovskiy. In November 1950, he scored four victories – all against B-29s. (This photograph was provided by I. Seidov)

the gunner – Staff-Sergeant Harry J. Lavene – was credited with having shot down a MiG.

On 10 November, fighters from the 151st Guards Fighter Air Division again encountered Superfortresses. Six MiGs (around half of the 10 fighters in Major Bordun's group) attempted to attack a pair of B-29s. In contrast to the previous day, the bomber escort acted more decisively and the MiGs were attacked by two flights of Shooting Stars. The pilots of the 72nd Guards Fighter Air Regiment had to abandon their attack on the B-29s and engage the F-80s in battle. The arrival a few minutes later of two flights from the 28th Guards Fighter Air Regiment did not help to break through to the 'Fortresses' either. An hour-and-a-half later, MiGs from the 28th Fighter Air Division encountered bombers. At 1126 – following an order from the divisional Command Post – two flights led by Squadron Commander Major Kharkovskiy took to the skies.

Twenty minutes later, Kharkovskiy and his group were already over Andung at an altitude of 6,500 m. Following an order from the ground, the group turned onto a heading of 100° and descended down to 5,000 m. East of Sinuiju, Major Kharkovskiy noticed seven B-29s ahead and to the left at a distance of up to 16 km – flying in close echelon formation. The Superfortresses were escorted by four fighters identified as F-47s:

> After they noticed our fighters the enemy bombers began to turn back to their own territory. Major Kharkovskiy decided to manoeuvre the group to attack the enemy bombers using a left hand turn and in a combat formation consisting of attack and escort groups (the escort group would be 500 m above them, while the flights would be in pairs at right echelon).
>
> Major Kharkovskiy, who led the attacking group, attacked the two right-hand outer B-29s in a pair with Lieutenant Akimov from a distance of 600–400 m from behind and below and from both the left and right flanks at an aspect angle of 1/4–2/4. After this first burst of gunfire the B-29, which was attacked by Major Kharkovskiy began to fall behind the rest of the group. Major Kharkovskiy repeated the attack from below and from the starboard side, as a result of which the B-29 caught fire and began to descend in flames, crashing in an area 25 km north-east of Antung, which was confirmed by the Antung ACP, the crews within the group, and the gun camera films.
>
> Lieutenant Akimov opened fire on a B-29 using the same manoeuvre and with an aspect angle of 1/4–2/4 from a distance of 600 m, and noticed that the tracer hit the tail and the aft section of the bomber's fuselage. He stopped firing, turned the aircraft and opened fire again with the same aspect angle from a distance of 400–300 m. The shells hit the centre section of the B-29. Before breaking off the attack Akimov noticed that sections of skin had begun to fall off the aircraft. He broke off the attack from a distance of 50 m in a steep climb, using a left turn to fall in beside Major Kharkovskiy.
>
> As he commenced his next attack Lieutenant Akimov noticed that the port flank of the B-29 that Lieutenant Kharkovskiy had attacked was on fire. On breaking away from this attack Akimov noticed that the B-29 he had just attacked was descending and trailing smoke.
>
> The B-29 attacked by Lieutenant Akimov was shot down, which was confirmed by the Commander of the

escort group Snr Lieutenant Zhdanovich, and by Major Kharkovskiy, as well as the gun camera films.

As he commenced the first attack the B-29's gunners fired at Major Kharkovskiy and Lieutenant Akimov with concentrated fire, but the formation had been destroyed after the first attack, which also disrupted the firing plan, and the gunners did not open fire on the second attack.

The group led by Snr Lieutenant Zhdanovich attacked the five remaining bombers from above and behind and from a considerable distance, after which two B-29s broke away from their group and descended beneath the clouds while the other three turned for home at an altitude of 4,000 m. The pilots were not able to confirm that the B-29 they had attacked had crashed due to poor visibility as well as their distance from the aircraft. The enemy aircraft were not pursued further to prevent the fighters from crossing the front line.

During their attacks Major Kharkovskiy and Lieutenant Akimov had tried to direct the leader of the second attack group Snr Lieutenant Kapranov onto four F-47s. Lieutenant Kakurin repelled the enemy attack after which the F-47s headed back to their own territory without engaging the MiGs in combat. At the end of the battle at 1053 [1153] Major Kharkovskiy regrouped and returned to base on the orders of the PCA on Antung airfield.[10]

It is worth noting that the B-29 escort fighters mentioned in the document are incorrect, in that 'Thunderbolts' never saw action during the Korean War; Kharkovskiy and Akimov were credited with shooting down one B-29 each. The Americans acknowledged that one bomber had been lost from the 307th Group, which had only just arrived.

On 12 November, 32 fighters from the 151st and 28th Fighter Air Divisions took off to counter a raid on the railway bridge over the Yalu River. For six pilots from Captain Korobov's squadron in the 28th Guards Fighter Air Regiment, the battle was over before it had begun: the undercarriage failed to retract on their MiGs after take-off. The first pilot was able to land at Liaoyang and another at Anshan. As a result, of the eight fighters from this squadron that took off, only the lead pair reached the combat zone. As soon as they were visual with nine B-29s 20 kilometres south of Antung (escorted by six F-80s), Captain Korobov and his wingman attacked the bombers. The pilots only managed to attack once – after which they themselves came under attack from a group of Shooting Star escort fighters that had caught up with the bombers. Having engaged an enemy with a numerical advantage of three to one, the pilots of the 28th Guards Fighter Air Regiment were forced to abandon a second attack on the bombers – and turning away from the attacking 'eighties', they headed for Antung. Captain Korobov and his wingman were the only pilots to actually get through to the bombers that day;

10 Fund of the 151st GvIAD, inventory 152691s, file. 8, pp. 57-58.

The Deputy Commander of the 28th Guards Fighter Air Regiment, Boris Mukhin (12 personal and three group victories in the Second World War, with one victory in Korea) and Flight Commander of the 28th Guards Fighter Air Regiment, Sergey Korobov (16 victories in the Second World War, with one victory in Korea), 1951.

the rest were engaged in combat with the escort fighters and the group of ground attack aircraft that hit the bridge. While the MiG pilots did not score any victories that day, Western historians state that a B-29 from the 98th Bomb Wing that was damaged by MiGs on 12 November only just made it back to Gimpo, where it made an emergency landing.

The following day, the American bombers employed a different tactic: over the course of two hours, three groups of up to 40 B-29s were detected on radar flying towards Sinuiju. The first two groups turned south-east 60 km short of the Sino–Korean border – leaving the third one to continue onto the target. The Americans thought that this tactical approach would keep the risk of encountering MiGs to a minimum, and make it harder to identify the individual groups that were actually going to hit the target; this approach was very successful. At 0956 the third group of nine Superfortresses emptied their bomb bays over the city – approaching from an altitude of 3,000 m – and the bridge was also damaged. The eight MiGs from the 72nd Guards Fighter Air Regiment that had taken off to counter the raid met with a B-29 that was already over the target, although they were not able to intercept the bomber due to aggressive opposition from escort fighters and a lack of time.

This new trick was employed again on 14 November, but this time it failed to work. Our leadership took the simplest of decisions in this case: to scramble fighters in pursuit of any prominent target. At 1047, 12 MiGs from the 72nd Regiment took off to intercept the same number of 'Fortresses'. Although only seven fighters reached Sinuiju (since five pilots were forced to return because their undercarriage failed to retract), the arrival of the MiGs was enough to force the enemy to abandon the bombing mission and turn back. At 1156 the Andung ACP once again detected up to 50 B-29s with fighter escorts heading for the Sino–Korean border at a distance of 110 km. They were met at midday 30 km north of Sinuiju by 14 fighters from the 28th Fighter Air Division under the command of Major Kharkovskiy:

> Major Kharkovskiy's group ... flying at an altitude of 6,000 m ... encountered 30–40 B-29s ahead and to the right at an altitude of 7,000 m, flying head-on towards the fighters in echelon formation (consisting of up to 4–5 aircraft each) disposed in depth and escorted by up to 20 F-80s.
>
> Once the enemy had been located our fighters gained height in a right hand turn in two groups (the attacking group was led by Major Kharkovskiy while the escort group was led by Snr Lieutenant Zhdanovich and was 200 m higher than the attacking group) and took up an initial position from which to attack the bombers. As they approached Sinuiju Major Kharkovskiy led his flight in the first attack on two groups of B-29s, attacking from the right hand side and from below at an aspect angle of 2/4–3/4.
>
> Kharkovskiy himself with his wingman Lieutenant Akimov opened fire from a distance of 600–800 m on the lead group and on the outer B-29 on the left hand side of the formation. As a result the B-29 attacked by Major Kharkovskiy caught fire. Lieutenant Akimov observed the aircraft descending in flames.
>
> The second group in Major Kharkovskiy's flight: [sic] flown by Kapranov and Kakurin attacked the next group of B-29s. They were not able to observe the outcome of their attacks. Major Kharkovskiy and Lieutenant Akimov broke off the first attack diving to the left and attacked the next group of B-29s from behind after initially climbing to an altitude of 7,000 m, and from a distance of 300–200 m and at an aspect angle of 3/4 Kharkovskiy fired at the lead aircraft, and Akimov attacked the port side of the outer B-29. As they broke off the attack they noticed that the lead B-29 had begun to turn to the left and was trailing smoke. Breaking off the attack in a 180° turn Snr Lieutenant Kapranov and Lieutenant Kakurin again took up their initial position and attacked the next group of B-29s. They were not able to observe the results of their attack. They broke off the attack in a left hand turn and returned to their rendezvous point.
>
> Major Kharkovskiy and Lieutenant Akimov broke-off this second attack in a dive, taking up their position again in a left hand climbing turn, and from a distance of 600–400 m they attacked the second group of B-29s from behind, slightly below and to the right, at an aspect angle of 3/4. They did not see the outcome of their attack. An F-80 came onto Major Kharkovskiy's tail as he was taking up position for the fourth attack. Noticing this, Major Kharkovskiy turned and shook off the attack, flying towards the sun. He gained altitude in a left hand climbing turn and from a distance of 400–800 m and at an aspect angle of 2/4 he attacked the fourth group of B-29s from above, behind and to the right hand side from out of the sun. As a result the left hand outer B-29 caught fire and departed to the left descending sharply. Lieutenant Akimov, who was following Major Kharkovskiy saw this B-29 crash in flames. At the end of the fourth attack Lieutenant Akimov broke away to the left ahead of Major Kharkovskiy and departed back to the assembly point.
>
> The F-80 that was on Kharkovskiy's tail was shot down by Captain Sokolov the leader of the second group. The flight led by Snr Lieutenant Zhdanovich provided cover for the duration of Major Kharkovskiy's attack.
>
> Major Kharkovskiy broke off the final attack in a left hand climbing turn and gave the order to "join up" They re-grouped and returned to the airfield on the orders of the ACP.
>
> The dogfight was completed in co-operation with six fighters from 74454 field post office unit [the 67th Fighter Air Regiment] led by squadron commander Captain Sokolov. The pilots in Major Kharkovskiy's group watched the F-80 that was attacked by Captain Sokolov catch fire and descend haphazardly.
>
> Major Kharkovskiy was credited with three personal B-29 kills, and this is confirmed both by field cameras, and by the crews within the group.
>
> The B-29s operated at a distance of 2 km between flights, interleaving "diamond" and "wedge" formations.[11]

A group from the 67th Fighter Air Regiment also attacked the B-29s – and during the attack, Captain N. Podgorniy ran into some defensive fire from the bomber's gunners. The tracer hit the MiG-15's nose compartment in front of the windscreen and one bullet hit a pressurised oxygen cylinder. As a result, the latter exploded – blowing off the compartment cover. Podgorniy was forced to break off the attack, but he was credited with having shot down a B-29. The bombers were able to reach the bridge, but were not able to carry out precision bombing.

In a letter to a colleague, I. Seidov, G.I. Kharkovskiy wrote that he had only shot down two B-29s in November – and one of those was on 14 November – thus, in spite of the archive records, there were only two successful attacks that day by Major Kharkovskiy and Captain Podgorniy. According to American sources, two B-29s from the 19th and 307th Bomb Wings were seriously damaged near Sinuiju on 14 November. In this battle, gunner Staff-Sergeant Richard W. Fisher was credited with shooting down one MiG-15. This was the last encounter between MiGs and Superfortresses in November 1950. On 16 November, 38 MiGs from the 28th and 151st Fighter Air Divisions were scrambled to intercept bombers, only for the enemy to turn away as our fighters approached Antung; there were no further sorties for two weeks due to

---
11 Fund of the 151st GvIAD, inventory 152691s, file. 8, pp. 63-64.

bad weather.

No bombers were encountered at all on the final combat sortie flown by the 28th Fighter Air Division on 26 November; archive documents state that the bombers did not dare come within 50 km of Sinuiju. Data from the opposing side states that bombers from the 19th and 307th Bombardment Groups destroyed two bridges across the Yalu River close to Manpo and Ch'ongch'on on that day.

On 28 November, the 151st and 50th Divisions were merged to form the 64th Fighter Air Corps. The 50th Fighter Air Division was the last to join the war – its pilots completing their first sortie on 30 November. The following day – at 1309 – a group of six MiG-15s from the 29th Guards Fighter Air Regiment under the 50th Fighter Air Division were scrambled from Antung airfield. The aim of this sortie, which was led by Senior Lieutenant Orlov, was to intercept B-29s in the area around Antung. At 1324 our fighters arrived over the target at an altitude of 7,000 m in line-abreast formation. One minute later, the order came through from the ACP: 'Heading 120°, altitude 5,000 m, time 5 mins'. The group, led by Orlov, failed to encounter the bombers at this altitude and they returned to Antung. At 1330 the ACP gave an alternative heading for the bombers: 'Heading 70°, altitude 5,000 m'. After flying for three minutes on this new heading, Orlov saw three B-29s flying in a 'wedge' formation at a distance of 3 km without fighter cover. The MiGs manoeuvred for the attack in a right-hand turn.

The following is an extract from the 50th Fighter Air Division's *Air Combat Log*:

At 1235 [1335] the first attack was carried out in right echelon at the same altitude as the enemy and using an aspect angle of 2/4–3/4 and the MiGs opened fire with medium bursts on the lead and right hand B-29s ...

... the pair led by Snr Lieutenant Orlov [who was Senior Lieutenant Volodkin's wingman] broke off the attack in a 90° left hand turn, climbing to 1,000 m above the enemy, while the pair of MiGs led by Bogatyrev [the lead pilot was Captain I. Bogatyrev, while his wingman was Senior Lieutenant G.I. Grebenkin] broke off the attack in a descending right hand turn. Having made a 150° descending turn to the right pulling out at the same altitude as that of the bombers, the pair of aircraft led by Snr Lieutenant Orlov made a second attack at an aspect angle of 2/4 firing on the lead B-29 in short bursts from a distance of 1,000–600 m.

During the course of the attack the B-29s dropped their bombs haphazardly. The pair of MiGs led by Captain Bogatyrev, having made their right hand turn, attacked from underneath the bombers at an aspect angle of 1/4–0/4 using medium bursts of fire from a distance of 1,200–400 m. It was during this attack that the pilot's cockpit, the port side of the stabiliser and the starboard side of Snr Lieutenant Grebenkin's aircraft were holed by the gunner in the top turret of the B-29 on the right hand side of the formation. After this Snr Lieutenant Grebenkin broke off the attack in a right hand combat turn and departed back to base.

The next two attacks by three of our fighters were the same as the first.

The escorting pair (Snr Lieutenants Derdienko and Lyubimov) were above the bombers at an altitude of 1,000 m.

After the fourth attack the pair led by Snr Lieutenant Orlov and Captain Bogatyrev broke off the attack in a right hand combat turn and returned to base. The escorting pair followed suit.

The B-29s flew in close formation, climbing sharply in response to attacks from below, which afforded the gunners in the upper turrets an opportunity to open fire. During the course of the attack the pilots noticed that the starboard inboard engine on the lead aircraft was trailing smoke while the aircraft on the right hand side of the formation was trailing smoke from the outboard port engine, which was confirmed by the gun cameras on Snr Lieutenant Grebenkin's aircraft.

At 1335 [1435] six MiG-15s landed back at Anshan airfield.[12]

The cartridges from the gun cameras on Senior Lieutenant Grebenkin's aircraft confirmed what the pilots, who reported that two bombers were trailing smoke as a result of their attacks, had observed. There were plumes of smoke on the gun camera films coming from the starboard inboard engine on the lead Superfortress, and from the port outboard engine of the wingman's aircraft. On the basis of the photo analysis – as well as the pilot's own observations – Senior Lieutenants Orlov and Grebenkin were credited with having shot down a single B-29 each.

In reality, all three B-29s probably returned to base. Neither the pilots, nor anyone on the ground, actually saw the aircraft crash. The cartridges from the gun cameras, which were an addendum to the description of the battle, provided a panoramic view of the entire group of B-29s – that is to say that in reality, the firing distances were much greater than those described by the pilots. There is no direct confirmation that the aircraft were actually shot down in the descriptions – and even the pilots themselves, as the division's *Operations Log* confirms, reported that only the pair of Superfortresses were damaged. American researchers have not provided any information concerning losses on 1 December.

On 6 December at a little after 1300, MiGs from the 29th Guards Fighter Air Regiment again engaged the B-29s in combat – as a result of which, three pilots were credited with victories. Lieutenant N.N. Serikov failed to return from his sortie and was supposedly shot down by defensive fire from

---

12 Fund of the 50th IAD, inventory 539809c, file. 4, pp.129-130.

The highlights from the sun on the wings of B-29 Superfortress of the US Far East Air Force forms a vivid contrast to the reflection from the snow on the rugged mountainsides as the formation wings its way to attack Anju – an important supply and communications centre in Korea. The city was firebombed with 32 tonnes of incendiary missiles in the attack on 4 December 1950. (Courtesy of the US National Archives)

The Deputy Squadron Commander of the 29th Guards Fighter Air Regiment, Major Stepan Ivanovich Naumenko. He scored five victories in Korea – including one B-29; 6 December 1950. (This photograph was provided by I. Seidov)

the gun camera films. The films showed that the distances involved were again considerable, as the field of vision of the lens encompassed almost the entire group of Superfortresses.

Mistakes in judging range during initial encounters with B-29s were very widespread. We will refrain from listing these in chronological order, but cite the Deputy Commander of the 18th Guards Fighter Air Regiment, 303rd Fighter Air Division, Aleksandr Pavlovich Smorchkov. Pilots in his division first encountered Superfortresses six months after the events described above, but the mistakes remained the same:

> In Korea the firing distances were 200–400 m for fighters and 400–800 m for bombers. Let's say they decoded the film. A distance of 300 m now that's acceptable, but you still need to check the aspect angle …
>
> I remember this sad incident with one of the pilots:
> "Hey … I shot a Fortress down!"
> "Well" I said … "Let's have a look at the film."
> I load the film onto the projector and ask him:
> "What was the distance?"
> "5,100."
> "Listen … You're kidding me about this bomber … The pilot is sitting back at base now with a cup of tea! … 5,100! Come on … it's got a 43 m wingspan and the crew would be used to fighters by now. It would appear close but that's … 3 km."
> He said nothing.
> A full-size model was then manufactured so pilots could get used to the dimensions of a B-29. This was actually a crudely manufactured wooden model covered in percale that was glued on. The model was fitted with a sight for training purposes and pilots were able to see how the aircraft was projected over a range of distances.

The Raids on the Bridges

On 15 December, the US Far East Air Force announced the start of a new battlefield interdiction campaign. This was the first operation to have a pre-conceived plan; up until that point, sorties had been carried out on the orders of ground forces. A total of 172 targets behind the advancing Korean People's Army and the Chinese People's Volunteer Army lines were selected, which if they were taken out of action, would reduce the flow of goods from the north considerably. There were 45 railway and 12 road bridges that were designated as targets, as well as 39 marshalling yards, 39 tunnels and 63 supply bases. Bomber Command were assigned the lead role in this campaign.

In a little over a week, the bombers completed around 50 sorties – in which they dropped 345 tonnes of bombs on supply bases and concentrations of forces in North Korean cities. On 21-22 October, the bombers hit four bridges north of the 37th parallel – and the following day, aircraft from all three groups bombed Pyongyang. From that day on – and up until the end of the war – Bomber Command threw everything they had at destroying North Korean cities. On 25 December, there was

a B-29; the American side did not declare any losses that day. It is therefore unlikely that records were manipulated in any way, since pilots were credited with victories on the basis of

B-29 Superfortresses of the US Far East Air Force's Bomber Command wing their relentless way over Anju – the supply and communications centre in North Korea – plastering the town in a firebomb attack on 4 December 1950. The rugged, mountainous terrain completely surrounding the stronghold is typical of that confronting United Nations troops battling the enemy through the bitter cold North Korean winter. A total of 32 tonnes of firebombs fell on the city in the attack. (Courtesy of the US National Archives)

A long distance from its home base, this mighty bomber of the US Far East Air Force's Bomber Command approaches the target area. This beautiful scene shows a roofless world of tranquillity and beauty, which the bomber's crew are able to view, but often this peaceful picture is changed. Enemy flak bursts and speedy, swept-wing MiG-15s offer a fighting challenge to the B-29 Superfortress' crew, which battles for its life; January 1951. (Courtesy of the US National Archives)

Their long noses pointed towards the target; their bays filled with high-demolition bombs; their powerful engines echoing a steady roar high above the earth, these bombers of the US Far East Air Force's Bomber Command are on their way to leave a target smouldering in ruins. By means of radar, the bombs will be dropped through the heavy overcast skies that lie below. It will be another devastating attack by B-29 Superfortress medium bombers, January 1951. (Courtesy of the US National Archives)

a massive raid on Sariwon, while the final day of the year saw 69 Superfortresses dropping incendiary bombs on Pyongyang. The fiery raids on the North Korean capital continued on 3 and 5 January, when 63 and 60 Superfortresses bombed the city respectively. As a result, up to 35 percent of residential buildings were burnt to the ground. US Far East Air Force analysts concluded that only a thick layer of snow, which lay on the roofs of the buildings, saved Pyongyang from disappearing in a huge fireball.

In January 1951, the majority of B-29 sorties were focused on tactical bombing. On tactical fighter-bomber missions, the enormous B-29s did not really have sufficient service life to carry out bombing raids behind enemy lines. As a result, the battlefield air interdiction mission was not as effective as it could be. On the other hand, the Superfortresses were inaccessible to the MiGs all the time they were over the front line. The only encounter between MiG-15s and B-29s to take place that month occurred on 10 January:

On that day ...

At 1135 [1235] Mikhaylov's squadron, comprising ten MiG-15s, took off to counter up to eight enemy fighters and were sent to an area close to Anju at an altitude of 5,000 m, where Mikhaylov's squadron encountered a single B-29 heading North-East at an altitude of 3,500 m flying below and to the right hand side of them. The B-29 was subsequently attacked from above and behind at an aspect angle of 1/4–2/4 initially by pairs of MiGs and then by the entire squadron individually. After a

B-29s of the US Far East Air Force speed to dump tonnes of bombs on the military targets, January 1951. (Courtesy of the US National Archives)

A long hard day is over for the crew members of the giant B-29 Superfortress, which are framed by the still props of a sister ship as they break formation after a strike against the enemy, February 1951. (Courtesy of the US National Archives)

series of attacks the pilots noticed plumes of black on the starboard side at the wing fuselage joint after which the crew of the B-29 stopped firing at our fighters and descended below the cloud rocking from side to side. Captain Mikhaylov was not able to pursue this aircraft further due to a lack of fuel and dense cloud cover.

The description of the air battle states that the pilots opened fire from a distance of 800 to 1,200 m using a fixed graticule, even though pilots needed to fire using a mobile graticule – and from a distance of no more than 800 to 600 m – to ensure they hit the target. Nevertheless, on the basis of the reports submitted by the combatants and the gun camera films, as well as data from the ACP (which stated that the B-29 had crashed 15 km north-west of Anju), Captain Mikhaylov was credited with shooting down one Superfortress. The American version of events differs from ours – stating that on 10 January, 15 MiGs crossed the Yalu River and attacked a lone B-29. The pilots of the MiGs, however, lacked persistence and broke off the attack one minute later. Fortunately, the bomber escaped damage and returned to base.

By February, the front line had stabilised and the B-29s reverted to taking enemy communications out of action – principally by destroying bridges.

Following the February respite, 10 MiGs from the 28th Guards Fighter Air Regiment were scrambled once again at 1125 – under the command of Major Ovsyannikov – to intercept B-29s escorted by fighters. At 1134 the ACP at Andung received a message: 'Enemy bombers 30 km ahead'. A pair of MiGs led by Lieutenant-Colonel Kolyadin (operating independently) set off on the given heading – and a short time later, the lead aircraft encountered eight B-29s. Lieutenant-Colonel Kolyadin made the first head-on attack on one of the bombers – opening fire from a distance of around 1,200 m (after which he headed towards the sun in a steep climb).

The B-29s put up a coordinated defence – dropping their bombs whilst under fire. Kolyadin was attacked by a

This neat formation of B-29 Superfortresses of the US Far East Air Force Bomber Command provides a vivid example of how the air war is being carried to the enemy fighting in Korea. This is only a small part of a formation, which recently sealed off several important rail and highway links in the communications network near the Manchurian border, February 1951. (Courtesy of the US National Archives)

flight of F-80s while he was breaking off his attack, but the MiGs evaded the Shooting Stars in the vertical. He turned away from them and attacked another B-29 – opening fire from a distance of around 1,000 m. The group of eight F-80s prevented the MiGs from completing a third attack, as they got on their tails. Kolyadin's pair broke off the attack in a descending turn and headed back to base. During the second attack, Senior Lieutenant Bushmelev's wingman noticed that a fire had broken out on board one of the B-29s. On the basis of photo analysis, as well as confirmation from the ACP, this bomber was recorded as having been shot down and was credited to Lieutenant-Colonel Kolyadin; we did not come across any reference to this battle in the material we studied. It is possible that all the B-29s returned to base, since Kolyadin had opened fire at relatively long range, and both his attacks

The Commander of the 28th Guards Fighter Air Regiment, Viktor Ivanovich Kolyadin (15 victories in the Second World War and five victories in Korea – including two B-29s). (This photograph was provided by I. Seidov)

The Squadron Commander of the 28th Guards Fighter Air Regiment, Porfiry Borisovich Ovsyannikov (two victories in the Second World War and four in Korea – including one B-29). (This photograph was provided by I. Seidov)

B-29s of the Okinawa-based 19th Bomb Group are pictured on their way to strike for the 115th time during the Korean War. At times, the 19th joins groups of the US Far East Air Force's Bomber Command (stationed in Japan) to deliver their combined tonnage on strategic Korean targets, February 1951. (Courtesy of the US National Archives)

were made head-on under threat from escort fighters, which left little time for him to aim accurately.

The B-29s appeared several times on the radar screens at Andung over the next few days, although they only encountered MiG-15s some 10 days later. On 25 February, a group of four B-29s without fighter escort were attacked by two flights of MiG-15s from the 28th Guards Fighter Air Regiment under the command of Major Ovsyannikov. Following this battle, a record appeared in the *151st Guards Fighter Air Division Operations Log* stating that 28th Guards Fighter Air Regiment pilots shot down two B-29s after three attacks, which was confirmed by the gun camera films, as well as by the observations of Colonel Isayev (an officer at the ACP). Pilots witnessed direct hits on the two remaining aircraft as well, but they began to descend and continued to head south; the MiGs were unable to pursue them any further due to a lack of fuel. There was a bullet hole in the starboard side of Captain Pronin's MiG-15 and the aileron control rods were damaged. Subsequently, 'Citizen of the Democratic People's Republic of Korea Pak Kii Koeul and the Commander of the Combined Air Division, Korean People's Air Force comrade Lieutenant-General Li'[13] reported that four bombers crashed in the mountains close to the city of Goseong – and the 28th Guards Fighter Air Regiment pilots were credited with shooting down all four B-29s. According to American researchers, all the Superfortresses returned to base undamaged.

By 10 February, UN forces were able to halt the Chinese and North Korean Army's advance south, and after mounting a counterattack, they were able to push them back to the edge of the Han River – liberating the airfields at Suwon and Gimpo. It was these two airfields that were closer than any others to

---

13 Fund of the 151st GvIAP, inventory 152691s, file. 8, pp.124-125.

These three B-29 Superfortresses of the US Far East Air Force's 19th Bomb Group present a stair-step appearance as they head towards a target in Korea from their Okinawa base. The hard-hitting Superfortresses of the 19th were the first medium bombers to strike a blow against the North Koreans – and they have been at it steadily ever since, February 1951. (Courtesy of the US National Archives)

Sharply silhouetted against the hazy snow-covered mountains of Korea, a flight of B-29 Superfortresses of the Okinawa-based 19th Bomb Group are shown on their way to bomb another stronghold, February 1951. (Courtesy of the US National Archives)

Its powerful engines momentarily making huge 'X' marks of its propellers, the B-29 Superfortress (at first glance) seems to be in the process of making a sharp bank, but this is an optical illusion due to the eccentricity of the camera angle. Actually, the bomber is on a straight and level flight during the transit from its Okinawa base to strike another sledgehammer blow at some target in North Korea, February 1951. (Courtesy of the US National Archives)

the border with North Korea that had runways long enough to accommodate the most modern F-86 Sabre fighter, which appeared in Korea in mid-December 1950. The 4th Air Group flew their first sortie from Kimpo in the F-86 on 17 December – and over the course of two weeks, its pilots reported eight aircraft kills, two probable kills and seven MiG-15s damaged for the loss of a single Sabre. The group subsequently departed for Japan, as the front line reached Kimpo, and an opportunity arose for Sabres to operate once again over the Yalu River with the liberation of Kimpo and Seoul. The airfields – which had been captured twice – were not in operational condition, although the engineers advised that Suwon could be repaired quickly. On 22 February, General Partridge, inspired by this news, transferred the 334th Squadron from the 4th Air Wing from Japan to Taegu airfield – expecting to transfer them to Suwon shortly afterwards; the Sabres were only able to reach the edge of Pyongyang as it is if they operated from Taegu.

Planning their next moves at the end of February, Bomber Command acted on the assumption that all sorties flown by Superfortresses to the Yalu River would be provided with a Sabre escort. By the time the new battlefield interdiction programme had been approved, it had become obvious that there would be no Sabre escort. It emerged that Suwon was badly damaged and any hope of repairing Gimpo in the near future turned out to be even more elusive.

Nevertheless, the Commander of Bomber Command US Far East Air Force, Brigadier General James E. Briggs (who had replaced O'Donnell in this post on 10 January), did not cancel the battlefield interdiction programme, but entrusted the fighter escort role to the F-80. The very first of these sorties

These giant bombers of the US Far East Air Force (better known as 'Superforts') pick their way high over the rugged countryside; their powerful engines droning like angry hornets. Although the target is not visible through the dense cloud deck, the radar operators of these B-29s from an air base in Japan will pick up the target in the scope and blast more of the enemy's supply lines; February 1951. (Courtesy of the US National Archives)

V.I. Kolyadin, P.B. Ovsyannikov and V.I. Pokryshkin (who was Kolyadin's wingman and the younger brother of A.I. Pokryshkin); China, 1951. (This photograph was provided by I. Seidov)

The Squadron Commander of the 28th Fighter Air Regiment, P.B. Ovsyannikov, in the cockpit of his MiG at Tolmachyovo in 1956. (This photograph was provided by I. Seidov)

– on 1 March 1951 – almost ended in catastrophe.

This battle became one of the greatest mysteries in the history of the confrontation between the MiG-15 and the B-29. According to our version of events, this is how the battle unfolded: at 1346, eight MiG-15s – led by Major Ovsyannikov – took off on the orders of the 28th Guards Fighter Air Regiment Command Post (CP), but the undercarriage on Lieutenant-Colonel Nikiforov's MiG failed to retract after take-off, and he and his wingman returned to base. Three minutes later, a further six MiGs – led by Lieutenant-Colonel Kolyadin – took off to make up the numbers.

Major Ovsyannikov's fighters were directed onto four B-29s by the ACP. The pilots sighted the enemy as they were climbing after eight minutes of flying time, and the flight of four B-29s were at 230° at an altitude of 6,000 m. At that moment, Ovsyannikov's wingman shouted: "Enemy fighters overhead coming out of the sun!" Ovsyannikov began to climb – and in doing so, he momentarily lost sight of the bombers. He found them again, however, one or two minutes later in a tight 'diamond' formation at 140°. After ordering the leader of the third pair of MiGs – Captain Motov – to cover him, Ovsyannikov attacked the lead B-29 using two pairs of fighters from the left-hand side, behind and slightly above the bombers. The B-29 attacked the leader of the second flight of MiGs, Captain Parfenov, while his wingman opened fire on the bomber in the centre of the formation.

Ovsyannikov's pair broke off the first attack in a right-hand turn, followed by a climb; they then came up behind the bombers and attacked once again. Major Ovsyannikov opened fire from a distance of 800–600 m on the lead bomber, while his wingman – Captain Pronin – fired at the B-29 to the right of the formation. Parfenov's pair maintained the attack.

By that time, Lieutenant-Colonel Kolyadin's group of three fighters had entered the fray. The Commander was without his wingman – Senior Lieutenant Bushmelev – who had returned to base because one of his drop tanks had failed to jettison. Kolyadin ordered Ovsyannikov: "Cover me, I'm going to lead my group in the attack," and attacked the B-29 in the centre of the formation from behind and to the right – opening fire from a distance of 800–600 m. The second and third pairs in his groups made two attacks each from above and behind the bombers – opening fire from distances ranging from 600–1,000 m.

During the course of the attack, the pilots noticed that three of the 'Fortresses' were trailing white smoke and observed that the B-29s held formation despite constant attacks – maintaining thick defensive fire in the initial attacks. Lieutenant-Colonel Kolyadin and Major Ovsyannikov were credited with shooting down one B-29 each, which according to the Commander of a self-contained Korean People's Army aircraft factory – Junior Lieutenant Kim Sek Te – crashed into the sea 15-20 km west of the city of Sonchon. All the MiGs returned to base.

Interestingly at first, the entry that appeared in the *Combat*

Log mentioned that the three Superfortresses were merely damaged. American researchers paint a picture which, in many ways, confirms our version of events. On 1 March, the target for the bombers was the bridge not far from Chongju (according to our documents, the battle took place close to Sonchon, which is just a few kilometres north of Chongju). B-29s from the 98th Bombardment Group suddenly encountered a powerful headwind in transit to the target. As a result, they were a good quarter of an hour late reaching their designated rendezvous point to formate with the escort fighters. The 22 F-80s escorting them were forced to abandon their charges a few kilometres short of the target, and the Superfortresses continued alone. Having dropped their bombs, they turned back to base (the headings given in the 28th Guards Fighter Air Regiment report that 140° and 230° to the south-west and south-east were the standard departure headings for B-29s). At this point, the group was attacked by nine MiG-15s (of the 11 MiGs scrambled, one pair would stay back to provide cover and would not engage the B-29s in combat at all) – and there is almost no contradiction at all in the two versions. They lie in the outcome of the battle, according to information from the Americans: 18 B-29s participated in the raid, and 10 were seriously damaged in the battle, moreover three of them failed to reach Japan, and were forced to make an emergency landing in Taegu in the southern part of the Korean Peninsula and were written off![14] The gunner – Sergeant William Finnegan from the 343rd Bomb Squadron – was credited with shooting down a MiG-15. People's Liberation Army Air Force MiGs were already operational in the period under discussion, although it is doubtful that the Chinese were involved in this battle, since they were either not scrambled to the target along with the Soviet pilots, or if they were scrambled, they would have been recorded in our combat reports.

It is difficult to believe that pilots from the 28th Guards Fighter Air Regiment attacked four B-29s without noticing the other 14 – and moreover, that they got into a *tight* formation, since they were bereft of a fighter escort according to American researchers. There is no way we are going to be led to believe that our pilots did not notice that they had inflicted damage on 2.5 times more bombers than they declared! We do not have a reasonable explanation of any kind for such a discrepancy in the assessment of the outcome of the battle, which can be backed up by any solid proof. We can only suppose that for some reason, Bomber Command included the losses from earlier battles – such as those incurred on 25 February – in the figures for 1 March.

If the Far East Air Force were not planning to accept these losses, they should have stepped up the battle for air supremacy over the Yalu River. A decision was taken to use Suwon airfield, which still resembled a runway churned up by ordnance in a sea of mud, as a staging post. On 6 March, F-86s from the 334th Bomb Squadron – flying from Taegu with a stopover at Suwon – began to patrol 'MiG Alley'. The working conditions for Sabre pilots at Suwon were awful. The runway was not only used for its primary purpose, but also as a taxiway, as Commander of the 4th Fighter Group, Colonel Benjamin S. Preston, recalled: 'We landed on one side [of the runway], swung around and taxied up the other side while aircraft kept coming in to land. Our wingtip clearance was maybe ten feet'.[15] The pilots were forced to land one behind the other, and were at risk of ending up in the wake of the aircraft landing in front of them. Moreover, some of the aircraft could be damaged, or have fuel tanks that were empty – remaining airborne only on a wing and a prayer. Working feverishly, Far East Air Force engineers restored Suwon to a respectable operational condition on 10 March, and the 334th Fighter Squadron were redeployed to Suwon – making it a permanent base. The neighbouring 336th Fighter Squadron redeployed to Taegu – from where they could patrol 'MiG Alley' via Suwon. From this moment on, Sabres would escort B-29s all the way to the Yalu River.

It was around this time that one of the finest fighter units in the Soviet Air Force – the 324th Fighter Air Division, led by Triple Hero of the Soviet Union I.N. Kozhedub, and consisting of the 176th Guards Fighter Air Division and the 196th Fighter Air Division – arrived to relieve the 151st Guards Fighter Air Regiment at DongFeng and Anshan airfields. Pilots were engaged in intensive training for almost three months – redeploying from Andun between 28 March and 2 April, from where they commenced combat operations immediately. Meanwhile, having recovered from the shock, Bomber Command once again sent their bombers into 'MiG Alley' on 23 March. Twenty-two B-29s from the 19th and 307th Bombardment Groups carried out bombing raids on railway bridges near Chongju and Yeoncheon-gun. A group of 12 MiGs from the 151st Guards Fighter Air Division took to the skies and engaged some two-dozen Sabres (American sources put this figure at 45) although there were no spare aircraft to break through the fighter escort and attack the bombers.

The most important target for the United Nations' air forces remained the bridges at Antung and the crossings at Uiju; the bombers visited these targets regularly at the end of March. Interestingly, B-29 raids on other bridges (with varying degrees of success) are mentioned in Western sources, but there is no mention of the bombing raids on the bridge at Antung. An explanation of two characteristic battles may serve to explain this:

On 29 March, Superfortresses escorted by F-80s and F-86s attempted to bomb the bridge at Antung; 18 MiGs from the 28th and 72nd Regiments were scrambled to intercept them. According to our own estimates, up to 30 B-29s and up to 70 fighters participated in this raid. Despite their overwhelming

---

14   This is pedalled (for example) by the authoritative historian Robert F. Futrell, based on trustworthy sources such as the Historical Records of Far East Air Force Bomber Command from February–June 1951 and Far East Air Force Intelligence Digest No. 26 for the period from 25 February–3 March 1951; Futrell, Robert F., *The United States Air Force in Korea 1950-1953* (New York: Duell, 1961), p. 294.

15   Davis, *Mig Alley*, pp.15-16.

A mission-bound Superfortress of the US Far East Air Force's Okinawa-based 307th Bomb Group taxi out for take-off. (Courtesy of the US National Archives)

This overall shot shows 'Heavenly Laden' – a B-29 Superfortress of the US Air Force's 98th Bomb Wing, which has just returned from its 60th consecutive combat mission over Korean targets without having a mishap for mechanical or other difficulties, April 1951. (Courtesy of the US National Archives)

numerical advantage, however, only one of the bombers was able to get through to the bridge itself, which emptied its bomb bay in a hurry (under fire from our fighters) and sought refuge in the clouds. Not one of the bombs hit the bridge. The rest of the 'Fortresses' – returning fire furiously – departed to the south-west without dropping their bombs. According to the photo-analysis unit, Major Korobov's flight from the 28th Guards Fighter Air Regiment damaged one Superfortress.

A subsequent raid by Superfortresses from the 19th, 98th and 307th Groups took place on 30 March. Twelve B-29s from each group departed on this raid – and according to Western authors, their targets were the bridges over Cheongsong, Manpo and Namsan. Fighter cover was provided by 32 Sabres from the 4th Fighter Wing, while Shooting Stars from the 8th and 49th Fighter Wings provided close air support. Some of the MiGs from the 151st Guards Fighter Air Regiment that were scrambled to intercept the bombers and fighters engaged the Sabres in combat, while the rest attacked the B-29s. This air battle above the Yalu River took place over a 50 km sector from the point at which the bombers were intercepted back to our own airfield; the Superfortresses never reached the bridge at Antung.

Following the battle, one B-29 and one F-86 were presumed shot down on the basis of photo interpretation from the gun camera films, although they were not subsequently confirmed; all the MiGs returned to base. The opposing side acknowledged that one of the B-29s from the 19th Bombardment Group was seriously damaged – and instead of returning to Okinawa, this aircraft was forced to make an emergency landing on Itazuke so that the injured crewmembers on board could be rescued. The gunners from the 28th Bomb Squadron were credited with shooting down two MiGs. It is interesting to note that there is no mention in Western sources about the attempt to bomb the bridge at Antung on 30 March – probably because it failed.

Low cloud over 'MiG Alley' prevented the B-29s from

The MiG-15 No. 125, serial No. 111025. The pilot is Senior Lieutenant Gogolev (two victories in Korea), the 2nd Squadron, 176th Guards Fighter Air Regiment; Andung, April 1951.

undertaking any sorties to this area for the next few days. In the meantime, pilots from the 151st Fighter Air Division completed their last combat sorties. The division was pulled back to the rear and was transferred to Anshan airfield, while the 324th Fighter Air Division commenced operations from Antung. The weather only lifted at the end of the first week of April – and on 7 April, B-29s from the 98th and 307th Bomb Wings and 48 F-84s from the 27th Fighter Escort Wing took off to bomb the railway bridges close to Sinuiju and the road bridge near Uiju. All the targets lay within sight of Antung, where the 324th Fighter Air Division was based. That morning, Kozhedub's pilots encountered the 'Fortresses' for the first time.

Aircraft activity over 'MiG Alley' began at 0800 – and at 0803 radar operators detected a group of targets, which was identified as a bomber escorted by four fighters. Three minutes later, six MiGs from the 176th Guards Fighter Air Regiment – led by Captain Sheberstov – had scrambled to intercept them. These aircraft, which were probably looking to survey the area

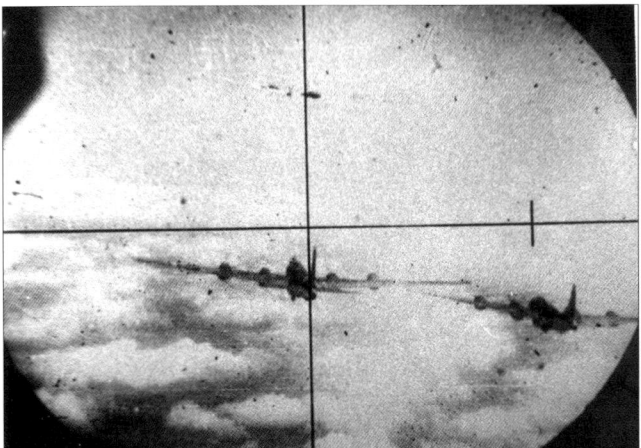

A frame from Captain Ivan Suchkov's gun camera, 176th Guards Fighter Air Regiment; 7 April 1951.

Captain Ivan Suchkov (10 victories in Korea), 176th Guards Fighter Air Regiment.

for the Superfortresses, set off in the direction of Pyongyang as our fighters were scrambled. Fighter aircraft were tracked by radar for almost the next two hours before the ACP reported that 40 'Fortresses' – escorted by 20 fighters – were on their way to Antung at 0955.

Six MiG-15s from the 176th Guards Fighter Air Regiment – led by Captain Vasko – were scrambled at 0953. Six minutes later, they were followed by two flights led by Captain Murashev – and one minute after that, by a further eight led by Captain Antipov. At 1018, six fighters from this same regiment took off under the command of Senior Lieutenant Bokach. At 1005 one of our pilots reported to the 324th Fighter Air Division CP that he had sighted enemy aircraft south-west of Sinuiju. Kozhedub, who was at the Command Post, gave the order: "All fighters: intercept the enemy bombers and attack them." At 1011 Captain Vasko engaged the fighter 'shield' – formed of F-86s – in combat, while the rest attacked the B-29s and the F-84s that were escorting them. One minute later, up to 16 of the bombers broke through to the Yalu River and ' ... bombed the bridge in a single approach and in level flight from an altitude of between 6,500–7,000 m. In all up to 24 bombs were dropped, of these two hit the bridge'.[16]

To begin with, the divisional combat report stated that ' ... as a result of the air battle two B-29s are presumed shot down on the basis of the gun camera data as well as the testimony of the pilots'.[17] Subsequently, the three pilots were credited with shooting down two B-29s and one F-84. Senior Lieutenant B.A. Obraztsov opened fire on one F-84 at a range of 500 m and ' ... the crew watched the F-84 turn as it began to trail smoke from its port side. The loss of the aircraft was confirmed by the gun camera film'.[18] Captain A.I. Suchkov ' ... concentrated his fire on one of the B-29s. The crew saw the shells explode along the port side of the aircraft, and the loss of the B-29 was confirmed by the gun camera film'.[19] As he made his attack, Captain S.B. Subbotin noticed ' ... one of the aircraft's components broke off

flying up and to the left. The loss of the aircraft was confirmed by the gun camera film'.[20] Our losses that day were one MiG-15 from the 196th Fighter Air Regiment; fortunately the pilot, Senior Lieutenant Andrushko, ejected.

According to American data, the F-84s did not concede any losses – and through their combined efforts, they shot down one MiG-15. On the whole, despite the MiGs' considerable advantage over the Thunderjets, the latter's pilots were so effective that only one of the MiGs was able to break through to the bombers – and it was this aircraft that destroyed a single B-29 from the 371st Bomb Squadron, 307th Bomb Wing.

Bomber Command's 'Big Day'

By the end of the first week of April, the bridge across the Yalu River at Sinuiju remained the only active crossing – and despite all the efforts of UN aircraft, there was no reduction in the flow of troops and equipment over it. The bridge once again became a target for the B-29s from the 19th, 98th and 307th Bomb Wings – and 39 Thunderjets from the 27th Fighter Escort Wing were allocated to the bombers to provide close support. Sabres from the 4th Wing provided high altitude support.

That very day became the first of Bomber Command's 'Big Days'. The problems began right from the beginning of the sortie, as nine bombers experienced different technical failures and they were forced to either abandon the mission, or return to base shortly after take-off. The remaining 39 aircraft were not able to form up into a close formation – arriving at the fighter escort rendezvous point in three disparate groups: the first of these were eight B-29s from the 19th Bombardment Wing; behind them were 12 B-29s from the 307th Bomb Wing; 19 B-29s from the 98th Bomb Wing brought up the rear. As a result, not only did they weaken their coordination of defensive fire amongst themselves, but they also dispersed the escort fighters ...

Events from our perspective unfolded as follows: at 0856 a single bomber was detected 120 km south of Antung, which was escorted by a flight of fighters. Eight MiG-15s from the 196th Fighter Air Regiment – led by Senior Lieutenant

---

16 Fund of the 324th IAD, inventory 152706ss, file. 7, p.7.
17 Fund of the 324th IAD, inventory 152706ss, file. 7, p.7.
18 Fund of the 324th IAD, inventory 152839s, file. 2, p.10.
19 Fund of the 324th IAD, inventory 152839s, file. 2, p.10.

20 Fund of the 324th IAD, inventory 152839s, file. 2, p.10.

The 'Blue Tail Fly' B-29 Superfortress of the US Far East Air Force's Okinawa-based 19th Bomb Group. Master Sergeant Constantine Profers, maintenance crew chief, gives the blue-tailer a pat on the back after he gets a lift from fellow maintenance crewmen. The pat on the back, however, rightfully belongs to the crew members themselves, who are responsible for the 'Superfort's' impressive combat record, April 1951. (Courtesy of the US National Archives)

Bokach – were scrambled to intercept them at 0900. The enemy changed course immediately after the MiGs took off – increasing speed and turning south-east. Senior Lieutenant Bokach was then given a new heading towards the area above Sinmi-do Island. The aircraft in that location began to descend to a low altitude – disappearing from radar screens at high speed as our fighters approached. It is likely that the enemy were carrying out initial reconnaissance of the target area prior to the main raid.

At 0945 the ACP radar detected a group of aircraft consisting of 20 B-29s near Hwanghae. To begin with, the group tracked west heading for Nampo, but at 0948 they turned north. The bombers, anticipating a fighter escort, began a turn to the left 30–40 km south of Sinmi-do at 0953 and at 1000 – having completed a full left-hand circuit – they rendezvoused with 30 escort fighters. The entire group then set course for Sinuiju at an altitude of 7,000–8,000 m.

At 0951 the ACP radar detected a second group of enemy aircraft consisting of between 16-20 B-29 bombers and a large number of escort fighters 28 km south of Nampo. The group moved in the general direction of Sinuiju, and 25 km south-south-east of Sinmi-do, they completed a right-hand circuit just to kill some time – returning to their previous heading at 1007.

At 0959 a third group were detected – consisting of around 20-24 bombers moving at an altitude of 7,000–7,500 m and with a large fighter escort at 11,000 m (some 30 km west of Pyongyang). To begin with, the group maintained their westerly heading, but at 1006 they set course for Sinuiju. By the time the bombers had been detected, the 324th Fighter Air Division had one squadron consisting of eight MiG-15s at first readiness, and two each at second and third readiness, while another squadron was refuelling following a sortie.

The Commander of the 324th Fighter Air Division, N.I. Kozhedub – describing the subsequent turn of events – wrote:

> After the first group of enemy fighters had been detected I brought the units, which were at second and third readiness up to first readiness. After it became clear that the enemy was heading in our direction at 0852 [0952] I decided to scramble 2 more groups of fighters – eight and six fighters from the 55702 field postal unit [the 196th Guards Fighter Air Regiment] under the overall command of Captain Shelamonov, with the aim of

The pilots of the 176th Guards Fighter Air Regiment. Seated are P.S. Milaushkin, K.Ya Sheberstov, S.A. Rodionov, P.F. Nikulin, and B.G. Reytarovskiy. Standing are I.A. Zyuz, I.S. Kutomanov, N.K. Serdyuk, G.A. Nikolayev, A.F. Golovachev, G.I. Ges, I.V. Lazutin, D.M. Fyodorov, A.P. Gogolev, I.A. Suchkov, and N.P. Kravtsov. (This photograph was provided by I. Seidov)

countering the raid by enemy bombers. These fighter groups took off at 0854–0855 [0954–0955].

Between 0900–0902 [1000–1002] I ordered another two groups of fighters to scramble – eight and six MiG-15s from the field postal unit 49772 [the 176th Guards Fighter Air Regiment] under the overall command of Captain Sheberstov (Captain Murashev was the wingman for the second group) in order to intercept the second wave of enemy bombers.

After taking off and gaining altitude our fighters were vectored onto the enemy bombers from the command centre and at 0910 [1010] one of our fighter pilots reported that they were visual with a column of B-29 aircraft.[21]

Captain Tkatskiy's MiGs encountered the lead column – consisting of eight B-29s from the 19th Bombardment Wing – 45 km south-west of Antung. At 1011 the Commander of the flight, Captain Lev Ivanov, attacked the Superfortresses – and one of the most famous battles to be fought in the air over Korea had begun ...

Captain Ivanov opened fire from a distance of 600–700 m with two short bursts, but the shells passed underneath the target. After reducing the distance to 300–400 m, Ivanov gave another two short bursts ' ... after which he noticed flashes on the B-29's fuselage ... '[22] Breaking off the attack, he began to follow his wingman, Senior Lieutenant Kochegarov, who was firing at a second Superfortress and observed ' ... smoke coming from the B-29's flank, which began to descend, turning towards the sea ... '[23] The pair of MiGs, led by Ivanov, subsequently engaged the Shooting Stars in combat.

The two aircraft under the command of the leader of the group – Captain Tkatskiy – engaged B-29s, F-80s and F-86s in combat. Following one of these attacks, Tkatskiy's wingman, Senior Lieutenant Vasilyev, who had fired on a B-29 from a distance of 600–700 m observed ' ... smoke coming from the B-29's starboard flank ... '[24]

The pair of MiGs led by Senior Lieutenant Gorshkov, who attacked a B-29 with defensive fire, were themselves attacked by a flight of F-80s. His wingman, Senior Lieutenant Fukin – after he had beaten back this attack – broke away from his wingman and was able, by continuing the battle on his own, to get onto the tail of one of the Shooting Stars – giving three bursts of concentrated fire from a distance of 150–200 m at an aspect angle of 2/4. He saw ' ... the shells explode as they hit the tail and the fuselage of the aircraft, and the starboard undercarriage door fell off ... '[25]

Shelamonov's squadron was initially directed to the Cholsan area up to an altitude of 11,000 m to engage enemy

21 Fund of the 324th IAD, inventory 152706ss, file. 7, p.19.
22 Fund of the 324th IAD, inventory 539839c, file. 1, p.5.
23 Fund of the 324th IAD, inventory 152839s, file. 2, p.5.
24 Fund of the 324th IAD, inventory 152839s, file. 2, p.6.
25 Fund of the 324th IAD, inventory 152839s, file. 2, p.9.

The Flight Commander of the 1st Squadron of the 196th Fighter Air Regiment, Captain Lev Ivanov (seven victories in Korea).

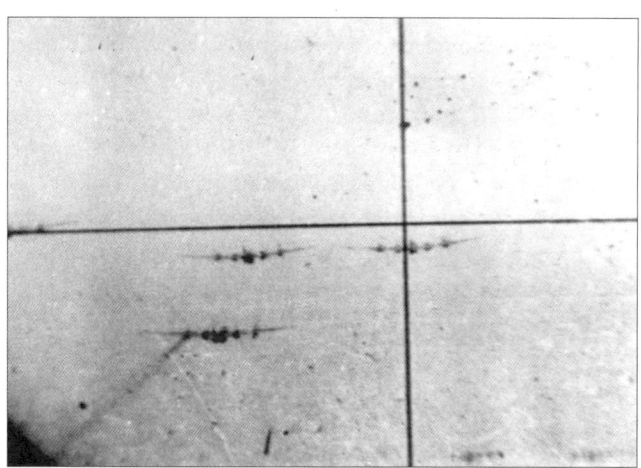

A frame from Senior Lieutenant Kochegarov's gun camera from the 196th Fighter Air Regiment, 12 April 1951. Smoke can be seen emanating from the outer engine on the port side of a B-29, which had previously been attacked by Kochegarov's lead pilot, Captain Ivanov.

fighters in combat. The latter, however, were not to be found at that altitude, and the fighters were re-directed to attack the bombers. As they descended, the squadron encountered two groups of Superfortresses flying in close formation. The MiGs caught up with the first group, and Shelamonov and Soskovets' group broke away from each other and attacked the B-29s three times – opening fire from a distance of 600–300 m. After the first attack by four of Soskovets' aircraft, the B-29 – which had been attacked by the Flight Commander – ' ...

The Squadron Commander of the 196th Fighter Air Regiment, Captain Nikolay Shelamonov (five victories in Korea).

Pilot of the 196th Fighter Air Regiment, Senior Lieutenant Fyodor Shebanov (six victories in Korea).

began to fall towards the ground out of control ... '[26] Another bomber 'departed – turning away to port'.

After the third attack on the 'Fortresses', a single Shooting Star got behind Shelamonov's flight, but after a long burst of fire from Captain Dostoyevskiy from a distance of 300–400 m at an aspect angle of 1/4, the F-80 ' ... began to descend sharply trailing smoke ... '[27] As he completed a 180° turn, Shelamonov noticed a second group of bombers and led his flight in a head-on attack – after which he set course to return to base. At that moment, Senior Lieutenant Samusin noticed an F-80 ahead and above him, and attacked him from behind and below with a long burst of fire at an aspect angle of 2/4 – ' ... after which the F-80 descended trailing smoke ... '[28]

Following the first attack, Senior Lieutenant Iovlev broke away from the group and transited to the area over the bridge at Antung, where he rendezvoused with a single MiG – and together they attacked the lead aircraft in the group of Superfortresses. As a result, the latter ' ... turned away descending ... '[29] and Iovlev saw ' ... four parachutists bail out of the stricken aircraft ... '[30]

Sheberstov's group attacked the lead detachment of the second group of Superfortresses 30-35 km south-west of Antung at 1018 – opening fire from a distance of 1,000–300 m and at bank angles ranging from 0/4–3/4. The combat report

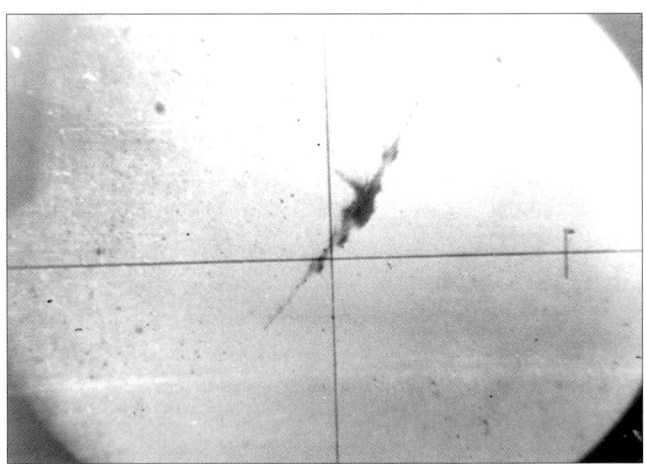

A frame from Senior Lieutenant Fyodor Shebanov's gun camera from the 196th Fighter Air Regiment, 12 April 1951.

stated that two B-29s attacked by Captains Sheberstov and Subotyn were shot down, while a further bomber, which had sustained fire from Captain Suchkov, was seriously damaged. The lead detachment of Superfortresses broke formation and dropped their bombs without reaching their target. During subsequent attacks, Captains Ges and Suchkov, and Senior Lieutenant Milaushkin shot down a further three B-29s.

Following on from Sheberstov's group, Captain Murashev's squadron attacked the rear detachment of the first group of 'Fortresses' 30 km south-west of Antung in pairs. Captain Shpitsin and his wingman carried out two attacks on the outer B-29 on the starboard side of the formation. As a result, they noticed that ' ... the outboard starboard engine

26 Fund of the 324th IAD, inventory 152839s, file. 2, p.9.
27 Fund of the 324th IAD, inventory 152839s, file. 2, p.9.
28 Fund of the 324th IAD, inventory 152839s, file. 2, p.9.
29 Fund of the 324th IAD, inventory 152839s, file. 2, p.9.
30 Fund of the 324th IAD, inventory 152839s, file. 2, p.9.

Pilots from the 3rd Squadron, 196th Fighter Air Regiment on leave; China, 1951. (This photograph was provided by I. Seidov)

Major Serafim Pavlovich Subbotin (nine victories in Korea), 176th Guards Fighter Air Regiment.

The Commander of the 1st Squadron, 176th Guards Fighter Air Regiment, Captain Grigoriy Ges (two victories in the Second World War and eight victories in Korea).

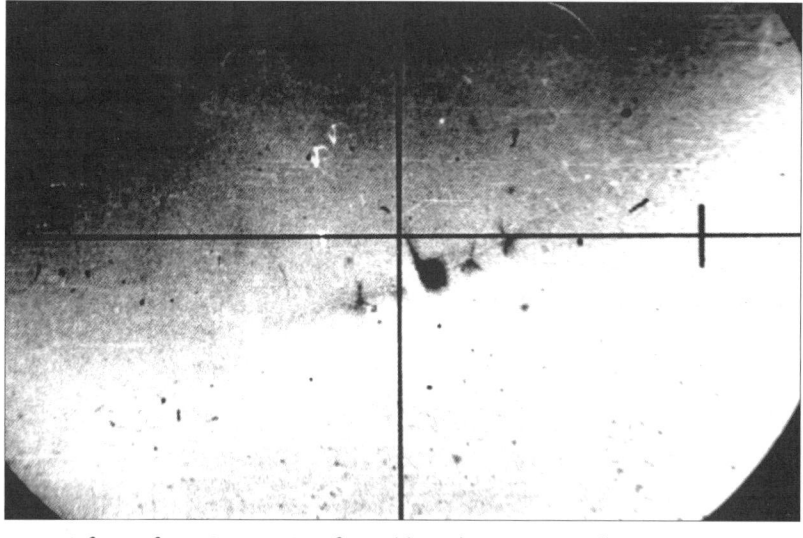
A frame from Captain Serafim Subbotin's gun camera from the 176th Guards Fighter Air Regiment, 12 April 1951. An explosion can be seen emanating from the left-hand side of a B-29's centre wing section.

on the bomber they attacked was on fire ... '[31] The attack by a pair of MiGs – led by Senior Lieutenant Plitkin – w as also successful. The leader opened fire from a distance of 600–300 m at a bank angle of 1/4–0/4 – giving two long bursts – and the ' ... pilots noticed smoke and flames coming from the lead enemy aircraft, which broke formation turning to port, as they broke off the attack the pilots watched the parachutists, that had bailed out of this aircraft descend to the ground ... '[32] Captain Plitkin's wingman, Senior Lieutenant Obraztsov, ' ... shot down a B-29 from above, behind, and slightly to the right from a distance of 1,200 m and at a bank angle of 1/4 ... "[33]

At 1013 – when the air battle had only just begun – four MiGs from the 176th Guards Fighter Air Regiment were scrambled in order to augment the groups heading into battle under the command of Captain A.F. Vasko. They encountered eight B-29s, escorted by fighters, 15 km south-east of Antung. Vasko's pair of MiGs attacked the bombers, but they opened fire from a distance of 1 km and did not see the outcome of their attack. The second pair in this flight, led by wingman Captain Kramarenko, engaged the fighters in combat – and on the basis of the outcome of this battle, both S.M. Kramarenko and his wingman, Senior Lieutenant Lazutin, were credited with one kill each.

Eight MiG-15s took off for the battle zone at 1023 led by Senior Lieutenant Bokach; these represented the division's last reserves. By the time he had encountered four B-29s and two groups of eight fighters 15 km south of the bridge, the MiGs

---

31 Fund of the 324th IAD, inventory 152839s, file. 2, p.14.
32 Fund of the 324th IAD, inventory 152706ss, file. 7, p.21.
33 Fund of the 324th IAD, inventory 539839s, file. 2, p.14.

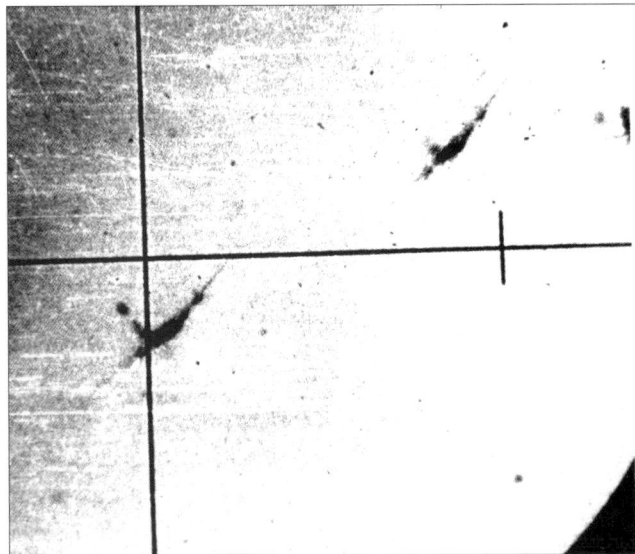

A frame from Captain Ivan Suchkov's gun camera from the 176th Guards Fighter Air Regiment, 12 April 1951. A B-29 can be seen falling towards the ground in the right-hand side of the frame.

Senior Lieutenant Pyotr Milaushkin (one victory in the Second World War and 11 victories in Korea) from the 176th Guards Fighter Air Regiment.

Senior Lieutenant Obraztsov (four victories in Korea), 176th Guards Fighter Air Regiment.

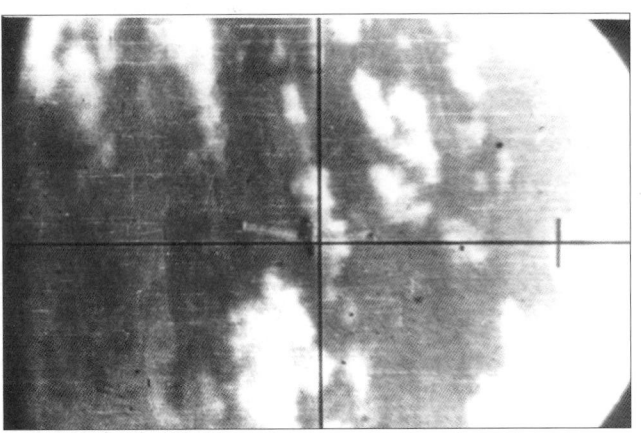

A frame from Captain Serafim Subbotin's gun camera from the 176th Guards Fighter Air Regiment, 12 April 1951. In the sight is an F-84 Thunderjet.

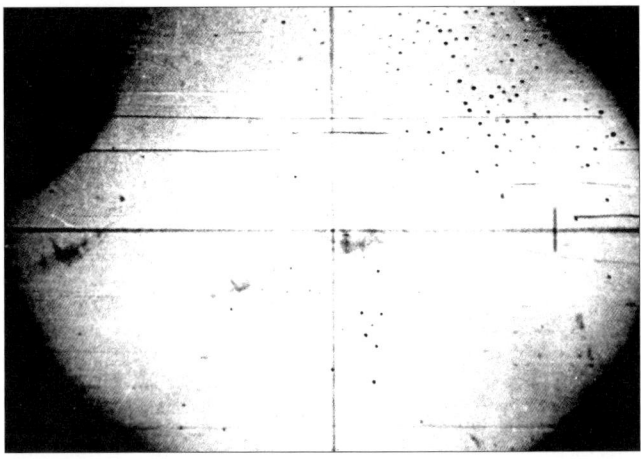

A frame from Senior Lieutenant Obraztsov's gun camera from the 176th Guards Fighter Air Regiment, 12 April 1951. It is evident that the B-29 Obraztsov is firing at is breaking away from the formation.

led by Boris Bokach had not climbed to the required altitude and attacked the enemy aircraft head-on and from below. After making this attack, Bokach's squadron broke away and got onto the tails of the bombers whilst under fire from two groups of eight Sabres and Shooting Stars. The Squadron Commander ordered Senior Lieutenant Abakumov's flight to engage the fighters in combat, whilst he himself headed for the 'Fortresses'. As he fired at a B-29, Bokach ' ... saw the shells explode around the two starboard engines, after which he noticed traces of smoke emanating from the aircraft ... the lead B-29 was descending and began to head north'.[34] Bokach's wingman, Senior Lieutenant Larionov – having beaten back the Sabres that were attacking his wingman – noticed a further quartet of B-29s approaching the bridge and fired on one of them from a distance of 400–500 m at an aspect angle of 0/4–1/4. The bomber ' ... began to emit smoke and headed south, turning sharply to port with one of its port engines trailing smoke ... '[35]

The leader of the second pair of MiGs, Captain Nazarkin, gave a Superfortress three bursts of fire from a distance of 600 m and an aspect angle of 0/4 and noticed ' ... how both starboard engines caught fire, after which he began to fire at the flight deck from a distance of 100–150 m giving a final

34 Fund of the 324th IAD, inventory 539839s, file. 1, p.7.

35 Fund of the 324th IAD, inventory 539839s, file. 1, p.7.

The Commander of the 2nd Squadron, 176th Guards Fighter Air Regiment, Captain Sergey Kramarenko (two victories in the Second World War and 13 victories in Korea).

S.M. Kramarenko, with his ground crew, standing next to MiG-15bis No. 729 (serial No. 0715329). Kramarenko fought in this aircraft from the end of April 1951 to January 1952. On 12 April 1951, he flew MiG-15 No. 133 (serial No. 111033) fitted with an RD-45 engine. (This photograph was provided by I. Seidov)

The Squadron Commander of the 196th Fighter Air Regiment, Captain Boris Bokach (two victories in the Second World War and six victories in Korea).

Senior Lieutenant Boris Abakumov of the 196th Fighter Air Regiment (five victories in Korea).

three bursts and using all his ammunition. After this the burning B-29 began to fall away turning to port'.[36] On hearing the Squadron Commander's order – "Anyone who has run out of ammunition: carry out simulated attacks" – Nazarkin ordered his wingman, Senior Lieutenant Vermin, to go forward and attack the Superfortresses. Vermin attacked one Fortress twice – closing to a distance of up to 300 m – and the 'B-29 descended sharply and departed away from its group trailing smoke'.[37] Breaking away, Vermin fired at the rearmost aircraft in the quartet of bombers departing to the south-east and 'Saw the shells explode as they hit the fuselage and the flight deck'.[38]

The flight led by Senior Lieutenant Abakumov engaged the fighters in combat, and the Flight Commander's pair was subjected to an attack by F-84s. The leader of the second pair – Captain Yakovlev – however, was able to save his colleagues. Getting onto a Thunderjet's tail, he gave it a short burst of fire from a distance of 400 m at an aspect angle of 2/4 and ' ... the F-84 began to fall, descending and rolling about its longitudinal axis and at that moment Captain Yakovlev opened fire using all his guns from a distance of 200 m and an aspect angle of 0/4. The F-84 aircraft turned sharply to starboard and fell away trailing smoke ... '[39] Slipping past the Thunderjets, Yakovlev's pair re-joined the group attacking the bombers.

Abakumov's pair – having escaped the Thunderjet attack – approached a group of Superfortresses heading towards the

36 Fund of the 324th IAD, inventory 539839s, file. 1, p.7.
37 Fund of the 324th IAD, inventory 539839s, file. 1, p.7.
38 Fund of the 324th IAD, inventory 539839s, file. 1, p.7.

39 Fund of the 324th IAD, inventory 539839s, file. 1, p.7.

bridge. Abakumov fired on the lead B-29 and then attacked the outermost trailing aircraft. He fired from a distance of 600–400 m at an aspect angle of 1/4–2/4 and noticed that the 'starboard engine was trailing smoke but the B-29 maintained formation'.[40] Abakumov gave the bomber three bursts on the second attack and ' ... the trailing B-29 began to bank away from its group with a steep 30° bank angle to port ... '[41] As he continued to pursue the bomber, Abakumov used the rest of his ammunition –firing from a distance of 400 m – and returning to base once the guns had gone silent.

❦

We note that the documents, first and foremost, refer to escort fighters as F-80s. On the gun camera films taken by some of our pilots, it is obvious that they have, in fact, engaged Shooting Stars in combat, although American researchers state that it was only Thunderjets from the 27th Fighter Wing and Sabres from the 4th Fighter Wing that provided close air support.

Once the MiGs had broken through the F-86 'shield' and ignored the Thunderjets, they would attack the B-29s – and the F-84s were no match for them in any respect; both in terms of speed and their rate of climb, they would concede hopelessly to the MiGs. Even worse was the fact that having let the MiGs slip away over the Yalu River, the Sabres would be scrambled to intercept them and would enter the fray. On top of everything else, this over-complicated the work of the Thunderjets. In the heat of battle, it was very difficult to distinguish a MiG-15 from an F-86 – and before long, F-84 pilots would fire away at random at any swept wing aircraft that would pass them by ...

We went into such detail over the description of the battle (although this has been abridged significantly in comparison with the archive documents) so that the reader is able to picture the enormous jumble of aircraft, cannon and machine gun fire – as well as the smoke and flames – that raged over a small sector of North Korean territory leading up to the Yalu River in the space of almost 40 minutes. This helps the reader to understand the reasons for such significant discrepancies in the assessment of the losses on either side in one of the largest air battles of the Korean War.

To complete the picture, we need to show how the battle looked from the enemy's point of view. As Sergeant Billy G. Beach – a gunner in the 28th Bomb Squadron, 19th Bomb Wing –remembers:

> It was my 19th mission and the 3rd on the "No Sweat."[42]
> Our targets were the bridges over the Yalu near Sinuiju, within sight of the MiG base at Antung. Twelve B-29s were assigned to the mission, all loaded with 2,000 lb bombs. We were to get fighter cover from F-84s and F-86s before entering "MiG Alley."
>
> We took off at dawn into a bright clear day - perfect for flying. About 40 minutes out we test-fired our guns and then settled down for a long ride. Two hours later we started to climb to our assigned altitude and leveled off. A few minutes later, we picked up our fighter cover.
>
> About noon we were alerted that we were approaching the target area. We were less than five minutes away from the bridges - and the MiGs. Suddenly the tail gunner shouted into his mike: "MiGs, about 30 of 'em, coming in at 6 o'clock!"[43] They were MiGs alright, coming in fast at 6 o'clock and breaking away at four - right in line with my sights. I watched as they shot at the tail first then swung to hit us amidship.
>
> They were coming so close that I could see the muzzle-blast from their 23 mm cannon. I started firing as soon as I got one in range. I caught my first MiG on his breakaway.
>
> I tracked him and kept firing short bursts until he went out of control about 900 yards out. He went straight down, spinning like crazy.
>
> Three minutes and four passes later, I spied this other guy coming in low at 1:30. I picked him up about 1,200 yards out and chopped into him with short steady bursts. That MiG got out about 400 yards, keeled over on its side and went into a headlong dive. I watched it crash and explode on the mountainside. That was my last shot at the MiGs as the fighters moved in on them.
>
> But they'd hurt the "No Sweat" plenty bad. Number 2 and 4 engines were shot out and feathered. The right aileron was shot out. The interphone was out and No.2 fuel tank caught fire. Our formation was broken up as two of the four aircraft had been shot down. The third ship had to turn back for Okinawa, so we were all alone.
>
> The AC rang the alert bell to prepare to bail out and all of a sudden I got scared.
>
> I'd never jumped before and I didn't want to start now. The Commies were throwing flak up at us now. I could see the little black puffs all along the wings and engines. But the bailout signal never came and it dawned on us that we were going to try to make the bomb run anyway.
>
> The AC tried to catch the flight up ahead of us, but with two engines out, it was impossible. So we went it alone. It seemed we were suspended in space. Like a bird with a broken wing, we limped in over the bridges. When we left, we could see that the bridges were gone.
>
> The next hour was the longest of my young life. We lost altitude and the AC had to depressurise the cabin. It got so cold we nearly froze. Each minute we dropped

---

40 Fund of the 324th IAD, inventory 539839s, file. 1, p.8.
41 Fund of the 324th IAD, inventory 539839s, file. 1, p.8.
42 'No Sweat' was the name given to a B-29 with the serial No. 44-87618.
43 American crews use the 'hour hand' method to describe the direction a target is approaching from. They imagine their aircraft to be in the centre of a huge dial, with the nose of the aircraft pointing towards the '12 o'clock' position. Therefore, a target approaching from behind would be at 'six o'clock', or from the left at 'nine o'clock' and so on.

A Boeing B-29 Superfortress parked in the dispersal area at an air base somewhere in Okinawa, Ryuku Retto. (Courtesy of the US National Archives)

closer to the mountains. It was the most spectacular flying I've ever seen. We were just barely in the air when we broke out over an advanced fighter base near the Han River.

The runway was way too short, but we went in anyway. When we touched down the main gear collapsed and we slid in on the belly and nose wheel. The old "No Sweat" came to a halt with her nose over the road near the strip. It was 1400 and she disrupted traffic.[44]

❦

What was the outcome of the air battle on 12 April? The 234th Division's archive documents state:

The first group of bombers incurred significant losses as a result of the actions of our fighters, and dropped their bombs before reaching their target.

The second group of bombers, which were also attacked by our fighters, also incurred heavy losses and dropped their bombs along the southern edge of the Sinuiju Mountains.

The third group of bombers did not encounter sufficient resistance from our fighters and were able to drop their bombs on the railway bridge. As the third group of bombers approached, our forces were principally engaged in beating back the first two groups...

The fighter pilots employed all the right air combat tactics, exploiting the enemy aircraft's weaknesses...

In total 40 MiG-15 fighters fought in the air battle... while on the enemy's side from 52–60 B-29s and 60–75 F-80s fought in the battle... As a result up to 11 B-29s, and two F-80s, were shot down, and up to 14 B-29s and five fighters were damaged. All our pilots returned from the air battle, and five aircraft had sustained between two and seven bullet holes.[45]

A few days later, N.I. Kozhedub wrote in his combat report that according to the North Koreans, the crews from three B-29s had been taken prisoner. Apart from that, the crew of another of the bombers had abandoned the aircraft at 1100 over Sinmi-do Island and had crashed into the sea, which was confirmed by the Chief of Police at Sonchon. Subsequently, 10 B-29 kills and four fighter kills were confirmed.

The Americans confirmed that only three bombers were lost, but the details in the information taken from different sources do not correspond – thus, according to R. Futrell, for example:

... Three minutes before they reached the target, the 19th Group's eight B-29s were attacked by 40 to 50 MiGs. One B-29 crashed in flames and five others were damaged.

Next, about 20 MiGs jumped the 307th Group's twelve B-29s. One of the bombers crashed in enemy territory and another badly damaged ship barely got back to Suwon.

Last over the target with 19 bombers, the 98th Group met a few wary MiGs and sustained no

---

44 Davis, *MiG Alley*, p.17.

45 Fund of the 324th IAD, inventory 152706ss, file. 7, pp.18-24.

The MiG-15 No. 108023 from the 324th Fighter Air Division that was damaged in combat on 12 April 1951. The aircraft has been dismantled to enable repairs to be carried out.

damage ... the loss of three medium bombers was a prohibitive loss ... [46]

It is worth noting that Robert Futrell obtained this information from reputable sources such as the 'Bomber Command Far East Air Force report no. 382' dated 12 April 1951 – and 'message AX-6514' to the Committee of the Joint Chiefs of Staff (dated 19 April 1951) and 'AX-6287' to the Commander-in-Chief of Strategic Air Command (dated 14 April 1951) from the Commander-in-Chief Far East Air Force, and so on.

On the other hand, we have information concerning losses obtained from the American representatives of the Joint Russian-American Commission for Prisoners of War and Missing in Action. According to these figures, Bomber Command also lost three bombers on 12 April: one B-29 (serial No. 44-62252) from the 307th Bomb Wing and two from the 19th Bomb Wing. Moreover, of the two latter aircraft, one of them (serial No. 44-69682) was shot down by the MiGs and crashed in the mountains, while a second (serial No. 44-68370) was damaged and had attempted to ditch. Wreckage and oil slicks were discovered in the area close to where the aircraft ditched.

According to Sergeant Beach, it is also clear that only one of the flights in the 19th Bomb Wing in which he served lost no fewer than two bombers. Apart from that, although we treat confirmation from eyewitnesses on the ground with great caution, it is worth noting that the crewmembers from the three bombers that were taken prisoner look very convincing. Therefore, according to our own assessment, losses can be put at six aircraft:

- Crews bailed out of three aircraft over the target – one each certainly from the 307th Bomb Wing and the 19th Bomb Wing – while a third probably belonged to the 19th Bomb Wing
- One crashed close to Sinmi-do Island from the 19th Bomb Wing
- One was written off following an emergency landing at Suwon from the 307th Bomb Wing
- One was written off following a landing at Kimpo; this was 'No Sweat' from the 19th Bomb Wing. Sergeant Beach gave a very graphic description

of this aircraft's arrival at this airfield, and it was probably beyond repair

As far as our official figures are concerned, 10 Superfortresses were shot down – and this has clearly been overstated. If this were true, then daily B-29 raids into 'MiG Alley' would have ceased in April – not six months later after the truly devastating 'Black week'.

By way of a consolation, the gunners on the B-29s were credited with shooting down seven MiGs, whilst Sabre pilots recorded four shot down and six damaged; F-80 pilots reported three probable kills. As we have seen, our side did not incur any losses in this battle at all. It is worth noting (in the interests of fairness) that on the afternoon of 12 April, one squadron from the 196th Fighter Air Regiment that had been scrambled to intercept RB-45s entered into a sufficiently complex battle with the Sabre escort fighters. In this battle, Captain Yakovlev's MiG was damaged. After he had sustained injuries from three 12.7 mm bullets, the pilot made an emergency landing 20 km east of Sinuiju – and the damaged aircraft was sent to an aircraft repair base at Dalniy for repair work. Western researchers, although clearly referring to the victories attained by F-86 pilots on 12 April, also list their victories in the second battle. (Judging by one comprehensive description of the battle from an eyewitness on board a B-29, the Sabres were nowhere near active enough for us to be able to discuss any victories they may have attained whatsoever.)

❦

Further B-29 operations into 'MiG Alley' seemed unreasonable. Morale in bomber squadrons fell to its lowest level, and crews dreaded hearing that their target for the next sortie would again be Sinuiju. On 12 April, Far East Air Force Headquarters received a message from Bomber Command stating that 25 B-29s had been lost or damaged in the raids on the bridges over the Yalu River, or one in four of the Superfortresses that Bomber Command has (or had) at its disposal! These figures went way beyond the acceptable 10 percent casualty rate, and the Commander of the US Far East Air Force – General Stratemeyer – banned any B-29 sorties to the Sinuiju region until truly effective escort fighters could be found to accompany them; they were probably never found. After 12 April, no further attempts were made to bomb the bridges at Sinuiju.

---

46 Futrell, *The United States Air Force in Korea*, p.298.

During the April air battles, UN pilots expressed concern that the enemy had raised their standards appreciably. Their discipline in the air had improved, and the MiG pilots became aggressive and unpredictable. The fact that this was happening as Bomber Command was launching a new campaign to take North Korean airfields out of action was of particular concern. The first sortie of this new campaign, however (which took place on 17 April), was successful – and the MiGs that had been scrambled to intercept them were engaged in combat with the F-86 'shield'. By 23 April, repeated raids on nine key airfields had taken them out of action for several weeks – and all the B-29s reverted to battlefield interdiction operations.

'A Smart Weapon' and Operations behind the Lines

From autumn 1950, the B-29s bombed their targets as if they were on a bombing range. They would drop their bombs from altitudes of up to 3,000 m and crews were able to carry out as many raids as were required to ensure that their target had been completely destroyed. If they were bombing a bridge, for example, the bomb-aimer would drop a series of four bombs in a single bombing run – and on average, a little more than 13 runs were required to destroy a bridge. Naturally, this latter figure illustrates how inaccurate the bombs were, but the Superfortresses from the five groups – around 150 aircraft – would constantly level the bridges so those designated as targets would not survive for long. A steady reinforcement of anti-aircraft artillery sites, however, meant that the bombing altitude had to be doubled – and the threat of MiGs left no time for a second bombing run on the target; bombing would have to be carried out in level flight, which put additional pressure on crews.

A new technique for destroying the bridges was developed, and three or five aircraft would approach the target at an angle ranging from 28°–37° to the axis of the bridge. Using this bombing pattern, the likelihood of just one bomb hitting the target increased, but in order to destroy the bridge, this would need to be a large-calibre bomb. Interestingly, it was only the 19th Bomb Wing aircraft that had bomb racks for the heavy 454 kg and 908 kg bombs. Aircraft from the 98th and 307th Bomb Wings arrived from the United States with bomb racks for weapons with a calibre of up to 227 kg – even though both these groups came under Strategic Air Command and their principal armament was a nuclear bomb (considered more than ponderous!) The bombers were only fitted with new bomb racks in 1951.

As an experiment in March of 1951, a flight of B-29s bombed a bridge with 1,800 kg high-explosive bombs with a thin walled outer skin, and explosives designed to detonate in the air. The aim of this test was to establish whether the bridge could be destroyed using just a single blast wave, which would not require such accurate bombing. More than seven tonnes of TNT would significantly alter the landscape in the area around the blast – and once the dust settled, it was only recognisable by dint of the bridge, which used to stand in that location. The most reliable method for destroying bridges remained a flight of four bombers with 454 kg and 908 kg bombs.

In an attempt to improve bombing accuracy, the 19th Bomb Wing started to conduct experiments using guided bombs. The first of these was the 454 kg 'Raisin' bomb developed during the Second World War, and which was radio-controlled. If they were to use this bomb, a crew would need to drop it very close to the target and then the bomb-aimer would guide it onto the target by sight. The first tests in autumn 1950 were not successful, but with additional training, bombing accuracy improved – thus, of the final 50 'Raisins' dropped, 48 of them hit the target. Testing with these weapons was concluded at the end of December 1950, and by that time, the 19th Bomb Wing had dropped 489 bombs – destroying 15 bridges. On average, four bombs needed to be dropped on each of the bridges – the reason being that the 'Raisin' was not sufficiently powerful.

In December, the 19th Bomb Wing began testing the new radio-controlled 'Tarzon' bomb, which was the heaviest weapon then in service with the United States Air Force. The 'Tarzon' was designed by the Bell Aircraft Company and was based on the British 5,450 kg 'Tallboy' bomb. The guidance system consisted of an AN/ARW-38 aircraft transmitter and an AN/URV-2 receiver installed on the bomb itself, as well as stabilisers controlled by actuators. In order to make tracking the bomb via the Norden optical sight easier, a light beacon was fitted to the tail section of the weapon. The large dimensions of the 'Tarzon' – a length of 6.22 m and a diameter of 1.37 m – required significant changes in the design of the bomber's fuselage. The forward and aft bomb bays were joined into one single bomb bay by modifying the sections between them. The radar sight, which used to be housed in this location, was transferred to the nose section behind the wheel well for the nosewheel undercarriage, after first removing the firing position. The wing centre section box, which passed through the centre section, meant that the bomb could not be fully enclosed within the bomb bay – thus part of the bomb protruded externally, which meant that the shape of the bomb bay doors needed to be changed. Finally, the lattice-style glazing on the bomb-aimer compartment was replaced with non-interlocking glass borrowed from a B-50.

In all, four B-29s from the 19th Bomb Wing were modified to accommodate the 'earthquake' bomb. The enormous weight of the bomb made it exceptionally bulky – thus out of the 10 'Tarzon' bombs dropped during December, only one of them hit the target. A sortie flown on 13 January 1951 was a notable success, when a bomb-aimer in the 19th Bomb Wing (who dropped the bomb from an altitude of 5,200 m) planted it on the span of a railway bridge in Kanggye, which UN aircraft had been bombing without success since the previous autumn. In March, two bridges were destroyed and a third damaged using 'Tarzon' bombs. On 29 March, three B-29s with 'Tarzon' bombs on board took off from Okinawa to hit the bridge at Sinuiju. The wheel of fortune, however, had stalled right from the outset when one of the bombers was forced to return to base due to engine failure; then for some unknown reason, two engines on 19th Bomb Wing Commander Payne Jennings' aircraft failed simultaneously and the bomber crashed into the East China Sea. All efforts to locate and rescue the crew proved futile. The remaining B-29 flew on to Sinuiju, but its 'Tarzon' fell some distance from the bridge. The following day, B-29s from all three Bomb Wings loaded with conventional bombs attacked the bridge. This raid produced a much better outcome – and the road bridge at Chongsongjin, the span of a railway bridge at Manpojin and a pontoon crossing were destroyed.

On 14 April 1951, out of those designated for interdiction, Bomber Command crews destroyed 48 bridges and 27 marshalling yards. Moreover (according to American figures), between the middle of March and the middle of April, combat losses among Superfortresses – both from anti-aircraft artillery and MiGs – amounted to eight aircraft, whilst a further 25 were temporarily grounded owing to damage they sustained. On the orders of Stratemeyer, the strain on the bomb wings was reduced to 12 sorties per day, which were divided between raids on airfields, air support for ground troops and battlefield interdiction operations; the 19th Bomb Wing continued to test the 'Tarzon' bombs.

On 20 April, one of the B-29s encountered a technical problem in flight and the crew dropped the bomb into the sea. The 'Tarzon' exploded on contact with the water, even though its detonator had not been primed. After this incident, all the bombs in the weapons stores were withdrawn for design modifications – but even after these modifications, they were not used for long. In all, 30 'Tarzon' bombs were dropped in the course of the war – of which eight bombs destroyed six and damaged one bridge, 19 of them missed their targets and three failed to explode.

At the end of May, the principal B-29 force was redirected onto marshalling yards and supply bases behind enemy lines. Raids on targets close to the Yalu River were envisaged, and the Superfortresses would come up against the MiGs once again.

✦

On 31 May, three flights of MiGs – at an altitude of 11,000 m – were heading for Anju when they sighted a pair of B-29s escorted by a quartet of Sabres. The Commander of the group – Lieutenant-Colonel Dzyubenko – attacked the first flight in a descending turn to port. Along with his wingman, Major Gulyayev, he fired at the right-hand Superfortress from a distance of 1,000–600 m. The second pair in his flight – flown by Senior Lieutenants Bobonin and Alikhnovich – attacked the bomber in the same way. Breaking off the attack, Dzyubenko sighted a pair of F-86s, which he attacked head-on and then got on their tail. The Sabres turned – evading the attack – and headed out to sea. His wingmen attempted to engage the other pair of F-86s, which had attacked the second flight in the bomb wing; however, they would not engage the MiGs – then Major Gulyayev, along with Senior Lieutenant Bobonin, attacked the B-29s again. Bobonin's wingman, Alekhnovich, was attacked by two F-86s during this attack and withdrew after his MiG sustained seven bullet holes.

Other flights of MiGs also attempted to attack the Superfortresses, but were forced to engage the Sabres in combat. The pilots were not able to see the outcome of their attacks on the bombers – and they were not successful in their attacks on the MiGs either. During the course of one of the attacks on the B-29s, Senior Lieutenant Semenenko jumped ahead of his leader, Major Perevozchikov – and after breaking off the attack in a combat turn, he lost sight of him. Major Perevozchikov was never seen again. As Lieutenant-Technician Nikolai Chepelev from the 176th Guards Fighter Air Regiment recalled – after travelling out to the location of the battle – the commission concluded that " ... he had bailed out and his parachute had come loose and fallen away from him and broke. Then they revealed that the parachute was not his, since the harness had not been adjusted ... "

On 31 May (according to American figures), 12 MiGs attacked two B-29s from the 19th Bomb Wing – escorted by a flight of F-86s – close to Anju, but the attack was not successful. One of the MiGs was shot down by a B-29, and a further two by Sabre pilots. This battle was noteworthy by dint of the fact that pilots from the Air Force Scientific-Research Centre participated for the first and last time. The reason for their coming to Korea is not given in 64th Fighter Air Corps documents, but veterans of the corps recalled that the test pilots were there to 'force a Sabre to land on one of our own airfields'. However, for all the pilots' excellent individual training, their collective formation flying and observation was unsatisfactory. After sustaining a casualty in an air battle (in which the enemy was at a numerical disadvantage) and subsequently losing Lieutenant-Colonel Dzyubenko in a MiG-15 as a result of a landing accident, the group returned to the Soviet Union. The following day (1 July) at 0923-0924, the corps' radar 25 km south-west of the city of Huichon picked up a group of bombers escorted by Sabres heading towards Anju from Taechon County at an altitude of 6,000–10,000 m.

Five groups of MiG-15s were scrambled from the 324th and 303rd Fighter Air Divisions to intercept the B-29s. Pilots from the 303rd Fighter Air Division first encountered the Superfortresses whilst they were still based in the Soviet Union, when on 26 December 1950 a pair of MiGs – flown by Captain S.A. Bakhayev and Senior Lieutenant N. Kotov from the 532rd Fighter Air Regiment, who had taken off from the Vozdvizhenka airfield on the coast – intercepted and shot down an RB-29.

The division, which comprised the 17th and 18th Guards (as well as the 523rd Fighter Air) Regiments, had arrived to augment Kozhedub's division in April 1951. After a month of intensive training, they began to fly combat sorties. To begin with, this only applied to the 18th Guards Fighter Air Regiment, but after the new airfield at Myaogou came on stream from the middle of June, this applied to the entire complement. Eight MiGs from the 176th Guards Fighter Air Regiment were scrambled at 0927 under the command of

Contrasting highlights and soft shadows on the aircraft and rugged mountainous Korean terrain blend to near-camouflage proportions as a B-29 Superfortress of the US Far East Air Force's Japan-based 98th Bomb Group heads for its targets, June 1951. (Courtesy of the US National Archives)

Native Okinawan labourers pause at their work to watch a US Far East Air Force B-29 Superfortress of the 19th Bomb Group come in for a landing, June 1951 (Courtesy of the US National Archives)

Colonel S.F. Vishnyakov. Following his group, six MiGs from this same regiment took off under the command of Captain G.I. Ges. One minute later, 10 MiG-15s from the 18th Guards Fighter Air Regiment – under the command of Captain P.N. Antonov – also received the order to scramble. A further three minutes later, Captain S.M. Kramorenko led a flight from the 176th Guards Fighter Air Regiment into the skies to intercept the bombers – and finally, at 0950, a group of nine MiGs from the 18th Guards Fighter Air Regiment (under the command of Lieutenant-Colonel A.P. Smorchkov) took to the air.

From the combat reports of the 324th Fighter Air Division:

Captain Stepan Bakhayev of the 523rd Fighter Air Regiment (11 personal victories and three group victories in the Second World War, and 11 victories in Korea). On 26 December 1950 – flying in a pair with Senior Lieutenant Kotov – he intercepted and shot down a reconnaissance RB-29. (This photograph was provided by I. Seidov)

Captain Antonov's group encountered four enemy bombers, which were yet to reach the KIDZYO (Kusong) region at an altitude of 7,000 m on a heading of 120°…

Captain Antonov – on hearing news of the bombers over the radio – put his group into a 90° turn and at that moment, he encountered a pair of F-86s… this pair flew towards our fighters head-on and subsequently tried to get behind Antonov's group. Captain Antonov made a climbing turn to port and ended up above the enemy, and the F-86s discontinued the air battle and departed to the south. At the same time, Antonov noticed four enemy bombers that were also heading south; one of these, the trailing aircraft on the port side, was on fire and began to break up in mid-air. Captain Antonov then received a report over the radio from his wingman, Senior Lieutenant Ageyev, that he was being attacked by an enemy aircraft. He made a climbing turn to port – after which he saw three aircraft that he did not recognise.

As he approached this group, the aircraft scattered in all directions and Captain Antonov lost sight of them. Snr Lieutenant Ageyev reported that the engine on his aircraft was beginning to run rough after the attack and he departed back to his airfield, where he fortunately made an emergency landing after his engine failed. He was unhurt, but the aircraft had sustained 21 bullet holes.

As they became visual with the bombers, the second pair in the guard's flight – led by Captain Kornienko, with Snr Lieutenant Stelmakh and his wingman, Captain Muravyev – attacked them independently and shot down one B-29 that crashed in flames close to Aidzyu (Wonju) after breaking up in mid-air. The loss

A tropical moon bathes a powerful instrument of war in the soft light, as this US Far East Air Force B-29 Superfortress of the 19th Bomb Wing – readied for night combat operations – awaits the guiding hands of its crew, June 1951. (Courtesy of the US National Archives)

Senior Lieutenant Yevgeniy Stelmakh of the 18th Guards Fighter Air Regiment (two victories in Korea). (This photograph was provided by I. Seidov)

The Deputy Commander of the 18th Guards Fighter Air Regiment, Aleksandr Smorchkov (four victories in the Second World War and 12 victories in Korea).

of the bomber was confirmed by battle crews, as well as operational staff at ACP No. 1. Before commencing his attack, Snr Lieutenant Stelmakh declared over the radio that he was "heading in to attack the bombers," but after his attack he said that he had " ... used all his ammunition and that the aircraft control surfaces were damaged" and he was returning to base. However, Snr Lieutenant Stelmakh never landed back at base. It is assumed that he made an emergency landing somewhere in North Korean territory. Search parties were organised to look for Snr Lieutenant Stelmakh.[47]

Other groups of MiGs did not come into contact with bombers at all. Documents from the 303rd Fighter Air Division do, however, contain a record stating that Senior Lieutenant Yevgeniy Mikhaylovich Stelmakh shot down two B-29s on 1 June, but that he himself was shot down by defensive fire from the bombers themselves and was killed on the ground in a gun battle with Chinese infantry. However, the Deputy Commander of the 18th Guards Fighter Air Regiment – Aleksandr Pavlovich Smorchkov – described the course of events slightly differently:

> Zhenya Stelmakh was one of the pilots in my regiment ... he was a footballer ... He was scrambled as part of Antonov's squadron ... it was very misty. Imagine, 12 guys are in the air but fail to notice a B-29 escorted by eight Sabres. But Stelmakh when we once drank cognac, argued ... say I will show you how to shoot down enemy planes ... we were just entering the fray at that stage ... we were not fully warmed up yet ... and he could see this "fortress" even in all the fog–it was below him–and he doesn't say anything to anybody but just dives straight in. He shoots this aircraft down and it turns out to be a North Korean Air Defence research aircraft. This aircraft allegedly had the capability to send information direct to Washington using Morse code. It had a colonel from US Army Headquarters on board. He bailed out and was immediately captured ... and was sent to Moscow for questioning ...
>
> Stelmakh was later named a Hero ... posthumously. He shot down a "fortress" and was in turn shot down by Sabres and there were eight of them and one of him. After he ejected, Chinese conscripts came running up to him and he took them for American partisans; he killed two or three of them and then shot himself. That was out first loss.

---

47 Fund of the 324th IAD, inventory 152706ss, file. 7, l.l. pp.160-161.

Over the course of the subsequent (almost) five months, sorties against the 'Fortresses' were rare and were not successful for pilots of the 64th Fighter Air Corps. Moreover, an attempt to intercept B-29s on 26 June ended in tragedy ...

On that day, Superfortresses attacked an airfield close to Sinuiju, and 24 Thunderjets – in the shape of 16 aircraft from the 182nd Fighter Squadron, 136th Fighter Wing and eight from the 27th Fighter Wing – provided a fighter escort. The F-84s, which took off from the Itazuke airbase in Japan, rendezvoused with their 'charges' close to Choodo Island and headed north in a single formation over the Gulf of Korea – crossing the coast at a point 75 km south of the Yalu River estuary. At that moment, the pilot of one of the Thunderjets reported technical problems with his engine and, escorted by his wingman, he set off for the area close to Sinmi-do Island. It was there that he ejected – and a few minutes later, he was taken on board an SA-16 hydroplane rescue aircraft. The remaining 22 fighters continued onwards at an altitude of 7,650 m.

A group of three squadrons from the 17th Fighter Air Regiment (consisting of eight, six and six aircraft) were scrambled to intercept the bombers. Our pilots though were not able to disperse the bombers, as the B-29s had crossed the coast late and the Sabres were effective in forming a 'shield' in the air above the Yalu River. The group of B-29s bombed the airfield's runway from an altitude of around 7,150 m almost uninterrupted – and according to the eyewitness accounts provided by the Thunderjet pilots, they almost completely destroyed it.

The Superfortresses turned for home and four minutes later (at around 1435), an F-84 pilot – 1st Lieutenant Joseph C. Chapman – reported a MiG attack from above and behind. 'Kings' – one of the flights of F-84s – turned on the enemy and dispersed the attack. Only one pair of our fighters, led by Senior Lieutenant Fokyn, managed to break through to the bombers. Approaching from a distance of 1,000 m, he gave the rearmost bomber two long burst of fire – after which he was attacked by a pair of escort fighters (shaking them off in a combat turn). At that moment, his wingman – Senior Lieutenant Agranovich, who was covering for his leader – himself came under attack from the Thunderjets. Evidently, the Americans held two principal trump cards which decided the outcome of the battle: a height advantage, together with the element of surprise. As leader of the 'Kings' flight, 182nd Fighter-Bomber Squadron, 1st Lieutenant Arthur E. Oligher remembers:

> When Joe [Lieutenant Chapman] reported the MiGs he added that they were directly below me. I turned the aircraft onto its back and saw a MiG attacking the bombers from their six o'clock position. As soon as he began to climb I opened fire on him, and continued to fire the entire time that he was moving upwards. He performed a half roll and pulled out into a descending loop. I dived after him. After firing about 1,200 rounds I noticed that the MiG's undercarriage had dropped

This 20th Air Force B-29 Superfortress of the 19th Bomb Group – named 'Rock Happy' after a favourite Okinawa-based airmen expression – is a seasoned veteran of more than 75 combat missions over Korea, June 1951. (Courtesy of the US National Archives)

Two 98th Bombardment Wing B-29 Superfortresses of the US Far East Air Force stand out sharply against a heavy undercast somewhere in Korea, 12 June 1951. (Courtesy of the US National Archives)

American sources state that on 1 June, the MiGs waited for the fighter escort to depart and attacked four B-29s from the 98th Bomb Wing. One bomber was shot down and a further two were seriously damaged; two of the gunners were credited with shooting down one MiG-15 each. A further two MiGs were shot down in a battle with an F-86 that had come to the aid of the bombers.

One of the first 20th Air Force medium bombers to start 'delivering the goods' in the Korean conflict was the 'Double Whammy' – a B-29 Superfortress of the 19th Bomb Group. The 'Double Whammy' had flown 99 combat missions since making her first aerial attack on the enemy on 28 June 1950. One MiG-15 jet had been shot down in flames by the .50 calibre machine guns of the 'Double Whammy' while on a bombing mission over North Korea, June 1951. (Courtesy of the US National Archives)

One of the 20th Air Force B-29 'Superforts' which has proved itself highly durable in combat is the 'South Sea Sinner' of the 19th Bomb Group. Hit six times by enemy flak in 94 combat missions over Korea, the 'Sinner' continues to deliver heavy attacks against the enemy; June 1951. (Courtesy of the US National Archives)

The MiG-15bis, serial No. 121082 (the 82nd aircraft in the 21st production run at Factory No. 1 in Kuibyshev) at the State Air Force Scientific-Research Centre of the Order of the Red Banner. The 21st, 22nd and 23rd production series aircraft, which bore only Korean markings (with red painted noses and tailfins above the stabilisers), formed the basis of the aircraft fleet for the 303rd Fighter Air Division in Korea.

The MiG-15bis, serial No. 122035 (the 35th aircraft in the 22nd production series at Factory No. 1 in Kuibyshev) at the State Air Force Scientific-Research Centre of the Order of the Red Banner. The 21st, 22nd and 23rd production series aircraft, which bore only Korean markings (with red painted noses and tailfins above the stabilisers), formed the basis of the aircraft fleet for the 303rd Fighter Air Division in Korea.

down from under his wings and at an altitude of around 6,000 feet [1,830 m] he pulled out to straight and level flight. I pursued him firing long bursts of fire and I could see my rounds were hitting the target. I fired from an angle of 15° to the horizontal [which corresponds to an aspect angle of 1/4] and what is more I could see the MiG pilot in the cockpit. The MiG began to turn, rolling to port and we completed three rolls, cockpit to cockpit. He then performed a high G slow roll and fell into a "spin." Andy [Captain Underwood] gave him a burst of fire from an angle of 15° and I continued to fire as he was spinning and followed him all the way to the ground. He exploded on impact and the explosion blew the tail section of the MiG a good 50 feet [15 m] away from the impact point.[48]

According to official documents, Lieutenant Oligher shared this victory with his squadron colleague, Harry L. Underwood, who recalled that: 'I engaged the MiG in combat and noticed that his starboard undercarriage leg was down. I opened fire and saw that I had scored direct hits around the cockpit and along the entire length of the fuselage, and I then followed him all the way down until the moment he hit the ground'.[49] Senior Lieutenant Agranovich's burning MiG crashed 17 km south-west of Wonju. The pilot was killed.

As the account of the battle – submitted by the Commander of the 17th Regiment to divisional headquarters – stated: ' ...

---

48 Dooner, William R., 'Thunderjets over Korea' *Air Classic Special*, Vol. 4, (1985).
49 Dooner, 'Thunderjets over Korea'.

A B-29 Superfortress of the 20th Air Force's 19th Bomb Group displays proof that it has lived up to the fighting motto of its unit: *'Inalis Vincimus'* ('Conquer with Wings'). While flying 68 combat missions against the enemy, the deadly .50 calibre machine guns of this medium bomber have blasted three enemy MiG-15 jets out of the skies over North Korea; June 1951. (Courtesy of the US National Archives)

Snr Lieutenant Fokin's gun camera film provisionally confirms that one B-29 type aircraft was shot down. Snr Lieutenant Fokin fired on the B-29 from a distance of 860 m and an aspect angle of 0/4 and the film shows six rounds hitting their target'.[50] Three days later (on 30 June), following an analysis of the films, the head of the Air Combat Service, 303rd Division wrote the following on a piece of paper he appended to the account of the battle: ' ... The recordings from the gun cameras enclosed in the description do not confirm anything ... '[51]

Foreign publications state that one B-29 was damaged on 26 June 1951 as a result of this one attack by MiGs. The pilot was forced to shut down one engine, but he did not break formation and brought the aircraft safely back to base. The MiGs of the 64th Fighter Air Corps would exact their revenge on the Superfortresses just four months later ...

※

Aside from our units, Chinese (and later, North Korean) pilots played their part in countering B-29 raids. A.P. Smorchkov remembers one of the interceptions carried out by Chinese pilots: "A Chinese pilot made a bumpy landing on our airfield. He jumped out of the cockpit – pale, his hands shaking – shouting: 'The film, the film!' We unloaded his gun camera and ran the film ... and there was the Fortress so close you could count the rivets!" Unfortunately, the date of this incident is not known.

Another encounter with Chinese pilots took place on 9 July 1951 when six MiG-15s from the People's Liberation Army Air Force took off for the Sinuiju region to intercept six Superfortresses from the 19th Bomb Wing. In order to provide cover for Allied aircraft, 10 fighters were scrambled from the 17th Fighter Air Regiment, led by Major Maslennikov. On approach to Anju, our pilots encountered three groups of Sabres totalling up to 20 aircraft. According to the account of the battle ' ... Major Maslennikov's group engaged all groups of enemy fighter aircraft in combat. During the course of the battle Major Maslennikov sighted two flights of B-29 bombers flying over the sea and heading further out, which were attacked by a flight of Chinese fighters. Major Maslennikov did not see the outcome of a battle fought against superior enemy forces'.[52]

Another witness to this battle was Squadron Commander Major Viktor Pavlovich Popov of the 523rd Fighter Air Regiment:

> ... I committed the Chinese pilots to battle, and flew with them four times at 6,000, 8,000, 10,000 and 12,000 m and committed them to battle as a regiment. They did not understand Russian at all and I didn't have the first clue in Chinese. I had to relay my order to the ground and a Chinese interpreter would translate it and relay it to their pilots.
>
> I landed at the end of one of these sorties and noticed that the Chinese were running around excitedly for some reason, making a fuss. It turned out that their Deputy Squadron Commander, while we were on our way back, had sighted a B-29 out over the sea. He crossed the coast and sped towards it. His speed as he approached the Fortress was very high. He deployed the airbrake, but it had no effect; he lowered the undercarriage, but this had no effect either. He deployed the flaps, he shot the B-29 down, but lost speed and the escort fighters shot him down ... The Chinese were celebrating their victory, and it was of no consequence to them that the pilot was killed. They really were making a fuss at that time ...

On the basis of the outcome of the battle, Sergeant Gus C. Opfer – a B-29 gunner serving with No. 30 Squadron – was credited with two MiG kills; and Captain Milton E. Nelson – an F-86 pilot serving with 335 Squadron – was credited with one MiG kill. All the Superfortresses were able to return to base.

There was something of an odd overhang to the events of 9 July. A Chinese MiG-15 crashed in shallow water close to the Yalu River estuary, which afforded the enemy a long-awaited opportunity to investigate the 'Korean mystery'. The United States Air Force, the US Navy and the US Army – as well as South Korean Army units and ships from Britain's Royal Navy – were involved in the operation to recover the MiG. The wreckage was successfully loaded onto a Royal Navy launch and was sent to the United States to Wright-Patterson (now Elgin) air force base for examination. The MiG, however, had

---

50 Fund of the 303rd IAD, inventory 539825s, file. 4, p.73.
51 Fund of the 303rd IAD, inventory 539825s, file. 4, p.69.
52 Fund of the 303rd IAD, inventory 539825s, file. 4, p.111.

A Boeing B-29 flying over Korea. (Courtesy of the US National Archives)

The 'Snugglebunny' – a famous B-29 Superfortress of the Japan-based 98th Bombardment Wing – is coming home. After 65 missions in the Second World War, the big US Far East Air Force's B-29 flew an additional 75 combat missions over North Korea and now returns to the United States for depot overhaul. Her last airplane commander, Captain Richard Oster, says: "The old gal has 140 missions and a MiG fighter to her credit – and almost 3,000 hours' flying time, most of which is time in combat. She's patched all over where she's been hit with flak and could use new bomb bay doors. I hate to see her go, but she needs the overhaul." Radio operator Sergeant James A. Stephens remarked: "They should send the old gal on a tour of the States and let the folks back home see her. They don't get to see one very often that has a record like hers." July 1951. (Courtesy of the US National Archives)

This huge B-29 Superfortress of the US Far East Air Force's 407th Bomb Wing lifts gracefully from the runway of the Okinawa base with the distinction of beginning the second year of bombing targets in Korea. Okinawan labourers pause to watch the big bomber as it takes to the sky, August 1951. (Courtesy of the US National Archives)

been severely damaged both in battle and in the crash itself – and American specialists were not able to retrieve anything of value from the wreckage. Unfortunately, we do not have any more detailed information concerning the results of battles in which Chinese or Korean units took on B-29s, and there are no B-29s featured in the short list of victories attained by the Sino-Korean Combined Air Army.

The Targets are the Airfields

In spring 1951, the front line stabilised at the Han River (north of Seoul). From that time onwards up until the end of the war, both sides would embark on countless large and small-scale offensives and counter-offensives. The flame of war was still consuming thousands and thousands of lives, but the dividing line separating the Korean Peninsula remained the 38th parallel. The principal force, which made it possible for UN troops to hold back a numerically superior Sino-Korean Army, was the air power provided by the US Far East Air Force. Small groups of storm-troopers, who knew the People's Liberation Army and Korean People's Army logistics areas like the back of their hands, would notice any change in the situation straight away and would attack without affording the enemy an opportunity to hide. There was no respite even for a moment from the threat of air raids on North Korea's roads either, and this only abated somewhat at night. During the day, it was impossible for even a single lorry to navigate the main roads, let alone a mechanised column. The Sino-Korean forces, who were practically cut off from their logistics units, experienced very acute shortages of even the most basic needs on the front line: fresh reinforcements, weapons, ammunition, provisions and medicines ... The 64th Fighter Air Corps was in no position to protect all of North Korea's communications from the air – and the following objective reasons could serve as an explanation:

- The complicated situation in the air – resulting from the enemy's considerable numerical superiority
- The need to protect highly-valued assets along a broad front using only our own forces without any support from Chinese or Korean aviation
- The lack of combat personnel in the corps that are sufficiently highly trained, which is expressed on average as follows: up until October 1951, there were 160 combat-capable MiG-15 crews and 20 La-11 crews, but from the beginning of October, this was at 100 combat-capable MiG-15 crews and 20 La-11 crews
- The very limited nature of the network of airfields in the combat zone, which prohibited any possibility of relocating airfields forward of or along the front line completely[53]

This last point (the lack of airfields in North Korean territory) really aggrieved Sino-Korean Army (SKA) Command. Aside from the MiG-15s, Yak-9s; La-9s; Il-10 ground attack aircraft and Tu-2 bombers were in service with the SKA. They could all (theoretically) have an impact on the battlefield and on communications behind UN lines. However, they needed to be escorted, and the MiGs operating from bases in Manchuria were not able to reach the front line – thus forward bases in North Korea would have helped in gaining air supremacy over the country's entire territory, which in the end, would have contributed to a fundamental breakthrough in the course of the ground war.

The Koreans tried to build one of their first airfields at Uiju on the southern bank of the Yalu River (very close to the Antung airfield complex). These attempts, however, were not successful, as James Johnson wrote:

> ... At the end of the 1950s the Russians and Chinese received reinforcements in the form of the first North Korean MiG-15 units to be based at Uiju, not far from the border with Manchuria.
>
> It was however short-sighted to locate the airfield at Uiju from the very beginning, since the Americans, who were constantly employing offensive tactics, and who were presented with the first opportunity to attack an enemy "jet" base, bombed the airfield day and night ... after about six weeks of pounding, North Korean

Staff Sergeant Jerry Webb – tail gunner on this US Air Force B-29 Superfortress of the US Far East Air Force's 307th Bombardment Wing – points out a shell hole which came uncomfortably close to his head while on a bombing attack over North Korea on 23 October 1951. Swarms of MiG-15 jet fighters pounced on formations of medium bombers, and a vicious air battle resulted. Sergeant Webb shot down one of the attacking planes, while a second gunner on this Superfortress downed another MiG and scored one as probable. The shell knocked out rudder controls, and another hit damaged the hydraulic system, but a safe landing was made at this Okinawa base. (Courtesy of the US National Archives)

aviation retreated to Manchuria, from where it would return only after the ceasefire had been signed ... [54]

By the end of September 1951, 'MiG Alley' had become a very dangerous place for any UN bomber aircraft if they were not provided with the requisite escort of F-86 fighters. There was, however, a catastrophic shortage of Sabres – thus the Commander of the 4th Fighter Wing, Colonel Herman A. Schmid, had just 44 Sabres at his disposal in June – and these were, for the most part, only on paper. In reality, the chronic shortage of spare parts and the difficulties in repairing damaged aircraft – as well as the scant replacement of the required technology – meant that, as Schmid put it: 'It took "maintenance miracles" to keep half of his Sabres in the air'.[55]

---

53 Fund of the 64th IAD, inventory 174045ss, file. 51, pp.10-11.
54 Johnson, James E., *Full circle. The Story of Air Fighting* (London: Chatto & Windus, 1964), pp. 271-272.
55 Dorr, Lake, Thompson, *Korean War Aces*, p. 28.

The commanders of the 5th Air Army bombarded Washington with requests to send a second wing of F-86 Sabres to Korea, or at least replace one of the existing wings equipped with Shooting Stars with Sabres. General Frank E. Everest, who became Commander 5th Air Army on 1 June 1951, was no exception. When his request for F-86s was again turned down in September, he cancelled all bomber sorties to the Yalu River – redirecting them to regions from Ch'ongch'on to Pyongyang. The North Koreans were afforded an opportunity to return to building their airfields.

At the beginning of October, reconnaissance aircraft (amongst others) began to bring back images showing 18 airfields that were nearing completion. Three of them had the potential to become the most up-to-date airfields and were, therefore, capable of supporting jet technology; these were Namsi, Taechon and Saamchan. The MiGs based at any of these airfields would be capable of escorting Il-10 ground attack aircraft, with the potential to attack UN assets behind enemy lines. If they were based at these airfields, the MiGs would have had the potential to expand their own 'Alley' to an area covering the entire territory of North Korea. The airfield complex immediately became a first-priority target for the US Far East Air Force.

For fighter-bomber pilots, the task of destroying the airfields would prove very difficult. A concentrated raid by a large strike force would be required to ensure that they were indeed taken out of action, and there were not enough Sabres to provide a fighter escort. The only force capable of destroying airfields remained the B-29; in terms of their firepower, the Superfortresses conceded nothing to a wing of ground attack aircraft. In the interests of safety, a decision was taken to bomb the airfields using relatively small groups of B-29s at night – utilising the SHORAN radio navigation system.[56] When the system is used for its intended purpose – that is to say, in pinpointing an aircraft's position – the onboard equipment receives a signal from two radio stations and calculates how far the aircraft is from each of them. The coordinates of the stations themselves were known and were pre-programmed into the bomber's navigational computer – therefore the bomber's position could be calculated accurately at any point in time. The feedback objective was solved when bombing using SHORAN in as much as each target could be plotted on a map by dissecting two arcs centred on the locations of the radio stations so that as it flew towards the target, the bomber would 'lock on' to one of the arcs (the main one) and follow it until it reached the point at which this arc dissected the auxiliary arc. The pilot would then navigate using the signal that the onboard equipment was giving him, which indicated how far the bomber was from the primary radio station. Apart from that, the armament and navigation system would also constantly calculate the distance from the auxiliary radio

---

56 SHOrt RAnge Navigation system.

Fire crews of the 67th Tactical Reconnaissance Wing spray the burning engine of a US Air Force B-29 Superfortress with chemical foam after the medium bomber tangled with enemy jet aircraft and anti-aircraft guns over North Korea. The daring aircrew brought this limping Superfortress back to this advanced air base with the use of flaps or rudder controls, and with two engines cut; none of the crew was injured, October 1951. (Courtesy of the US National Archives)

station – and as soon as this was equal to what had been fed into it, the system would start the bombing sequence automatically; the coordinates of the designated targets would be taken from images recorded by reconnaissance squadrons. The SHORAN system required crews to possess specific skills, and when it was used correctly, would produce excellent results at any time of the day or night – and in any weather. During the first two sorties flown by B-29s from the 307th Bomb Wing against Saamchan airfield on 13 and 14 October however, not one of the bombs fell anywhere near the target. The issue with the airfields needed to be solved immediately. With no alternative, Far East Air Force Headquarters decided on large-scale daylight raids. These raids were to put 'maximum pressure' on the jet fighter and ground attack aircraft providing an escort for the B-29s in the form of a defensive 'shield'.

The first of these sorties took place on 18 October. Bombers from the 98th Bomb Wing, which had been assigned the task of bombing Taechon airfield, were not able to rendezvous with their escort fighters and so bombed an auxiliary target. Meanwhile, the 19th Bomb Wing bombed Saamchan – the southernmost of the three airfields. On 21 October, the 98th Bomb Wing were again sent to bomb Taechon – and again they bombed an auxiliary target after missing their escort fighters. The task of destroying Taechon was transferred to the 19th Bomb Wing. Their sortie – which took place the following day on Monday, 22 October – heralded the most frightening week in the history of Bomber Command … This was a mass raid attacking several targets at once. According to our archive documents, at a little after 1500, 12 B-29s appeared over the Soviet zone of responsibility, as well as more than 50 [this ranges from 64 to 106 according to various sources] fighters of varying types transiting towards Anju in five groups. As

Dwarfed by the tail of their US Air Force B-29 Superfortress, pilot 1st Lieutenant George A. Jordan (left) points out the damage done to his plane by a flak battery to his bombardier and navigator, Captain Joseph H. Burke (centre) and 1st Lieutenant Sherman F. Butler. All assigned to the veteran US Far East Air Force's 19th Bomb Group on Okinawa, the officers discovered the six-inch hole during their post-mission inspection after a crew member had reported 'the Reds are using slingshots', October 1951. (Courtesy of the US National Archives)

the Sabres patrolled the Taechon–Pakchon–Anju region, the F-84s bombed the railway stations in the area around Sukchon–Anju–Sukchon. Fighters from the 303rd Fighter Air Division began to be scrambled at 1503 – and these comprised of 20 MiG-15s from the 17th Fighter Air Regiment, 14 MiG-15s from the 18th Guards Fighter Air Regiment and 20 MiG-15s from the 523rd Fighter Air Regiment. The pilots' task was to counter the raid by enemy ground attack and bomber aircraft; the target for the Superfortresses remained unclear at that time.

The groups from the 17th and 523rd Fighter Air Regiments soon engaged the ground attack aircraft in combat. The 18th Guards Fighter Air Regiment group climbed to an altitude of 10,000 m and set course for the B-29s, as A.P. Smorchkov remembers:

> The sorties against the B-29s were the most difficult. One of these remains for me the most memorable ... We were scrambled in inclement weather – and we were not exactly 'top-ranking' pilots. If there was a break in the clouds, we would go for it ... and it took us a very long time to climb to 10,000 m. We were then given an order to turn onto a heading, as apparently this was where the 'heavy bombers' were. We had to lose 5,000 m in altitude and descend beneath the cloud. How were we supposed to get through dense cloud cover? I could do it on my own, but we were flying as an entire regiment. You can't ask the ground controllers of course, as they would just say "Work it out for yourselves!" and would then cut in again.
>
> I looked round ... the entire regiment was behind me and the formation was holding up well. "We are going to dive," I told them. "Be very careful; don't 'hang around' in the cloud!" I dive down, and I'm scared to move. I look round at the wingman ... he is right there beside me, but I can't see anything else at all. My heart was heavy – what if there was a collision? Naturally as a commander, I bear a moral responsibility for all my pilots – and a legal responsibility as well. If just one of the pairs were to collide, I would definitely be held responsible!
>
> Nevertheless, we got through the cloud. It became clearer and clearer outside the cockpit and at last there were the 'Fortresses' beneath the cloud and 3,000 m in front of us. According to the Command Post's calculations, there were 12 bombers – and I counted them again myself – and up to 120 escort fighters. How was my regiment? I looked round, and love a duck – all my clever cookies were with me – and immediately I began to relax. I said to the guys: "Let's hit the 'big guys', but don't forget about the 'small fry'!" and we went on the attack. They reached straight for their boost, but their top speed was 500 km/h while ours was 1,100 km/h. In a similar way, they turned out to be cowards when it came to protecting the bombers. If you bore down on them with a pair or a quartet of MiGs, they would scatter in all directions – opening the way to the 'Fortresses'. That's good, I thought to myself; these guys are helping us.
>
> I gave them one burst of fire. I watched ... they were still some way away; the tracer passed underneath them. I quickly closed on them and my shells remained straight and level. I hit the starboard 'box' – the two engines – the engine interface and the fuel pump there in the wing, and the Fortress went down ... in a ball of red flame ... and then the 'parachutists' spilled out. I saw six parachutes. I had no time to look out for the rest of them, as the fighter escort had come to their senses.
>
> I always taught my guys that they should use all their ammunition on an aircraft like the B-29. If each one of us were to use their ammunition, and we all hit the target, then that's great. On this occasion, I had some ammunition left after hitting a Fortress and I shot down an F-84; then I said to Volodya Voistinnykh, my wingman: "Go on ahead, I will cover you." By that time though, the battle had already come to an end.

We received the order from the ground: "It's all over! Everybody land."

According to documents, Lieutenant-Colonel Smorchkov's flight attacked the trailing quartet of Superfortresses. A.P. Smorchkov opened fire from a distance of 900 m and only broke off his attack at a distance of 300 m. His wingman – Lieutenant Voistinnykh – fired on the trailing B-29 from a long way out, but without success. The second pair in our flight, Guards Senior Lieutenants Stepanov and Shabanov, attacked the second pair of B-29s in this flight. As they had fired at them, the bombers ' ... maintained their place in the formation, but crews noticed the shells exploding along the B-29's fuselage and along their flank ... '[57]

Two MiGs from the 18th Guards Fighter Air Regiment were slightly damaged (supposedly by an F-84 that was escorting the Superfortresses).

After this battle, the Commander of the 303rd Fighter Air Division – Kumanichkin – stated in the order he issued that:

On 22.10.51 fourteen crews from the 18th Guards Fighter Air Regiment, acting as fighter cover for troops in the Chongju region broke through cloud and confronted 12 B-29s at an altitude of 5,000 m with 12 F-84s and eight Gloster Meteor F.4s providing close air support. The lead group under the command of the Deputy Commander of the regiment Lieutenant-Colonel Smorchkov decided to contain the escort fighters and attack the bombers.

Five F-84s were shot down as well as one B-29 in this battle, and a further two B-29s were damaged. Lieutenant-Colonel Smorchkov personally shot down one B-29 and one F-84 in this battle.[58]

Subsequently, information came to light that the B-29s damaged by Senior Lieutenants Stepanov and Shabanov crashed into the sea – and they were credited with having shot them down. At the same time, the number of F-84s shot down by pilots of the 18th Guards Fighter Air Regiment was reduced to three. American sources stated that nine B-29s from the 19th Bomb Wing took part in the raid on the airfield and 24 Thunderjets provided close air support – and they only acknowledged the loss of one bomber in this battle.

'Black Tuesday'

If there really was an element of chance to the encounter between the MiGs and B-29s on the Monday, then on Tuesday the crews in the Superfortresses were anticipating a fierce, well-planned reception. All the veterans of the Korean War know about the battles that took place on 23 October 1951 and historians around the world make reference to it. We are

---
57 Fund of the 303rd IAD, inventory 152694s, file. 1, p.225.
58 Fund of the 303rd IAD, inventory 152694s, file. 1, p.225.

Senior Lieutenant Vasiliy Stepanov of the 18th Guards Fighter Air Regiment (five victories in Korea). (This photograph was provided by I. Seidov)

going to pay close attention to the events of this day, since they marked a milestone in the history of the war: 'Black Tuesday'.

From the 'Description of the Air Battle':

... Between 0810-0830 [0910-0930] our radar detected eight groups of enemy aircraft at altitudes ranging from 6,500–8,000 m on the edge of the Kaishu–Kinsen–Isen–Iotoku and comprising of between eight and 32 aircraft per group, with a total of up to 200 F-86, F-84, F-80 and Gloster Meteor F.4 fighters and two groups of bombers comprising 10 to 12 B-29s each that had carried out a concentrated bombing and ground attack raid between 0835-0904 [0935-1004] on the following regions: the ground attack aircraft had attacked Ansu, Pakchon, Taesu from an altitude of 4,000 m right down to low level, while the bombers had attacked Nansi airfield from an altitude of 7,000 m (the bombs fell some 2 km south of the airfield, but the airfield itself was undamaged).

A fighter "shield" consisting of 40 F-86s that patrolled the Goseong–Sonchon area at altitudes between 8,000–10,000 m as well as a close air support patrol consisting of up to eighty fighters at altitudes between 6,000–9,000 m provided protection for the ground-attack and bomber aircraft. In all up to 200 fighters and 22 bombers participated in the raid.

The Enemy's Plan:

The aim was to destroy the Sino–Korean Army supply lines and take the airfields at Taechon and Nansi out of action and to carry out a concentrated bombing and ground attack raid on the bridges, crossings, railway lines, as well as the airfields that were under construction. This raid would make use of a large number of ground attack and bomber aircraft operating under a powerful fighter escort.

The Commander's Decision:

Having assessed the situation the Commander of the 64th Fighter Air Corps decided: to counter the concentrated raid by bombers and ground attack aircraft with two of the Corps' divisions by engaging them consistently in combat.

In accordance with this decision the 303rd Fighter Air Division consisting of the 17th, 18th and 523rd Fighter Air Regiments (58 MiG-15s in total) made up the first echelon and were tasked with striking the principal alignment of enemy bomber and ground attack aircraft.

The 324th Fighter Air Division comprising the 176th and 196th Fighter Air Regiments (26 MiG-15s in total) made up the second echelon, and were tasked with augmenting tactical forces and of relieving 303rd Fighter Air Division units in combat. The 351st Fighter Air Regiment comprised the Corps Commander's reserve [in the period under discussion, the separate 351st Fighter Air Regiment – which was led by Regimental Commander Ivan Andreyevich Yefimov – was equipped with La-11s and carried out combat sorties at night].

... Between 0812-0816 [0912-0916] the Corps' units were at first readiness. Between 0824-0833 [0924-0933] under orders from the Fighter Air Corps' Command Post the 303rd Fighter Air Division consisting of the 17th Fighter Air Regiments (20 MiG-15s in total) and led by Major Maslennikov along with the 18th Guards Fighter Air Regiment (20 MiG-15s in total) and led by Lieutenant-Colonel Smorchkov, and the 523rd Fighter Air Regiment (18 MiG-15s in total) led by Major Oskin, were scrambled.

... Between 0840-0845 [0940-0945] under orders from the Fighter Air Corps Command Post the 324th Fighter Air Division consisting of the 176th Guards Fighter Air Regiment (14 MiG-15s in total) led by Colonel Vishnyakov and the 196th Fighter Air Regiment (12 MiG-15s in total) led by Major Mitusov were scrambled.

... The regiments that made up the 303rd and 324th Fighter Air Divisions grouped together making 90° and 180° turns over the right bank of the Yalu River. After climbing to an altitude of 5,000–6,000 m the units were directed onto a heading towards the Anju–Taechon region using the directional method. Our fighters were vectored onto their targets by the Fighter Air Corps and Fighter Air Division Command Posts, as well as ACP No. 2. In this case the focus was on vectoring them onto the bombers.

The 303rd Fighter Air Division formation consisted of groups of attack and covering aircraft, transiting in a formation divided into regiments six to seven kilometres apart at the limits of visual range. The attack aircraft came under the 196th Fighter Air Regiment while the covering aircraft came under the 176th Guards Fighter Air Regiment. Lieutenant-Colonel Smorchkov was named head of this divisional group.

The 324th Fighter Air Division formation also consisted of groups of attack and covering aircraft transiting as a "column" of regiments six to seven kilometres apart. The attack aircraft came under the 196th Fighter Air Regiment while the covering aircraft came under the 176th Guards Fighter Air Regiment. Colonel Vishnyakov was named head of this divisional group.

At 0940 [1040] the 18th Guards Fighter Air Regiment tracking at an altitude of 8,000 m at the head of the group of attack aircraft encountered the fighter "shield" heading both towards them head on and dissecting their path at a location 20-25 km east of Uiju. The shield consisted of up to 40 F-86s flying in an S-turn figure of eight formation with eight aircraft in "flight echelon", and the flights in "pair's echelon."

Meanwhile the Commander of the group Lieutenant-Colonel Smorchkov sighted eight B-29s ahead and to the left of him at an altitude of 8,000 m flying in "line abreast" formation with the aircraft 40-50 m apart, heading south. They were escorted by up to thirty F-84s that were located above, behind and to the left and right of them in groups of six to eight aircraft 600–800 m above the bomber formation.

After assessing the situation the Commander of the group Lieutenant-Colonel Smorchkov ordered the 1st and 3rd Squadrons (fourteen MiGs in total) to engage the F-86 fighters in combat and the 2nd Squadron (six MiG-15s in total) to attack the bombers. In accordance with the order given by the Commander our fighters followed the order engaging the enemy in combat. As a result of the battle on the basis of the pilot's own reports as well as the gun camera films two B-29s and two F-84s were confirmed shot down.

At 0943 [1043] the 523rd Fighter Air Regiment (totalling eighteen MiG-15s) and led by Major Oskin, flying at an altitude of 9,000 m as part of the strike

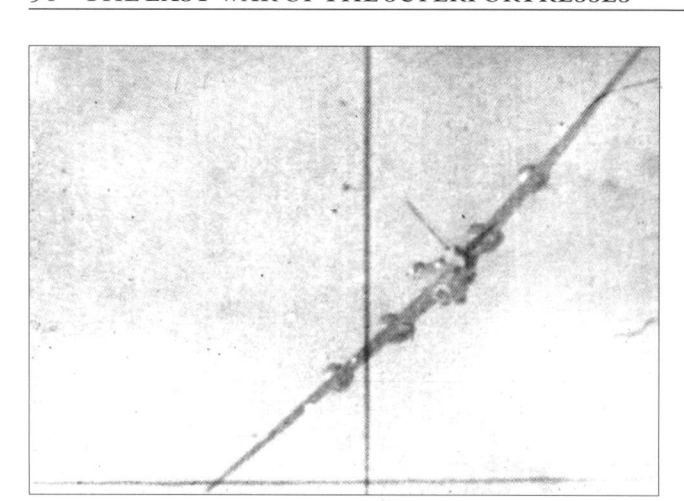

A B-29 on a frame from Lieutenant-Colonel Smorchkov's gun camera of the 18th Guards Fighter Air Regiment, 303rd Fighter Air Division, 23 October 1951.

Senior Lieutenant Lev Shchukin of the 18th Guards Fighter Air Regiment (15 victories in Korea – including two F-84s, which were shot down on 22 October 1951 and 23 October 1951). (This photograph was provided by I. Seidov)

Senior Lieutenant Nikolay Kornienko of the 18th Guards Fighter Air Regiment (five victories in Korea – including one B-29, which was shot down on 23 October 1951). (This photograph was provided by I. Seidov)

group behind the 18th Guards Fighter Air Regiment encountered eight F-86 aircraft at an altitude of 7,000 m some 20-40 km south-west of Taechon proceeding on a collision course towards them. After turning his flight 90° to starboard they encountered nine B-29s and up to forty F-84s, F-86s and Gloster Meteor F.4s at an altitude of 5,000 m.

The B-29 formation was as follows: the lead flight consisted of three aircraft and flew in a tight "wedge" formation, the trailing six aircraft flew at a distance of 4,000–5,000 m behind and to the right of the lead flight, in a "line abreast" formation (our fighters attacked a group of six B-29s). The escort fighters were: eight Gloster Meteor F.4s ahead of the B-29s at a distance of 2,000–3,000 m and positioned 1,000–2,000 m to the right and 600–800 m above the bombers, the F-84s were behind and to the left and right of the B-29s, each group consisted of four to eight F-84s. Two groups consisting of eight F-86s each patrolled behind and to the right of the B-29s at an altitude of 8,000 m at a distance of 10-15 km. On the orders of the Commander the regiment engaged the fighters and bombers in combat.

On the basis of the outcome of the battle, the testimony of the pilots and photographic analysis five B-29s were shot down as well as one F-84. In terms of our own losses 2nd Lieutenant KHRUTIN was shot down after he was attacked by four F-86s around 15-20 km north-west of ANDUN as he was returning to base ...

As the Senior Pilot of the 523rd Fighter Air Regiment Guards, 2nd Lieutenant Dmitriy Aleksandrovich Samoylov, remembers:

... I was Oskin's wingman [Guards Major Dmitriy Pavlovich Oskin was the Deputy Commander]. Filimonov was due to fly with him, but I was with Zykov in the second pair in the Oskin's flight. I look round and the Commander had taxied out, but his wingman was still on the hardstanding. The other pilots had already started to taxi out, but he was still there; then I told Zykov to stay where he was and I would join Oskin as his wingman.

As we approached the Anju area, we were attacked by a large group of Sabres. They pounced on us from above and we engaged them in combat. During the course of the battle, Oskin got behind one of the F-86s

Senior Lieutenant Georgiy Dyachenko and Captain Stepan Bakhayev of the 523rd Fighter Air Regiment, who shot down a B-29 each on 23 October 1951. (This photograph was provided by I. Seidov)

and closed in on it. He was almost within firing range – less than 800 m away – when I noticed a group of B-29s approaching us from below. I could be certain that there were nine of them, but not whether there were additional groups of bombers. I shouted to Oksin: "Heavy bombers below and to the right!" Evidently, he too had noticed them and broke off his attack on the F-86 – performing a half-roll and putting his aircraft into a dive; I followed suit.

He attacked the B-29s head-on and set the front of one of them ablaze, but as he was manoeuvring for his next attack, a pair of F-84s from the group of escort fighters tried to attack him from behind. I gave him a good burst of defensive fire without taking aim ... I had no time to take aim; I just had time to drive him away ...

We only had enough fuel to engage fighters in combat for a little over five minutes and then we had to turn for home. There were usually six of the Sabres, maybe more, on patrol over the Yalu River – and the Sabres caught us as we broke off combat. At that moment, the order came through to do just that. Oskin shot down two B-29s in that battle, Shevarev shot one down, while Dyachenko and one of the other pilots sustained one bullet hole in the tailfin – and that was the only damage from the gunners. Khutrin, however ... he was shot down after he crossed the Yalu River. He was already over Chinese territory, near Antung ...

From the 'Description of the Air Battle':

... At 0945 (1045) the 17th Fighter Air Regiment (totalling 20 MiG-15s) led by Major Maslennikov flying as part of a group of escort fighters encountered a group of up to 20 F-86s flying towards them on a collision course at an altitude of 8,500 m in columns of six or eight in "line astern" formation above and to the left of the MiG-15s. At that time the regiment's fighter crews were spotted by eleven B29s at an altitude of 7,000 m escorted by F-84s and Gloster Meteor F.4s. The formation the bombers employed was "line astern" divided into detachments (the first detachment consisted of three aircraft in a "wedge" formation while the second and third comprised four B-29s each in a "diamond" shaped formation). The escort fighters comprising up to 20 F-84s were above and behind the bombers, each group was made up of four to eight fighters. There were eight Gloster Meteor F-4s in front of the bombers at a distance of 1,000–2,000 m.

After assessing the situation in the air the Commander of the group made a decision: to attack the fighters in the "shield" (up to 20 F-86s) with the 2nd and 3rd Squadrons while the 1st Squadron would attack the enemy bombers. The regiment went on the attack in accordance with their orders.

On the basis of the results of the battle, the testimony of pilots and photo analysis three B29s and one F-84 were shot down while one B-29 was damaged. We did not sustain any losses. One of the MiG-15s flown by Snr Lieutenant Nikolayev sustained one bullet hole during the course of the battle.

The 176th Guards Fighter Air Regiment, which flew to the Anju area without encountering the enemy at an altitude of 8,000 m turned right and headed out towards Sinmi-Do Island.

At 1008 [1108] the regiment identified two F-80s and two F-86s that had been observed 10 km east of the island by Captain Suchov's flight. The battle however

Pilots in Captain Dokachenko's flight, 17th Fighter Air Regiment, 303rd Fighter Air Division: Captain Nikolai Volkov (seven victories in Korea), Senior Lieutenant Aleksey Nikolayev (four victories in Korea – including one B-29, which was shot down on 23 October 1951), Captain Vladimir Khvostantsev (four victories in Korea) and Captain Nikolai Dokachenko (nine victories in Korea).

Senior Lieutenant Vasiliy Shulev of the 17th Fighter Air Regiment (seven victories in Korea – including one F-84, which was shot down in combat on 23 October 1951) standing next to his MiG-15bis No. 177 (serial No. 121077) from the 17th Fighter Air Regiment, along with his ground crew. (This photograph was provided by I. Seidov)

was not successful since the enemy fighters disappeared into the clouds after the first attack.

The 196th Fighter Air Regiment that were flying over the Sinuiju area identified a single F-86 at an altitude of 7,000 m, which tried to attack a pair of MiG-15s from the 303rd Fighter Air Division as they left the combat zone. As the group made a corrective turn on the F-86 the latter broke off its approach and departed towards the sea at high speed. As they approached the Anju area at an altitude of 8,000–9,000 m the leader of the group was informed that the enemy was departing to the south. Although they set off in that direction the group did not encounter the enemy.

For the most part our fighters attacked the enemy fighters and bombers from the aft hemisphere, at an aspect angle of 0/4–3/4 opening fire from a distance ranging from 1,000–400 m with two or three medium bursts of fire, using a movable gunsight reticle. Attacks on enemy aircraft would be made both as a flight and in pairs, and crews cooperated with each other for the entire duration of the battle according to the principles of mutual support. Our fighters would engage the enemy in battle in the vertical manoeuvres. The group, squadron and flight commanders coordinated the battle.

At a time estimated to be between 0948-1008 [1048-1108] all the regiments were ordered to break off combat by the Corps' Command Post.

A total of 84 MiG-15s had been scrambled to counter this concentrated raid by enemy aircraft, 72 pilots had participated in the battle and 36 of them had actually opened fire. In total the units were engaged in air combat for 10-15 mins.

On the basis of the outcome of the battle, 14 enemy aircraft had been shot down, of those 10 were B-29s, and four were F-84s, while a single B-29 was damaged. Our own losses amounted to one MiG-15 pilot (Snr Lieutenant Khutrin).

The armament expended was as follows:

N-37 shells   865 rounds
NS-23 shells   2,619 rounds

The weather conditions: eight to ten oktas of cloud cover, with a 3,000–4,000 m cloud base and visibility of up to 10 km.[59]

Western researchers traditionally assess the outcome of the battle differently. Some authors attribute the loss of between three and five MiGs to defensive fire on the part of the Superfortresses, whereas officially, only two gunners attained one kill each; these were Sergeant Fred R. Spivey and Staff-Sergeant Jerry M. Webb – both of whom served in the 371st Bomb Squadron. One of the F-84 pilots from the group of fighters – 1st Lieutenant Farrie D. Fortner – was credited with shooting down one MiG. Apart from that, Sabre pilots Major Richard D. Creighton from the 336th Fighter Squadron and Captain Ralph E. Banks attained one kill each. In reality, our losses were as follows:

- From the 17th Fighter Air Regiment: a MiG-15 flown by Senior Lieutenant Nikolayev sustained one bullet hole from a B-29 gunner
- From the 18th Guards Fighter Air Regiment: MiGs flown by Lieutenant-Colonel Smorchkov and Senior Lieutenant Ustyuzhaninov were slightly damaged.

59 Fund of the 64th IAK, inventory 174045ss, file. 51, pp.147-154.

Both of these were attacked by escort fighters as they broke off combat with B-29s
- From the 523rd Fighter Air Regiment: Senior Lieutenant Khrutin was shot down by Sabres and killed on his way back to base

Let us now take a look at American losses; Robert F. Futrell wrote:

> ... The morning of 23 October found the Communist air force obviously briefed and prepared to engage the medium bombers in what would be one of the most savage and bloody air battles of the Korean War. South of the Yalu some hundred MiGs engaged and boxed in the 34 Sabres of the screening force. The Sabres dropped two MiGs, but the American swept-wing pilots were effectively out of action for the combat taking place to the south.
>
> On this morning three flights comprising eight 'Superforts' (one had aborted) of the 307th Bombardment Wing made rendezvous with 55 Thunderjets of the 49th and 136th Wings and headed for Namsi Airfield. As the leading "Charlie" flight turned on course to the target, some 50 MiGs circled the formation like Indians around a covered-wagon train.
>
> When the Thunderjets would not let themselves be decoyed away, the MiGs bored in with determined attacks.
>
> Red jets raked the lead ship of "Charlie" flight, but Captain Thomas L. Shields nevertheless held his burning bomber on course long enough to drop his bombs, thus fulfilling his duties as a leader. Between their initial point and the target all of the ships in "Charlie" flight were under attack, and as the bombers dropped their loads and broke left, some confusion on the part of escorting Thunderjets left them inadequately protected. Actually, however, the Thunderjets were so badly outclassed that they could not offer too much protection. Most of the attacking MiGs flew normal pursuit curves, but some of them dived downward through the bomber formation so as to deny the Thunderjet pilots or the Superfortress gunners much opportunity to fire. One flight of MiGs came straight up under the B-29s with all guns blazing.
>
> In the lead flight, Captain Shields coaxed his bomber back to the coast, where his crew bailed out, but Shields did not get free from the stricken ship in time to save his own life.
>
> While rallying to the left after bombs-away, "Able" and "Baker" flights each lost a bomber to the MiGs. In twenty minutes it was all over. Superfortress gunners claimed three MiGs destroyed, and Thunderjet pilots also claimed a MiG as shot down. All but one of the bombers which survived the attacks received major damage, and most of them had dead and wounded men aboard when they made emergency landings in Korea and Japan.
>
> One F-84 was also lost in the air battle.
>
> Describing the holocaust in its mission report, the 307th Wing praised the efforts of the Thunderjets, but it wryly observed that nothing less than 150 F-86s would have been an adequate escort for the bombers.[60]

We note that these separate episodes that took place during the course of the battle itself were somewhat embellished, and that the sequence of events has been changed. The impression that unfolds on reading the account of the battle is that the Sabres shot down a pair of MiGs in open combat when they were outnumbered three to one. We should bear in mind, however, that the strength of the 64th Fighter Air Corps was half of what the Americans claimed – and the only MiG to be shot down was on its way back to base after the battle. Moreover, it was not shot down 'south of the Yalu River', but in open combat in Chinese airspace that UN pilots were forbidden from entering. Furthermore, Captain Shields is worthy of respect – as is any fallen soldier in the war – but in reality, it is unlikely that he would have been able to execute his duties as leader with such triumph and heroism. There was no need, therefore, for bomber pilots to clench their teeth breaking through to the target in a hail of fire from the MiGs, since the *bombers were intercepted as they broke away from the target*. In our view, the official account of the battle set out above does not correspond to reality for one reason: namely that it is aimed not so much at painting an objective picture of the battle, as sweetening an extraordinarily bitter pill that Bomber Command swallowed on 23 October by any means possible – even lies. The pill in question contained far more than the loss of just three bombers.

Many Western historians advise that the losses incurred on 23 October forced Bomber Command to transfer exclusively to night-time operations – using B-29s in 'MiG Alley' right up until the end of the war – and 'Black Tuesday' was the last day that Superfortresses would fly to the Yalu River in daylight. In reality, bombers also appeared over the 64th Fighter Air Corps' zone of responsibility on 24 and 27 October; however, their losses that day were incomparably less – thus, the daylight raids by B-29s on 23 October 1951 really were a turning point in history. Why that day in particular however, when the outcome of the battles on 1 March and 12 April were, it would appear, no less tragic? In our view, this can be explained by the fact that actual losses were higher when compared with the official figures.

As Harold E. Fischer – who at that time, served as a Shooting Star pilot in the 80th Fighter-Bomber Squadron – remembers:

> On a particularly black day for our air force, a large formation of 12 airplanes, in beautiful weather, flew

---

60 Futrell, *The United States Air Force in Korea*, p.411.

over the North Korean area with an escort of F-86s. They were met as they pulled off the target by enemy MiG-15 fighters, who ignoring the fighter escort which was ineffective, flew in perfect four plane formation on fighter passes and fired their 20 and 37 mm cannon on the B-29 formation. There was little our B-29 gunners could do against these tactics since the aircraft would fire out of range. It was the meeting of World War Two aircraft and the modern jet at that time. The results were that eight B-29s were shot down and the remainder so shot up that they landed at forward air bases, in Korea, rather than make the long overwater trek to their base in Okinawa. It was our duty to fly the patrol from the friendly islands of Chodo to the mouth of the Yalu River in order to see if any of the crews of the B-29s were still in the water after bailing out of the crippled B-29s.

We flew on a scramble mission and flew line abreast all along the coast and to the mouth of the Yalu and returned, but not one life raft did we see. We flew a few feet above the waves and eagerly scanned the waves hoping that we could see something. Our search time was drastically cut down by the low altitudes that we were flying and we finally had to leave the area, much to our chagrin. The only other aircraft we saw was a 'Dumbo', a rescue aircraft that was looking for some of the crews also. The 'Dumbo' withdrew when we did because of the fear that the MiGs might return and shoot it down.

Just after we left and came home, our last swing was to the mouth of the Yalu, where I saw a light reflected from one of the buildings. It was either a reflected mirror or the flash of gun powder. We climbed towards home feeling sadder and realising that the tactics would have to change; that either the bomber would have to have better and more escort, or they would have to cease flying day missions and begin night missions.

It so happened that this was the last day mission of the war for the B-29s.

According to the testimony of one of the crewmembers in the Superfortresses shot down by anti-aircraft fire on 23 January 1952, in the space of one week in October 1951, Bomber Command lost Superfortresses on every sortie – and moreover, losses sustained from the MiGs on 'Black Tuesday' amounted to nine aircraft. These figures are supported by the fact that three B-29s shot down by MiGs on 23 October are recorded in the list of US Air Force aircraft losses in Korea, while a further six were written off the following day after sustaining serious damage.

To quote *Alice In Wonderland*, it gets 'curiouser and curioser'. We found another version of the outcome of the battle on 23 October – this time giving a figure of 10 bombers lost – in Larry Davis' work. His account reads as follows:

… … When the fight was over, all the B-29s had suffered major damage. Three were lost over the target, and four more crashed at bases in South Korea. The last three made it back to Kadena but were written off and scrapped. The MiGs had effectively wiped out an entire B-29 force. Orders came down that night – no more daylight missions in or near "MiG Alley" … [61]

Davis goes on to describe the total losses the B-29s incurred in North Korea, and writes:

Officially, their losses were very light – 17 aircraft lost over the three years of conflict – but these were only losses over North Korea or enemy territory. They were not considered 'lost in action' if the aircraft went down in the Yellow Sea, Sea of Japan, or crashed in South Korea. It also was not a loss if the aircraft was written off from damage inflicted by enemy air or ground forces.[62]

If we take this assertion into account, perhaps we can suggest that on 23 October 1951, between eight and 12 B-29s took off for North Korea – of which three were lost … while the others … we could say were deleted from Bomber Command's inventory. It sounds somewhat outlandish, but it is a very good compromise for both sides.

As far as the double discrepancy with 64th Fighter Air Corps documents regarding the numbers of bombers, it seems that we need to acknowledge that all three regiments from the 303rd Fighter Air Division attacked the same group of B-29s. Moreover, not one of the regiments was able to determine accurately whether the figures for the numbers of bombers were correct. This situation is more a rule, rather than an exception, in any conflict. Furthermore, it is wholly plausible that on a *regimental* level, the number of B-29s was determined accurately and the confusion arose in collating regimental reports into a divisional report, which is then summarised into a single account of the air battle compiled by the corps.

From the 64th Fighter Air Corps' account of the battle, it follows that the regiments in the 303rd Division that went into combat one behind the other encountered groups of eight, nine and 11 bombers respectively. As the numbers of B-29s increased, this gave the impression that they were flying in three different groups, but on the other hand, any group that 'ran the gauntlet' of the Soviet regiments should have been thinned out.

Let us start with the 18th Guards Regiment, which were the first to encounter the Superfortresses: the single account of the battle compiled by the corps states that the group consisted of eight B-29s in 'line astern' formation. If we are honest, this formation does not lend itself to mounting an effective defence. However, it would be wrong to take the enemy for a fool. The 18th Guards Fighter Air Regiment most likely encountered the bombers after they had turned for home

---

61 Davis, *Air War Over Korea*, pp.29-30.
62 Davis, *Air War Over Korea*, pp.29-30.

following their bombing runs. It is then possible that the B-29s were not counted properly, and some of them that were already out in front went unnoticed. This version becomes even more plausible when one considers that the conditions were not conducive to counting the numbers of bombers; the way in which the B-29s were identified in a head-on position; and the moderate visibility.

Three minutes later, the 523rd Regiment encountered a group of nine B-29s – and if we are to apply the logic of the single corps' account of the battle, this was a new group. However, according to the *divisional* account, the 523rd Fighter Air Regiment encountered nine bombers 'in a tight formation', while the lead flight was 'in a tight wedge formation'. The trailing group of six B-29s that had previously been attacked by Lieutenant-Colonel Smorchkov's group followed on behind and to the right at a distance of 4-5 km and at intervals of 400–600 m in "section line abreast' formation'.[63]

Two minutes later, the 17th Fighter Air Regiment went into combat – their designated target being a group of 11 B-29s. The divisional account of the battle, which is collated on the basis of the regimental account, initially mentions just eight Superfortresses. This figure is then corrected in pencil to read '11' – and this was how it migrated to divisional headquarters[64] – thus the number of B-29s in the group was still downgraded, which forms a basis to argue that there was only ever one group of B-29s.

According to A.P. Smorchkov, the commanders of the various regiments in the corps who returned from their sorties on 23 October:

> ... We're only able to speak with any certainty about their own group's activities. We analysed every sortie and we drew the necessary conclusions ... but strictly from our own regiment's perspective. We only had a vague idea about the actions of our neighbouring regiments. All this was done at regimental and divisional headquarters. In total, over the entire duration of the conflict, not once did I attend any meetings on aggregating combat experience, since we were permanently at a state of readiness for the next sortie; then for us, the war came to an end all of a sudden and we were sent back to the Soviet Union ...

The Final Daylight Sorties

Despite their defeat the previous day on Wednesday, 24 October the bombers again took off for 'MiG Alley' – and the target for eight B-29s from the 98th Bomb Wing was the railway bridge at Sukchon. The 4th Fighter Squadron put up a fighter 'shield' – and fighter cover over this region was provided by 16 Meteors from No. 77 Squadron, Royal Australian Air Force; 10 Thunderjets were assigned to provide close air support for the bombers.

At 1458, the 64th Fighter Air Corps radar detected the enemy over the Pyongyang–Nampo border – and three minutes later, the regiments forming the 303rd Fighter Air Division were put on first readiness. The fighters began to scramble at 1506 – and nine minutes later, 16 MiGs from the 523rd, 20 MiGs from the 18th Guards and 18 MiGs from the 17th Regiments were scrambled to intercept the enemy. Under the overall command of Lieutenant-Colonel Smorchkov, the group set course for the Anju–Gochon region. Once in the air, the commanders of the different groups received their orders: the 523rd Fighter Air Regiment were to engage the 'shield' in battle, while the 17th and 18th were to break through to the bombers. However, by that time, the B-29s had already dropped their bombs and had begun to leave the area – heading towards East Korea Bay. At 1522, the 523rd Regiment encountered the Meteors and Sabres from the 'shield' and engaged them in combat. The 20 MiGs from the 18th Guards Fighter Air Regiment did try to catch up with the B-29s – pursuing them at an altitude of 9,500 m in a south-easterly direction. At 1535, close to the town of Yandok, the pilots encountered the bombers (escorted by Meteors, Thunderjets and Sabres). Lieutenant-Colonel Smorchkov decided that the 1st Squadron would neutralise the fighters, while the 2nd and 3rd would attack the bombers.

This encounter took place very close to the Pyongyang–Wonsan line, which the fighters of the 64th Fighter Air Corps were not permitted to cross, so the pilots were only able to attack the bombers once. Moreover, the majority opened fire from a distance of 1,500–2,000 m or more.

The only successful attack was that carried out by Lieutenant-Colonel Smorchkov, who opened fire after closing to a distance of 700 m – breaking off the attack just 300 m from the B29 itself. As a result, the bomber caught fire. A.P. Smorchkov did not come out of the battle unscathed either, as he himself remembers:

> As soon as I had shot the B-29 down, something else came up ... I could see that a Thunderjet was shooting to a MiG. The 'Fortresses' were below and to the right of me, and all the guns were blazing. I flipped over in a combat turn to port and got onto his tail. The cabin depressurised and I had been shot in the leg, right on the bone, but my leg was in one piece ... I still sent him packing though.

The 17th Fighter Air Regiment were not able to take part in the battle, since the bombers managed to escape over the Pyongyang–Wonsan line. On the basis of the outcome of the battle, the pilots of the 18th and 523rd Regiments were credited with shooting down four F-86s, four Meteors and one B-29.

Western publications state that one Meteor was damaged by cannon fire from MiGs at the very start of the air battle, and this aircraft had entered a spin after the starboard engine failed. The pilot, Flying-Officer Hamilton-Foster, managed to regain control and landed the aircraft at Kimpo – despite the

---
63 Fund of the 303rd IAD, inventory 539825s file. 2, p.116.
64 Fund of the 303rd IAD, inventory 539825s file. 2, p.104.

Two pilots with five 'Fortresses' between them! The Deputy Commander of the 18th Guards Fighter Air Regiment, Aleksandr Smorchkov (four victories in the Second World War and 12 victories in Korea) and Commander of the 523rd Fighter Air Regiment, Dmitriy Oskin (15 victories in Korea); between 22–24 October 1951, these two pilots shot down five B-29s!

fact that the port engine also failed as he was on his glide path. One B-29 from the 98th Bomb Wing also became a casualty, and was so seriously damaged that it ditched in Wonsan Bay. Technical Sergeant Harold M. Setters from the 344th Fighter Squadron was credited with shooting down a MiG.

In reality, the MiGs did not incur any losses on the part of the Superfortresses, although 2nd Lieutenant Georgiy Khristoforovich Dyachenko – a pilot in the 523rd Fighter Air Regiment – was shot down by Sabres and was forced to eject. The only F-86 pilot to be credited with a kill that day was the Second World War ace Harrison R. Thing from the headquarters of the 4th Air Wing – a future Wing Commander and a Korean War ace. Apart from that, a further three MiGs from the 18th Guards Fighter Air Regiment were damaged: one of them sustained a bullet hole to the nose section, while a second was damaged by a 37 mm shell case; a third sustained a bullet hole in the wing as a result of shrapnel from its own shells.

We cannot ignore the fact that Hero of the Soviet Union Aleksandr Pavlovich Smorchkov shot down one bomber per day for three days in a row during the most demanding of sorties – and furthermore, all his bomber kills have been confirmed by the opposing side, which is an exceptionally rare occurrence!

༺༻

Saturday, 27 October marked the last day of 'Black week'. A sortie by nine B-29s from the 19th Bomb Wing against a railway bridge in the Anju area was supported by 32 F-84s from the 49th and 136th Fighter Wings, together with 16 Australian Meteors. Since it was common knowledge that the MiGs avoided flying over the sea, the route was planned in such a way that the bombers were over the waters of the Yellow Sea for as long as possible and only crossed the coast very close to the target. As usual, the Sabres put up a fighter 'shield' over the Yalu River.

Between 1002-1004, 22 MiG-15s from the 523rd Fighter Air Regiment were scrambled to intercept the B-29s and were under the command of Guards Major A.N. Karasev; this was the main strike group in the 303rd Fighter Air Division. Groups from the 17th and 18th Guards Regiments – each consisting of 20 fighters – were ordered to engage the escort fighters in combat, as well as those comprising the 'shield', as D.A. Samoylov remembers:

> ... I took off in my pair [his wingman was Senior Lieutenant Mikhail Zykov] as part of Popov's flight, who was the Commander of our 2nd Squadron. The 2nd and 3rd Squadrons were the attack squadrons, while we were the escort squadron and flew in the rearmost position in the regiment.
>
> As we approached the interception, I saw the whole picture: the 'Fortresses' were heading away to the right of us towards the coast, completely free, without any kind of escort. Behind them was a huge tangle of fighters. I said to Popov: "We probably need to attack the heavy bombers." He ordered us to "Attack!" and we immediately went after them. I was to the right of Popov, and the 'Fortresses' were heading away to the right of us. For some reason, I did not want to re-group the formation and I turned away myself sharply to the right. I had to use almost 90° of bank and I lost visual contact with Popov. I pulled in slightly and recovered the aircraft to level flight. I looked around me ... Zykov was cruising around to my right, but nobody else was there. I did not know where Popov had got to and I forgot to ask after the sortie was over.

At that time, Captain Popov's pair were engaging the F-84s from the escort fighters in combat. Of the six MiGs in the 2nd Squadron, only D.A. Samoylov and his wingman got through to the bombers. He continued:

> There they were: nine B-29s right in front of me. They were trailing smoke, using their boost to get to the coast, as they knew we would not fly over the sea. Nevertheless, my top speed was 1,000 something, while theirs was barely 700; I was closing on them rapidly. They were blazing away with their machine guns, but I could not see the tracer head-on, but I knew from the flames coming out of every gun turret that they were firing. I attacked them – setting one of them ablaze. I would overshoot above and beneath them, as many times as I wanted. My speed was high and I could still break away, and then turn and make a second attack: this time head-on. I did not want to attack them head-on; it was easier to attack from behind, since my closing speed was reduced. As soon as I had stopped firing, I would

Pilots from the 523rd Fighter Air Regiment: Right is Dmitriy Samoylov (10 victories in Korea – including one B-29, which was shot down in combat on 27 October 1951) and left, his wingman, Mikhail Zykov (four victories in Korea).

immediately initiate a climbing turn ... almost over their group. It was then that Zykov shouted out "I'm hit." They had caught him, as he was in the air above them. That was it: once you had been hit, you had to break off combat.

We turned away and noticed that the entire fighter pack was rushing towards the bombers, both MiGs and F-84s. I nailed one of the Thunderjets just like that ... it was approaching on a collision course at an aspect angle of around 3/4. I fired at him and watched as he went crashing down ... we then landed back at base and inspected our aircraft ... Zykov had sustained just one bullet hole, somewhere in the fuselage.

It has to be said that on the whole, the escort fighters managed to neutralise the activities of the MiGs. The report based on the outcome of the battle concluded: 'Our fighters hardly got near the bombers. Many of the flights and the pairs were distracted unnecessarily engaging the escort fighters in combat'.[65]

Pilots from the 523rd Fighter Air Regiment were credited with shooting down two B-29s and two F-84s. Apart from that, pilots from the 17th and 18th Guards Regiments escorting the fighters were credited with shooting down two F-86s and one F-84. All the MiGs returned from their sortie, but three had been damaged by F-84s. Western publications state that four B-29s were damaged by MiGs on 27 October – one of them seriously. Five gunners in the Superfortresses were credited with shooting down one MiG each, while a further example was reported as having sustained serious damage by Meteor pilot Flying-Officer Reading.

❧

During the October air battles, pilots from the 64th Fighter Air Corps finally worked out their tactics for dealing with

Two MiGs attacked this US Air Force Superfortress in the battle over Sinuiju, Korea on 27 October. When the battle was over, this rugged B-29 returned to its Okinawa air base with a damaged left wing, and with two destroyed MiGs under its belt. Sergeant Worle E. Goff (left), tail gunner (who destroyed two MiGs), inspects the damaged wing with 1st Lieutenant Bernard A. Stein, radar observer, October 1951. (Courtesy of the US National Archives)

the Superfortresses successfully. Using their experience they established that:

> ... A squadron of MiG-15s were capable of taking on a group of up to eight B-29s escorted by up to 12 F-80s and F-84s successfully. The attack would be carried out at maximum speed and as a flight either consecutively or at the same time. This kind of attack would not afford the escort fighters an opportunity to mount their defence since they would have no time to prepare themselves.
>
> The attack was carried out from behind the bombers at an aspect angle ranging from 0/4–2/4 using a movable gunsight reticle and aiming at the fuel tanks, engines, and cockpit. The MiGs would open fire from a distance of 800–300 m using long bursts. Once they had stopped firing the MiGs would overshoot the B-29s and then break off combat in front of them turning away at an angle of 20-30°. One and a half minutes later they would turn 180° in the opposite direction to the turn they would use to break off combat and would then attack again – this time head on using an aspect

---

65 Fund of the 303rd IAD, inventory 539825s file. 2, p.311.

62 THE LAST WAR OF THE SUPERFORTRESSES

The grave of Captain Timofeyev – a pilot from the 523rd Fighter Air Regiment (he scored five victories in Korea and was killed in combat on 28 November 1951); Port Arthur, May 1953. Standing next to the gravestone (from left to right) are: Major Popov (five victories in Korea), Lieutenant-Colonel Maslennikov (three victories in Korea), Hero of the Soviet Union Colonel Karasev (21 personal and nine group victories in the Second World War, and seven victories in Korea – including one B-29 on 27 October 1951), Hero of the Soviet Union Lieutenant-Colonel Oskin (15 victories in Korea – including two B-29s on 23 October 1951) and Hero of the Soviet Union Lieutenant-Colonel Pulov (eight victories in Korea).

angle of 0/4–2/4 opening fire from a distance of 1,300–1,200 m. This would be reduced to a distance of 400 m, after which the MiGs would slide away – breaking off combat without changing direction ... [66]

This experience, however, was no longer of any use. For the corps' pilots, the question of 'how to shoot aircraft down' was secondary to the question of 'how to find them', since 27 October was the last day on which the MiGs and B-29s would meet in daylight.

On 28 October, a meeting of the heads of Bomber Command and the 5th Air Army (held at Itakuze) concluded that it was impossible to prevent the MiGs from reaching the Superfortresses – even if they had all the escort fighters they could lay their hands on. The Thunderjet and Meteor pilots escorting a B-29 at altitudes in excess of 6,000 m flew at a Mach number that was almost at the limits of what their obsolete fighters were capable of – and any attempt to perform a drastic manoeuvre in combat with a MiG would end in the fighter pilots losing control of their aircraft. The only real defence for the B-29s could lie in the F-86 'shield', which had not yet been tested. The 5th Air Army, however, did not have enough F-86s at its disposal to form a 'shield' of this nature. This being the case, the head of Bomber Command – General Joe W. Kelly – suggested switching to night sorties. Given the level of radar equipment with which the bombers were fitted, a B-29 was capable of making five to seven bombing sorties per night using the SHORAN system; five to seven sorties using ground direction; and two 'psychological' sorties to drop leaflets and carry out reconnaissance as required. Kelly proposed that the priority should be to train crews how to bomb using SHORAN as quickly as possible; General Weyland agreed with Kelly.

Superfortresses would subsequently complete a series of daylight sorties to support ground troops in battle, but they no longer appeared north of Pyongyang. The pilots of the 64th Fighter Air Corps put an end to the career of the B-29 as a daylight strategic bomber – and the battle with the B-29s shifted to night sorties.

66 Fund of the 17th IAP, inventory 683351s file. 5, pp.51- 52.

Part 2

War from Sunset to Sunrise

On 26 August 1950, the aircraft carrier *Cape Esperance* left the quayside at San Diego naval air station. On the deck of the ship that was headed for Japan were F7F-3Ns from the 524th US Marines Corps' Night Fighter Squadron. On 11 September, the *Cape Esperance* put into the port of Yokosuka for discharge. The 524th Night Fighter Squadron became part of the 5th Air Army – and after disembarking from the carrier, they were sent to Itakuze airfield on Kyushu Island where the pilots kept watch at first readiness for a week – carrying out patrol flights periodically. On 19 September, the squadron transferred to Gimpo airfield, which had previously been used by UN forces. At sunset that evening, Tigercats lifted off the runway – heading north in the rapidly-gathering twilight. That night, the pilots of the 524th Squadron opened the air war that was to take place in the skies over Korea by night. The 523rd US Marines Night Fighter Squadron were soon to join the battle flying the F4U-5N.

As daytime fighter-bomber operations became more efficient, the North Koreans steadily transferred to supplying the army on the front line by night. At the same time, the North Korean air defence system grew stronger – and soon, UN aircraft began to pay a very high price for every 'foray'. The air force also transferred to night-time operations at around the time that the Pusan Perimeter was crossed in September 1950 – following on from the marine night fighter aircraft. Their use of Mustangs, as well as F-80 and F-84 jet fighters not designed for night-time operations, was short-lived and ineffective. The F-82 was more successful, however, out of all the air force's aircraft – it was really only the Invaders that were assimilated into night-time operations. In June 1951, the six bomber squadrons operating the B-26 – and which came under the 3rd and 452nd Bomb Groups – were officially re-organised and were renamed. These became bomber squadrons equipped with light intruder aircraft for night-time operations, even though prior to the re-organisation, more than 75 percent of B-26 sorties were carried out by night. Finally, in October 1951, Bomber Command joined the US Marine Corps and the air force. While all the lighter aircraft, such as the Corsairs and Invaders, would perform small-scale patrols, with the advent of the Superfortresses, the night war entered a new phase.

According to American reconnaissance, by the end of October – after the Superfortresses had been routed – the Sino-Korean Combined Air Army transferred some of their fighters to airfields on the south bank of the Yalu River. To begin with, 26 MiG-15s appeared at Uiju and then 64 piston-engine aircraft were transferred to Sinuiju from mainland China. Worse still was the fact that the final daylight sorties by Superfortresses had not succeeded in taking the North Korean airfields at Namsi, Taechon and Saamchan out of action for very long; the enemy employed thousands of workers to repair the damage quickly. It was these same forward bases that were the most dangerous for UN troops, so the Superfortresses continued to bomb them even though they had transferred to night-time operations.

Night raids on Uiju, Namsi, Saamchan and Taechon – using the SHORAN system – began on 4 November. Initially,

Two Superfortress gunners of the US Air Force's veteran 19th Bomb Wing examine the damage suffered by this rugged B-29 in a MiG air battle over Korea. In spite of its wounds, the B-29 stayed in the swirling air battle. Sergeant Robert Spenard (left gunner) and Pfc Harry E. Ruch (right gunner) look at the damaged wing and talk over the battle, November 1951. (Courtesy of the US National Archives)

While the other three engines remain idle, the newly-attached power plant is revved up for testing by the US Far East Air Force's B-29 bomber flight engineer prior to take-off on a combat mission over Korea, November 1951. (Courtesy of the US National Archives)

One Superfortress dramatically frames another at a US Far East Air Forces base on Okinawa, November 1951. (Courtesy of the US National Archives)

The US Air Force B-29 Superfortress in the background was picked up by the probing fingers of radar when it was returning to its home base in foul weather. Radar and electronic technicians of the US Far East Air Force's 98th Bombardment Wing manning the GCA (ground control approach) unit at night gave radio signals for turns, attitudes and airspeeds – and at the most precise moment, told the pilot to 'touch down'. This invaluable flying aid has taken most of the hazards of foul weather from daily operations of FEAF Bomber Command 'Superforts', December 1951. (Courtesy of the US National Archives)

these raids were carried out by single aircraft; however, as SHORAN began to be installed on more and more B-29s, the intensity of these raids grew. Admittedly, their accuracy left a great deal to be desired. The majority of crews had never touched SHORAN and were only able to gain experience on actual combat sorties. Since each of the crews were only given eight practice bombing runs, the statistics showed that they only gained confidence using this system after 35 sorties. Apart from that, it appeared that the locations of Namsi, Saamchan and Taechon airfields were not entirely accurate on the maps that the crews had been given. They had to adjust the point at which the bombs were dropped visually, and since the raids took place at night, crews were not able to do this. The lack of bombing accuracy needed to be balanced by a high 'payload' tonnage.

During November, 170 tonnes of bombs were dropped on Namsi in 26 sorties. For Taechon, this figure was 160 tonnes in 23 sorties and for Saamchan, 85 tonnes in 12 sorties. For Uiju, this was 80 tonnes in 12 sorties. The principal task was to take the runways out of action, as well as the taxiways and revetments, so 45 and 227 kg high-explosive bombs were used. At the same time, fragmentation bombs with explosives designed to detonate in the air were used against Uiju to destroy the MiGs, where according to US reconnaissance, the latter were already based. Despite the fact that during the raids on the first three airfields, circular error probable was 350–370 m by the end of November, they had been so badly damaged that they could no longer be considered viable as aircraft bases.

Uiju and Sinuiju were not taken out of action, and bombers would return to hit these airfields more than once right up until the end of the war – thus on one of these raids in January 1952, the B-29s set about bombing the airfield. As a result of this bombing raid, the airfield was taken out of action for 24 hours – and four La-9s, one Yak-11, one Yak-18 and three vehicles were destroyed; three La-9s, one MiG-15, one Po-2 and 85 mm anti-aircraft artillery were damaged. Three soldiers on the anti-aircraft battery were injured, up to 160 civilians were killed and more than a hundred were injured. Moreover, Anju – the largest of the airfield complexes – was located on the far side of the Yalu River, exactly opposite Sinuiju. It is hard to imagine how the B-29s achieved this success on a daylight raid right under the noses of the MiGs.

In the last few months of 1951, the B-29s flew more than 1,000 sorties – and in the first half of 1952, this figure stood at 1,500. Furthermore, the bombers would fly to the front line two or three times a night every night, where they would soften up the enemy's forward perimeter using ground guidance.

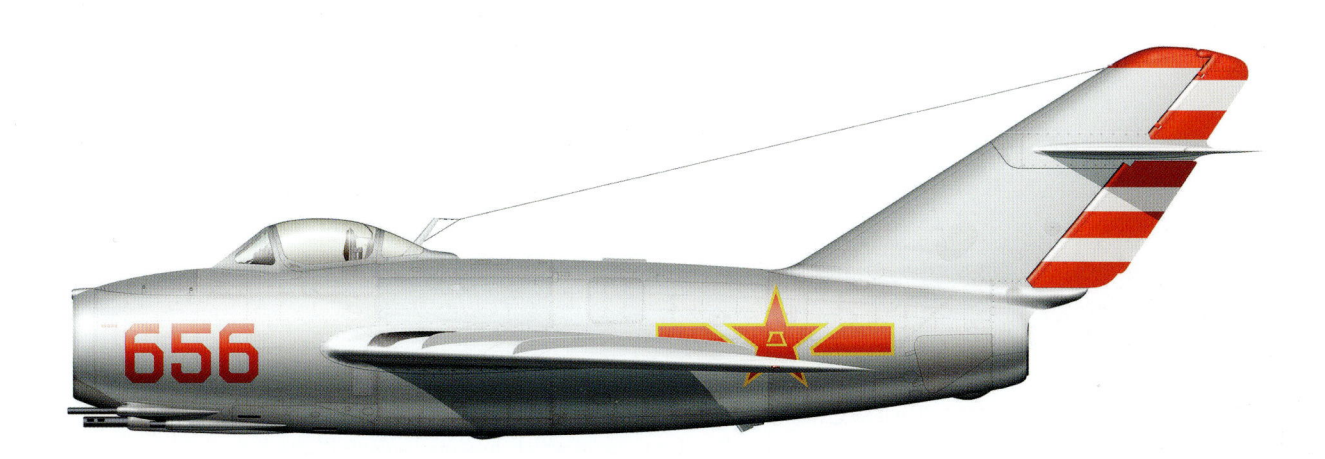

MiG-15 No. 656 (serial No. 0615356) flown by Major A.Z. Bordun of the 72nd Guards Fighter Air Regiment, 151st Guards Fighter Air Division. On 9 November 1950, Major Bordun – flying in a pair with Senior Lieutenant Dymchenko – attacked and seriously damaged an RB-29 from the 91st Strategic Reconnaissance Squadron, which was destroyed on landing at Gimpo airfield. This was the first encounter between MiG-15s and RB-29s in Korea.

MiG-15 No. 128 (serial No. 120128) flown by Major G.I. Kharkovskiy of the 139th Guards Fighter Air Regiment, 28th Fighter Air Division. Kharkovskiy participated in battles with B-29s on 10 and 14 November 1950 – scoring four B-29 kills.

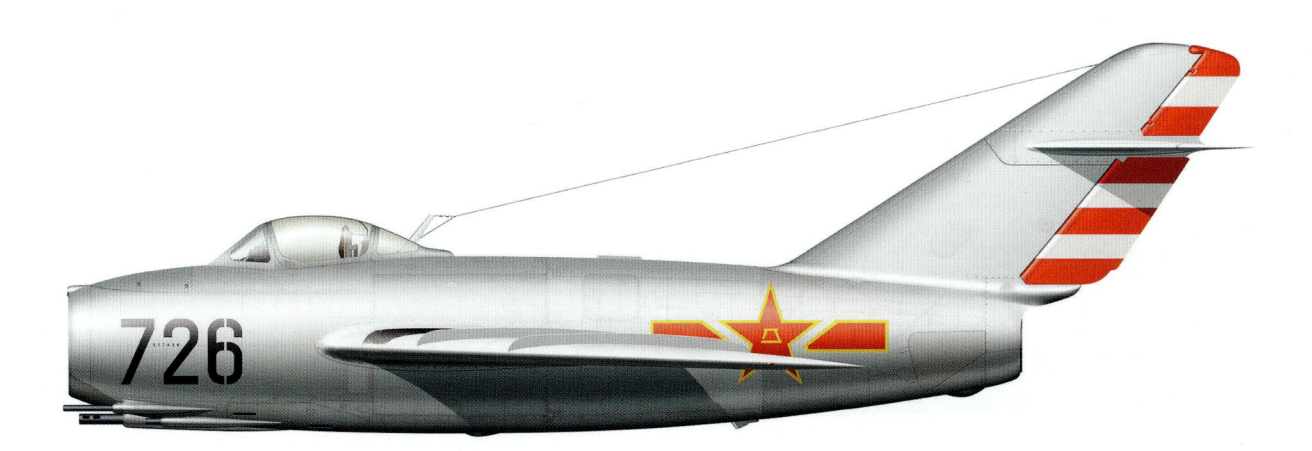

MiG-15 No. 726 (serial No. 117026) flown by Captain Korobov of the 28th Guards Fighter Air Regiment, 151st Guards Fighter Air Division. On 12 November 1950, Captain Korobov (along with his wingman) seriously damaged a single B-29 that made an emergency landing in South Korea.§

Colour views by Yuriy Tepsurkaev (MiG-15) and Andrey Yurgenson (B-29).

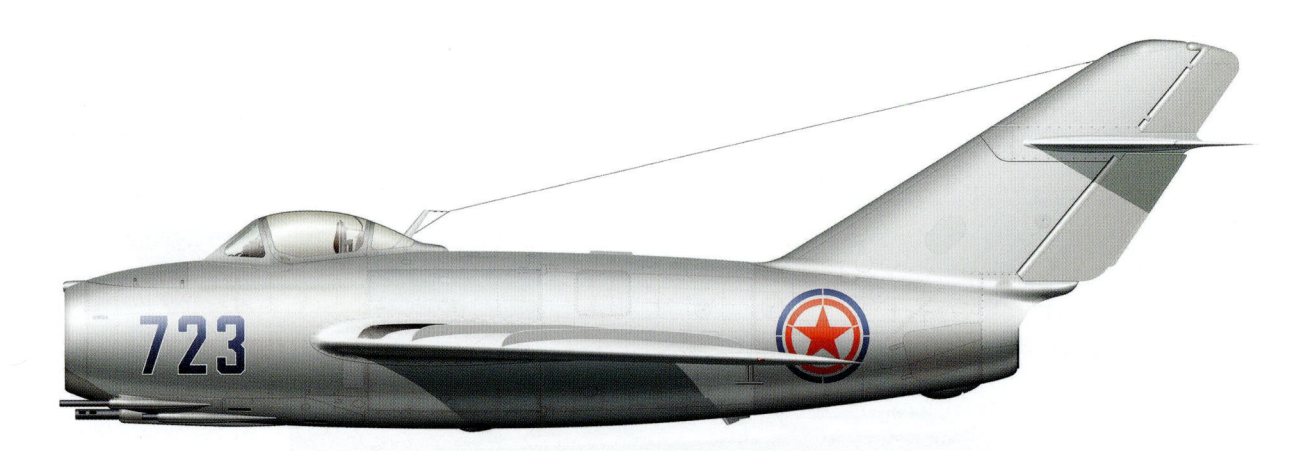

MiG-15bis No. 723 (serial No. 0715323) flown by Captain S.I. Naumenko of the 29th Guards Fighter Air Regiment, 50th Fighter Air Division. Naumenko participated in a battle on 6 December 1950 – as a result of which, he scored a single B-29 kill.

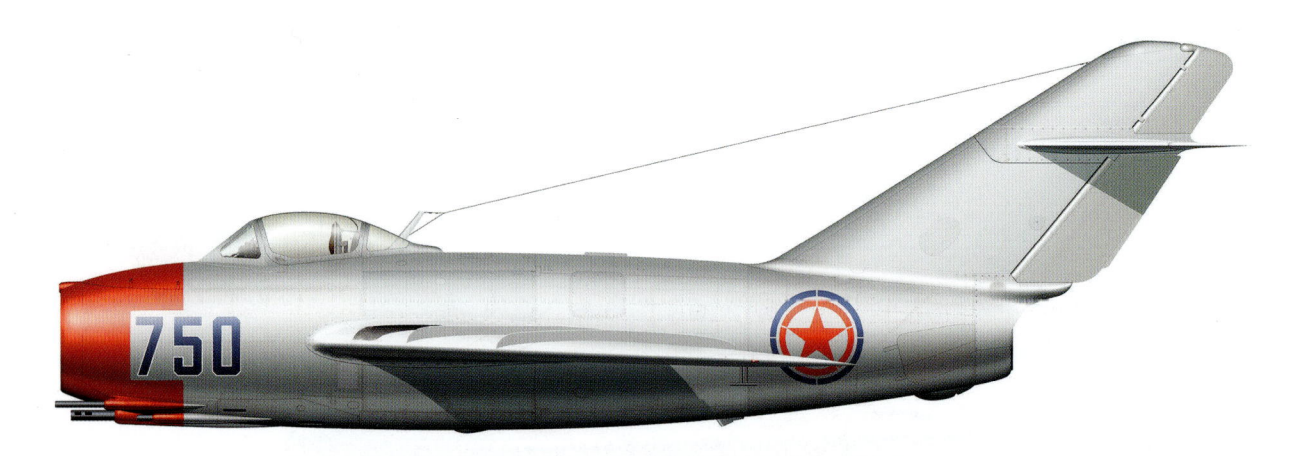

MiG-15bis No. 750 (serial No. 0715350) flown by Lieutenant-Colonel V.I. Kolyadin of the 28th Guards Fighter Air Regiment, 151st Guards Fighter Air Division. Kolyadin participated in battles with B-29s on 14 February and 1 March 1951, and scored two B-29 kills.

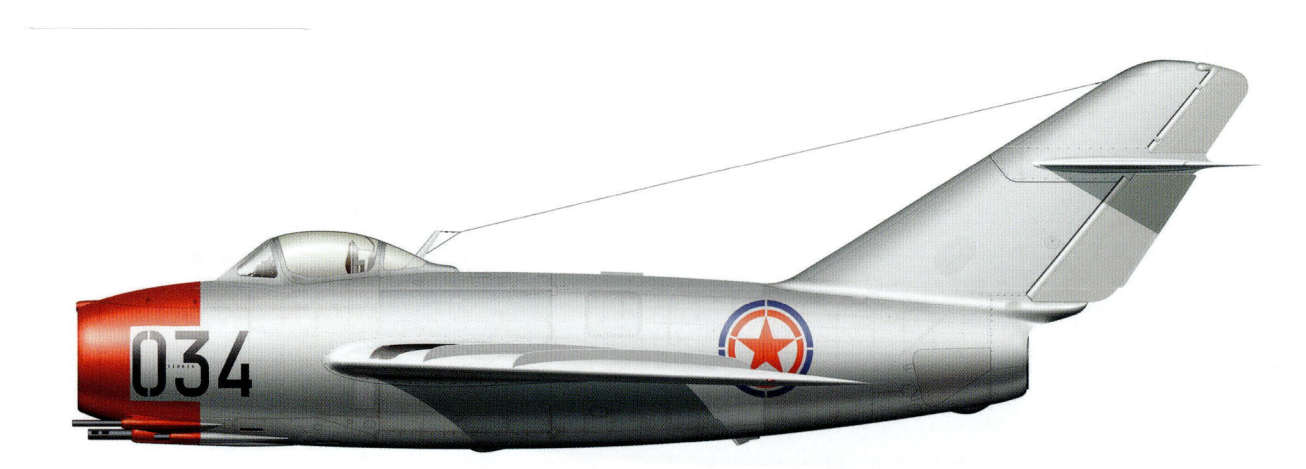

MiG-15 No. 034 (serial No. 110034) flown by Captain I.A. Suchkov of the 176th Guards Fighter Air Regiment, 324th Fighter Air Division. He participated in battles with B-29s on 7 and 12 April 1951, and scored two B-29 kills.

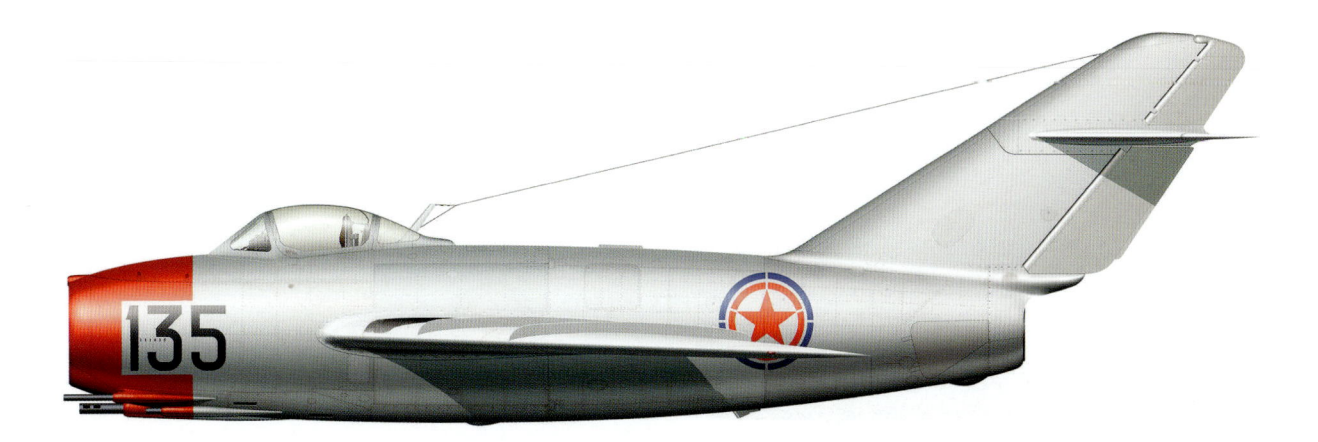

MiG-15 No. 135 (serial No. 111035) flown by Captain S.P. Subbotin of the 176th Guards Fighter Air Regiment, 324th Fighter Air Division. He saw action in combat with B-29s on 7 and 12 April 1951 – scoring two B-29 kills and one escort fighter F-84 kill.

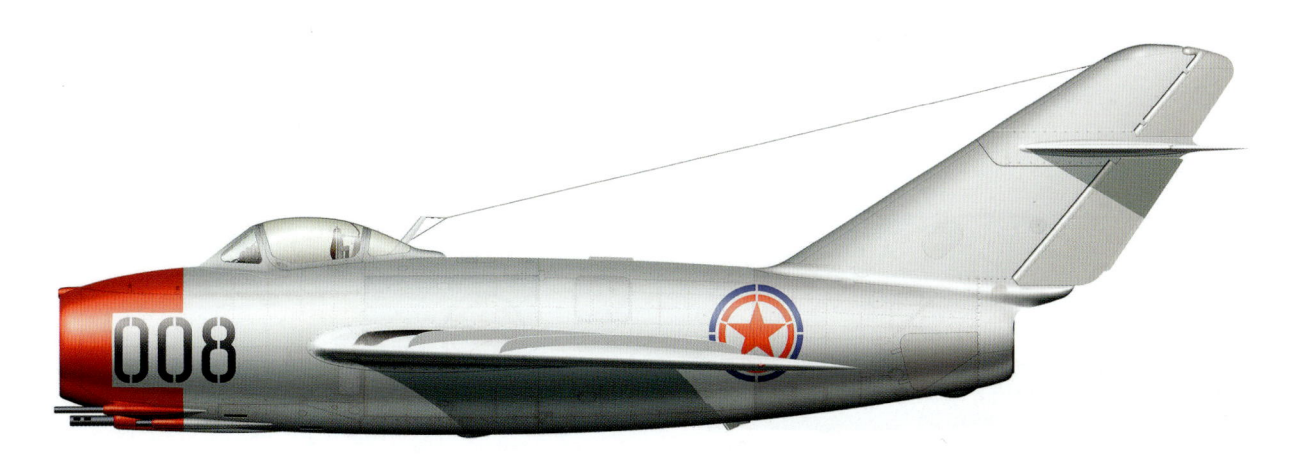

MiG-15 No. 008 (serial No. 110008) flown by Senior Lieutenant B.A. Obraztsov of the 176th Guards Fighter Air Regiment, 324th Fighter Air Division. He participated in battles with B-29s on 7 and 12 April 1951 – scoring one B-29 kill and one escort fighter F-84 kill.

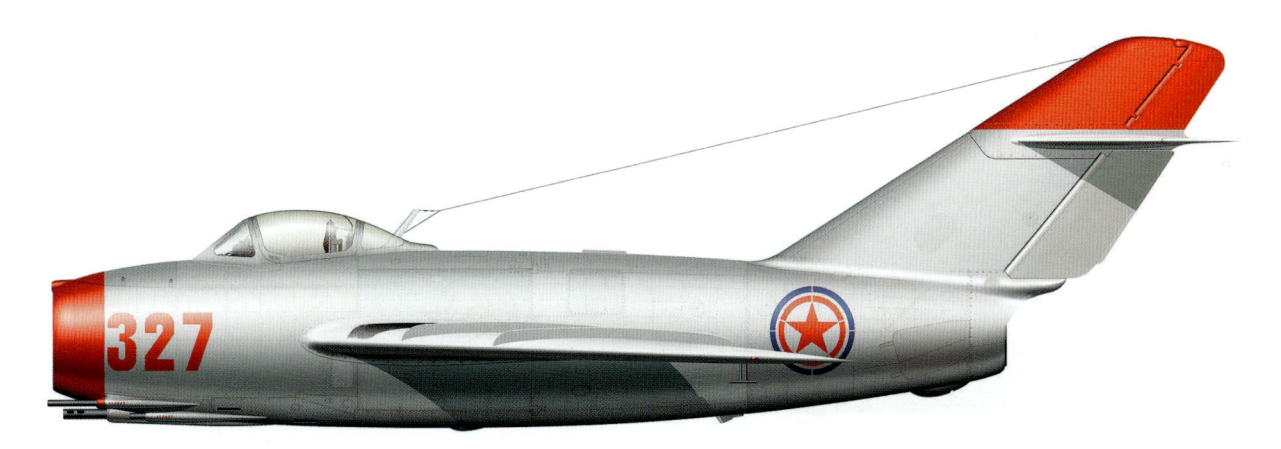

MiG-15bis No. 327 (serial No. 123027) flown by Senior Lieutenant E.M. Stelmakh of the 18th Guards Fighter Air Regiment, 303rd Fighter Air Division. In combat on 1 June 1951, he downed one B-29 on his own and seriously damaged a further two examples; he himself, however, was shot down by an F-86 escort fighter, ejected successfully, but was killed on the ground in a skirmish with Chinese volunteers.

MiG-15bis No. 345 (serial No. 123045) flown by Lieutenant Colonel A.P. Smorchkov of the 18th Guards Fighter Air Regiment, 303rd Fighter Air Division. It was in this aircraft on 22 and 23 October 1951 that Smorchkov shot down two B-29s; however, No. 345 was damaged in the latter battle, and Smorchkov saw action on 24 October in another aircraft.

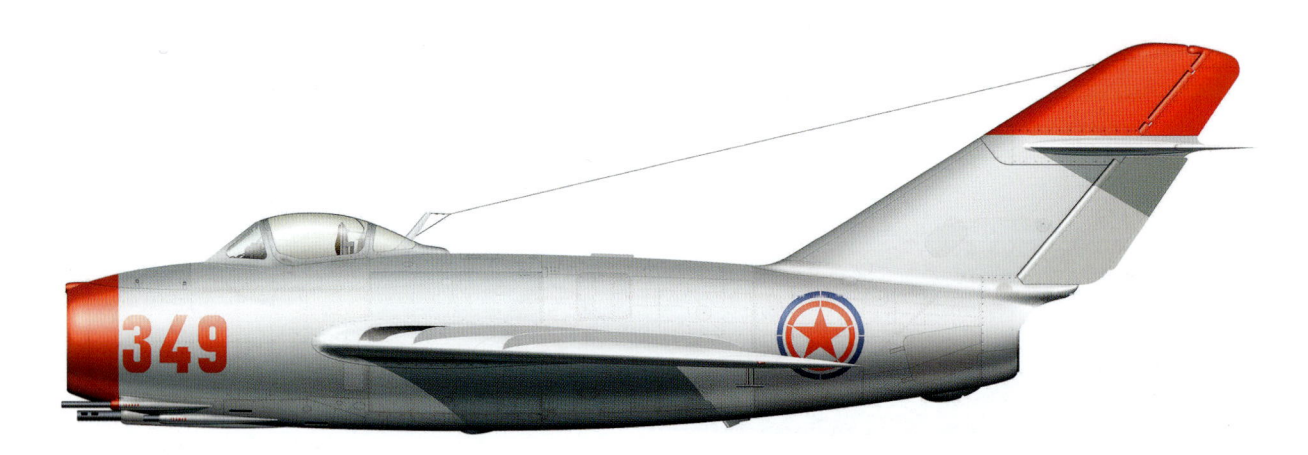

MiG-15bis No. 349 (serial No. 123049) flown by Lieutenant Colonel A.P. Smorchkov of the 18th Guards Fighter Air Regiment, 303rd Fighter Air Division. In view of the damage to his assigned aircraft (No. 345) that occurred on 23 October 1951, he saw action in combat on 24 October – flying aircraft No. 349. In this battle, Smorchkov shot down one B-29 and was wounded in the leg by fire from the aircraft's gunners.

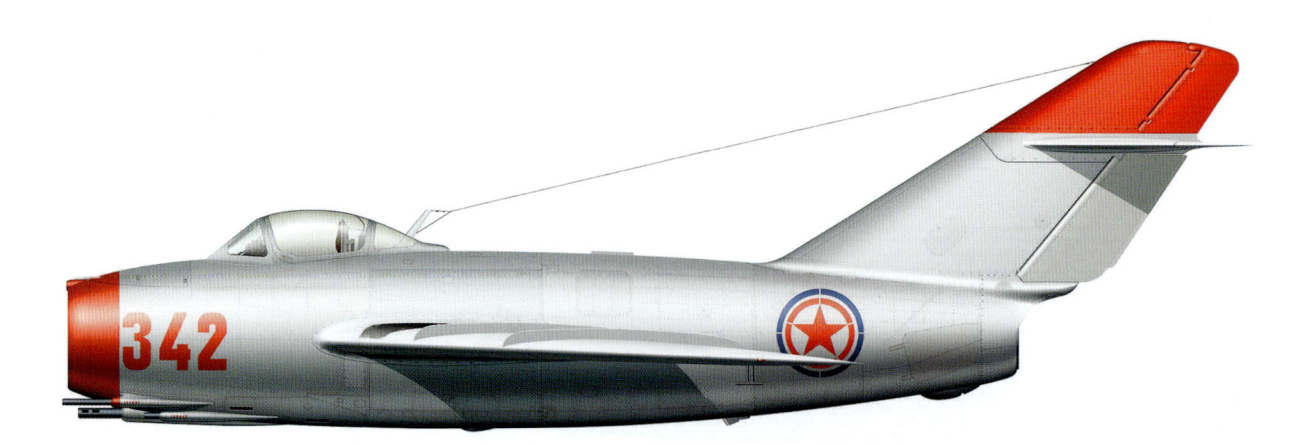

MiG-15bis No. 342 (serial No. 123042) flown by Senior Lieutenant L.K. Shukin of the 18th Guards Fighter Air Regiment, 303rd Fighter Air Division. In combat on 23 October 1951, Shukin shot down an F-84E (serial No. 50-1220) flown by John U. Shoemaker that was providing an escort fighter for the B-29s.

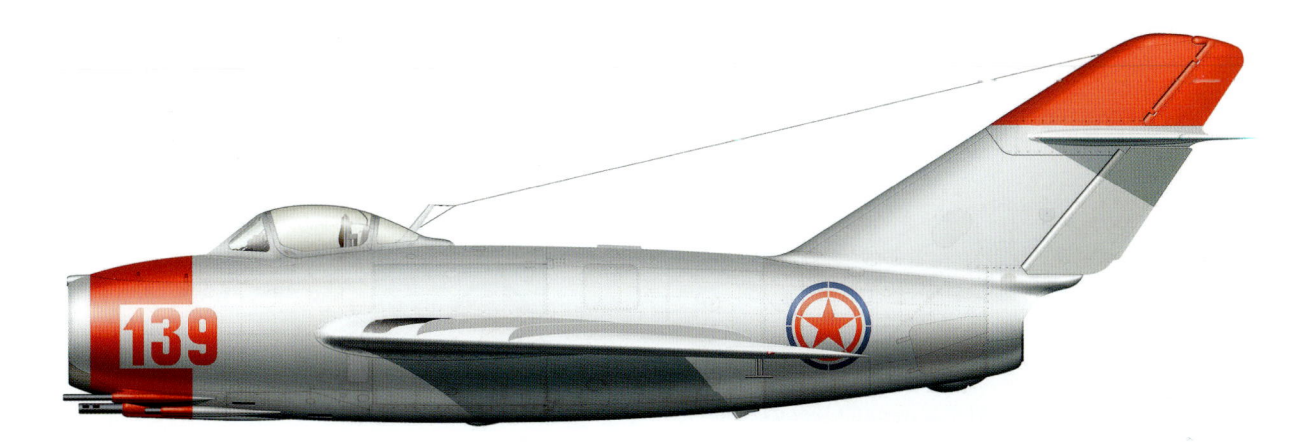

MiG-15bis No. 139 (serial No. 121039) flown by Captain A.P. Bychkov of the 17th Fighter Air Regiment, 303rd Fighter Air Division. Bychkov participated in battles on 23 October 1951 and scored one B-29 kill.

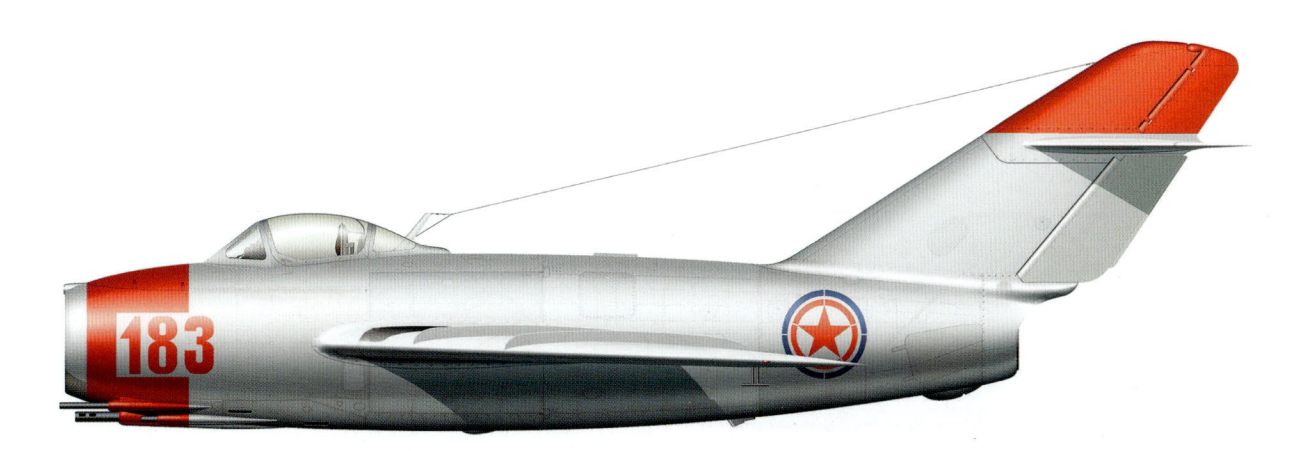

MiG-15bis No. 183 (serial No. 121083) flown by Captain A.P. Bychkov of the 17th Fighter Air Regiment, 303rd Fighter Air Division. Nikolayev participated in battles on 23 October 1951 and scored one B-29 kill; damaging another.

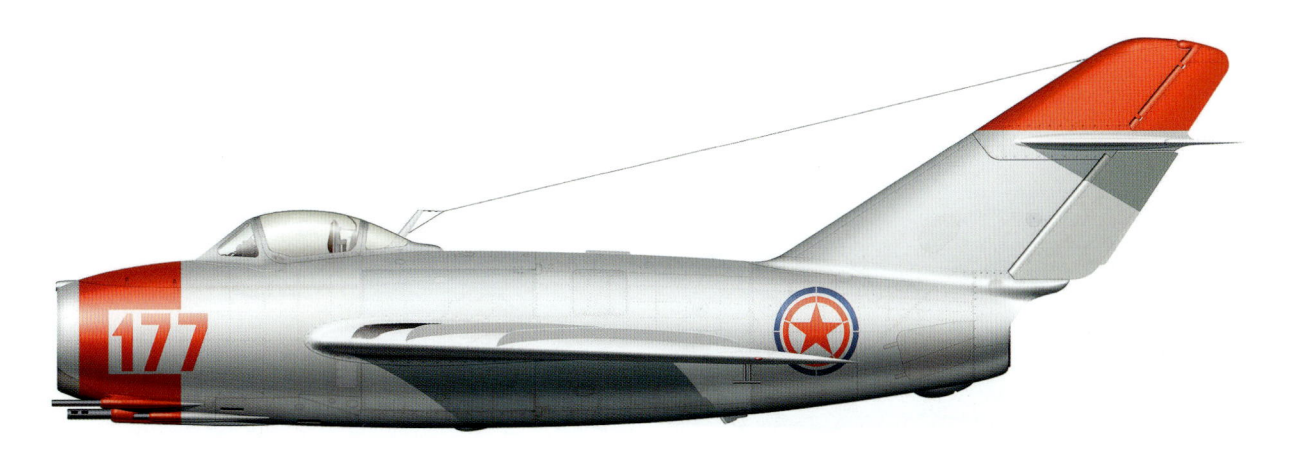

MiG-15bis No. 177 (serial No. 121077) flown by Senior Lieutenant V.F. Shulev of the 17th Fighter Air Regiment, 303rd Fighter Air Division. Shulev participated in battles on 23 October 1951 and scored a kill against an escort fighter F-84.

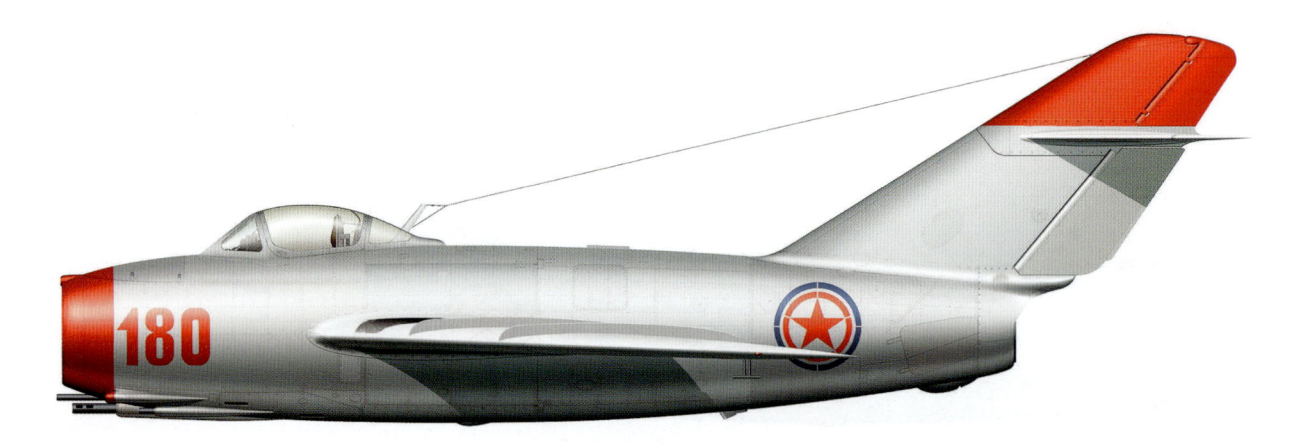

MiG-15bis serial No. 180 (serial No. 121080) flown by Captain S.A. Bakhayev of the 523rd Fighter Air Regiment, 303rd Fighter Air Division. In combat on 23 October 1951, Bakhayev shot down one B-29.

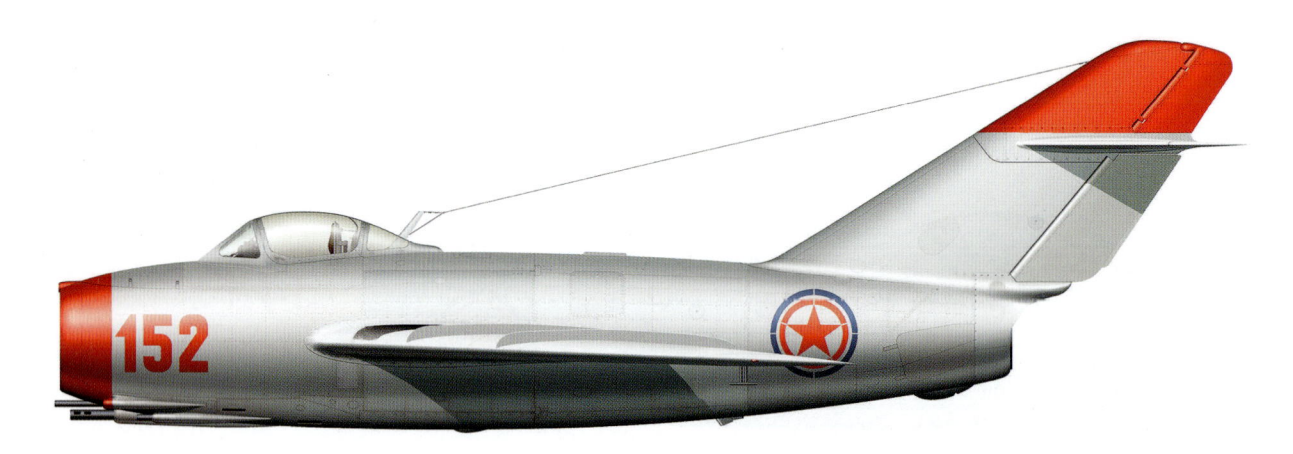

MiG-15bis serial No. 152 (serial No. 121052) flown by Senior Lieutenant Dyachenko of the 523rd Fighter Air Regiment, 303rd Fighter Air Division. He was Bakhayev's wingman during a battle on 23 October 1951 and scored one B-29 kill.

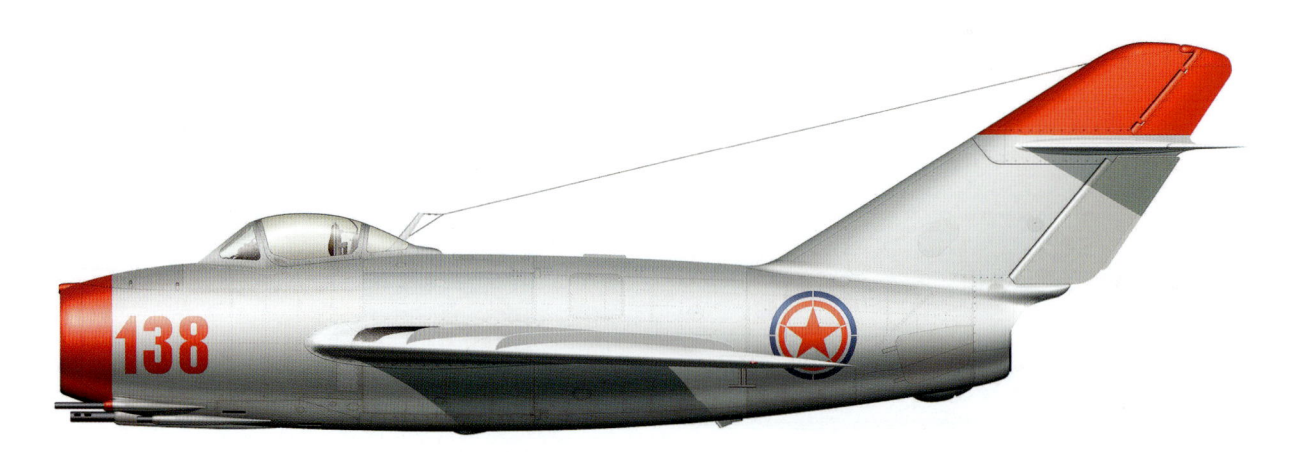

MiG-15bis serial No. 138 (serial No. 121038) – an aircraft from the tactical control flight of the 523rd Fighter Air Regiment, 303rd Fighter Air Division. It was in this aircraft that Major D.P. Oskin participated in a battle on 23 October 1951 – as a result of which, he scored two B-29 kills. On 27 October, Lieutenant Colonel A.N. Karasev took off in No. 138 and scored one B-29 kill.

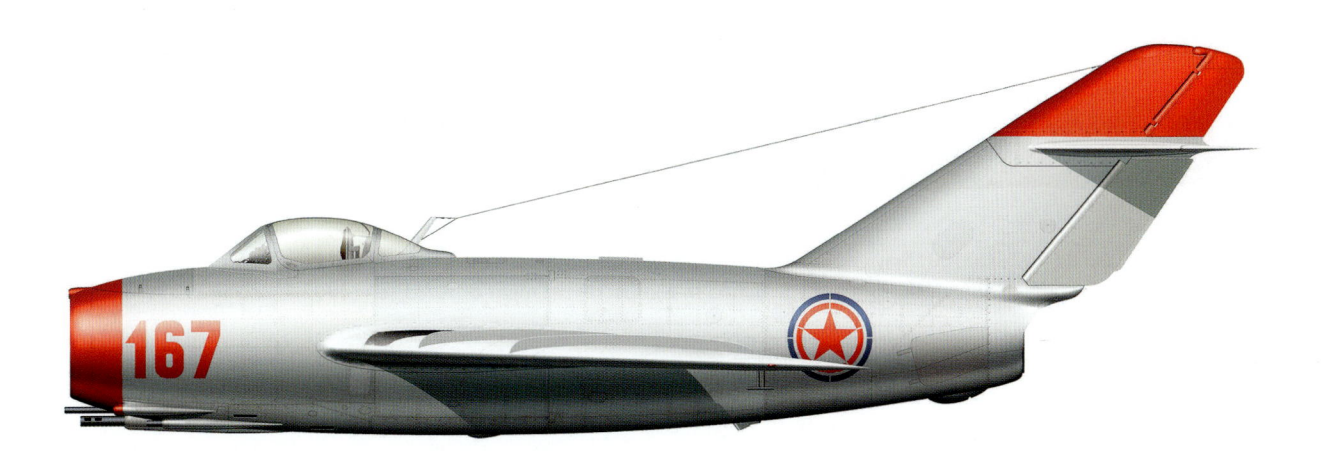

MiG-15bis serial No. 167 (serial No. 121067) flown by Senior Lieutenant Samoylov of the 523rd Fighter Air Regiment, 303rd Fighter Air Division. In combat on 23 October 1951, Samoylov was Major Oskin's wingman – and on 27 October (whilst flying as the lead pair), he scored two kills: one B-29 and one escort fighter F-84.

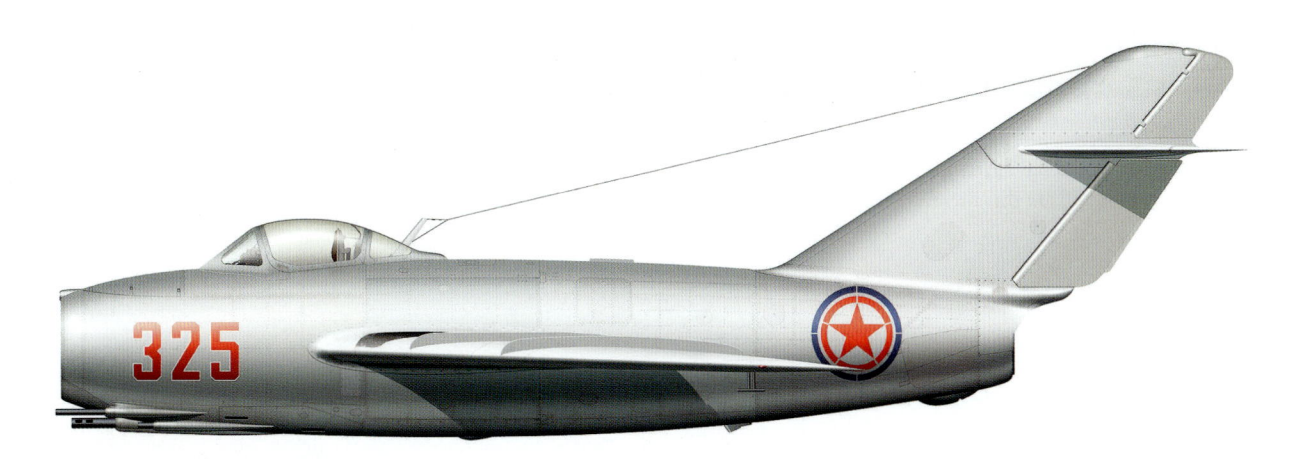

MiG-15bis serial No. 325 (serial No. 1315325) flown by Captain A.M. Karelin of the 351st Fighter Air Regiment. It was in this aircraft on the night of 10/11 June 1952 that Karelin shot down two B-29s and damaged another. No. 325 was the most 'successful' fighter aircraft in the 64th Fighter Air Corps. Aside from the two kills that Karelin scored in this aircraft, the Commander of the 196th Fighter Air Regiment, 324th Fighter Air Division (Colonel E.G. Pepelyayev) scored 17 victories in '325', whilst the Squadron Commander of the 16th Fighter Air Regiment, 97th Fighter Air Division (Captain P.V. Minervin) scored one kill – and Senior Pilot of the 415th Fighter Air Regiment, 133rd Fighter Air Division (Senior Lieutenant N.M. Sokurenko) scored two. It is likely that this is not an exhaustive list, since other pilots were able to fly aircraft '325' from the 16th, 351st and 415th Regiments and shoot down enemy aircraft. No. '325' fought up until the end of the Korean War and was transferred to one of the regiments of the 100th Fighter Air Division; then in November 1954, it was transferred (amongst other aircraft in the 64th Fighter Air Corps) to the Chinese People's Liberation Army Air Force.

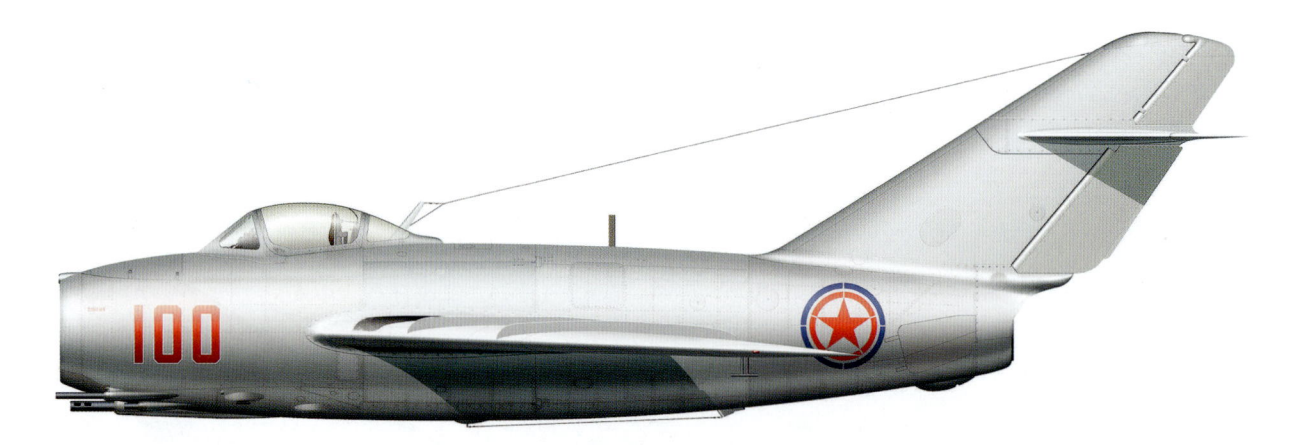

MiG-15bis No. 100 (serial No. 24153100) flown by Lieutenant-Colonel M.I. Studilin of the 147th Guards Fighter Air Regiment, 133rd Fighter Air Division. It was in this aircraft that Studilin saw action in combat on the night of 10/11 June 1952 – scoring a B-29 kill.

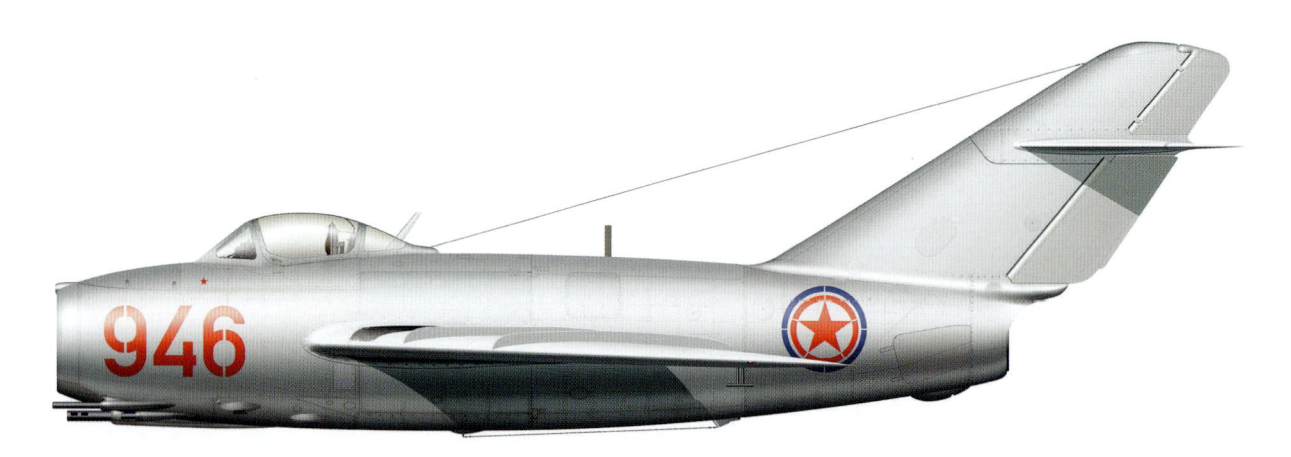

MiG-15bis No. 946 (serial No 2915346) flown by Senior Lieutenant Yu.N. Dobrovichan of the 147th Guards Fighter Air Regiment, 133rd Fighter Air Division. It was in this aircraft that Dorbovichan shot down one B-29 on the night of 10/11 June 1952.

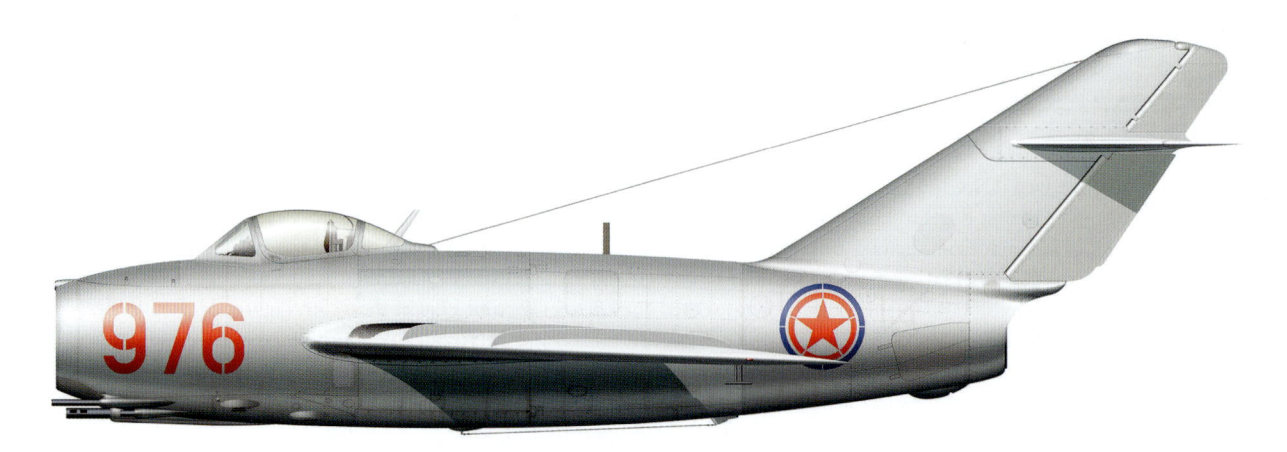

MiG-15bis No. 976 (serial No. 2915376) of the 351st Fighter Air Regiment at Andung airfield in September 1952.

MiG-15bis No. 546 (serial No. 53210546) of the 315st Fighter Air Regiment at Andung airfield in September 1952.

MiG-15bis No. 546 (serial No. 53210546) flown by Captain Goncharov of the 298th Fighter Air Regiment. In February 1953, the 351st Fighter Air Regiment returned to the Soviet Union after having transferred their aircraft (among which was No. 546) to the 298th Fighter Air Regiment that replaced them. At the beginning of 1953, No. 546 was repainted in the camouflage colours that characterised the 298th Fighter Air Regiment. It was in this aircraft on the night of 2/3 March 1953 that Captain Goncharov engaged an enemy fighter in combat – as a result of which, he scored a F-94 kill.

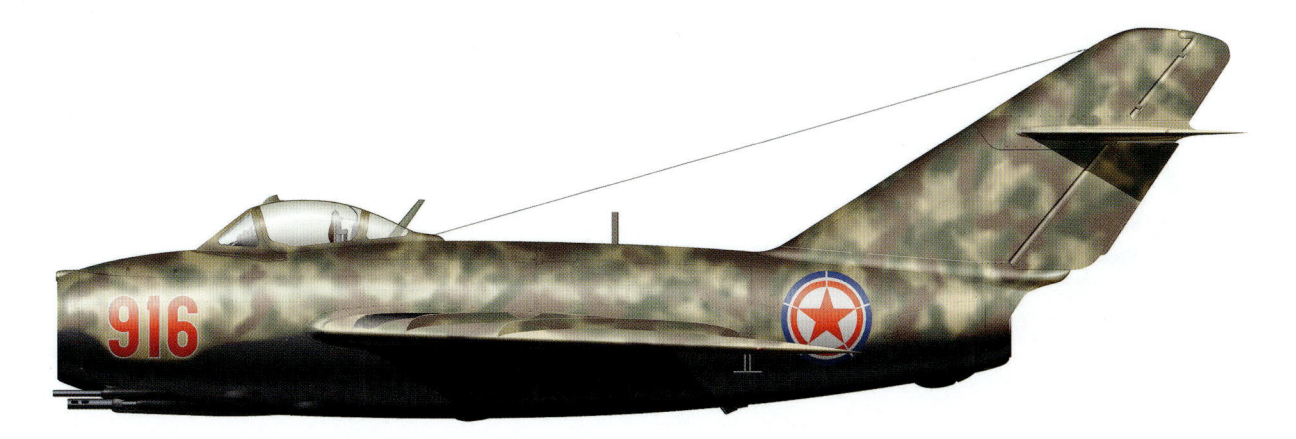

MiG-15bis No. 916 (serial No. 31530916) flown by Senior Lieutenant Ryabukhin of the 298th Fighter Air Regiment.

MiG-15bis No. 759 (serial No. 2715359) flown by Senior Lieutenant Ya.Z. Khabiev of the 535th Fighter Air Regiment, 32nd Fighter Air Division. In night battles during January 1953, Khabiev scored two kills – including on the night of 12/13 January when he downed RB-29 No. 44-62217 of the 91st Strategic Reconnaissance Squadron. This aircraft wears the livery it wore at the time it was found in the 236th Fighter Air Regiment, 37th Fighter Air Division. The reason for this is that judging by the condition of the paintwork, the aircraft was most likely not repainted after its transfer to the 236th Fighter Air Regiment.

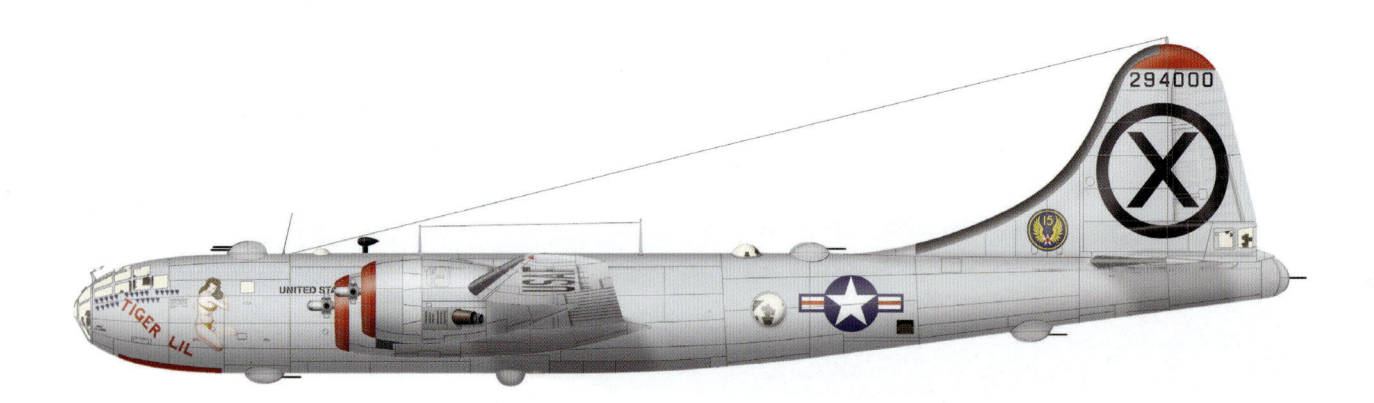

B-29A-20-BN of the 91st Squadron, 55th Strategic Air Reconnaissance Wing (based at Yokota airbase, Japan) in June 1950. This aircraft flew more than 50 sorties over North Korea – and on 7 November 1954, it was shot down by a pair of MiG-15s close to the Kuril Islands and crashed after it failed to make it back to Hokkaido.

B-29-65-BW 44-69805 'Deal Me In', 325th BS/92nd BG; Yokota, Japan 1950.

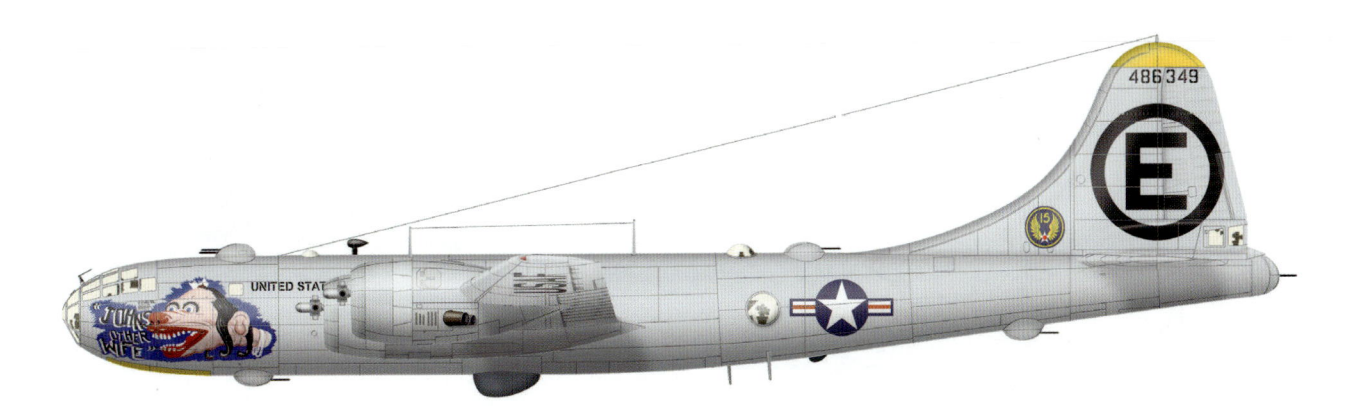

B-29-50-MO 44-86349 'John's Other Wife', 33rd BS/22nd BG; Kadena, Okinawa 1950.

B-29A-60-BN 44-62060 'Spirit of Freeport', 19th BS/22nd BG; Kadena, Okinawa 1950.

B-29, 42-65367, 28th BS/19th BG; Kadena, Okinawa 1951. This aircraft was the only one in 28th BS/19th BG not to be given a nickname.

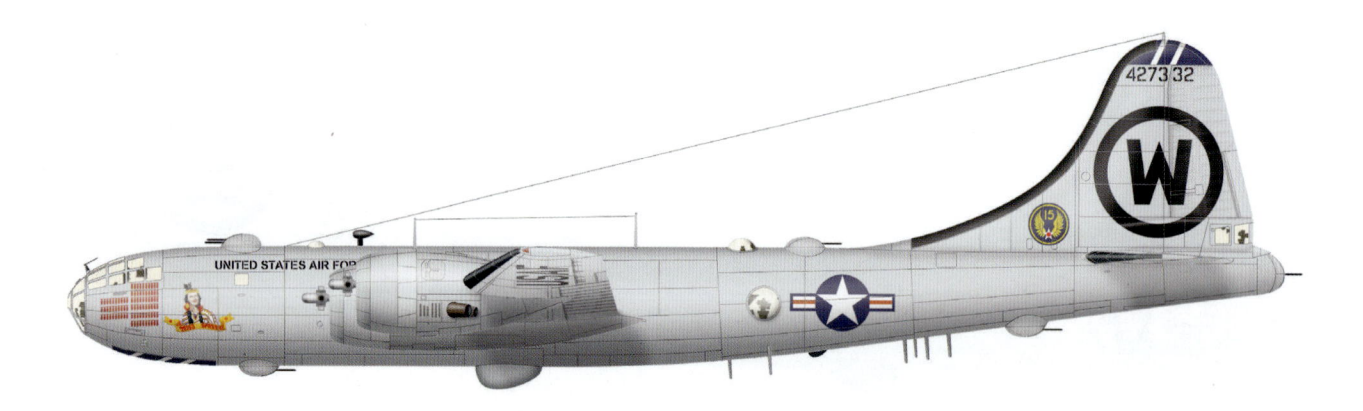

B-29-40-MO, 44-27332 'Miss Spokane', 326th BS/92nd BG; Yokota, Japan 1951.

B-29-55-BW, 44-69667 'Snugglebunny', 343rd BS/98th BG; Yokota, Japan 1951.

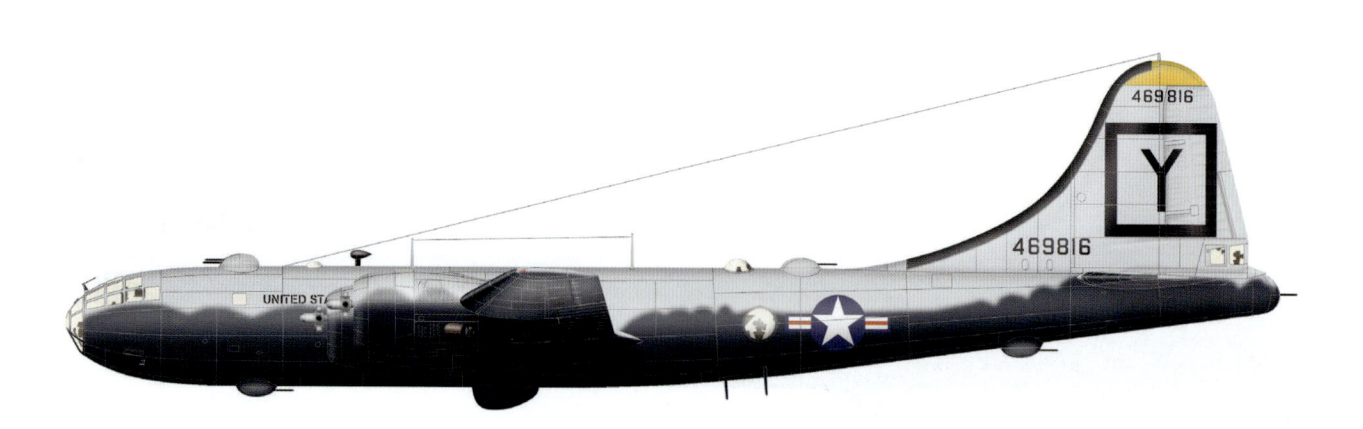

B-29-65-BW, 44-69816 'Sit 'n' Git', 371st BS/307th BG; Kadena, Okinawa 1951.

B-29-50-MO, 44-86323 'Four-A-Breast', 30th BS/19th BG; Kadena, Okinawa 1951.

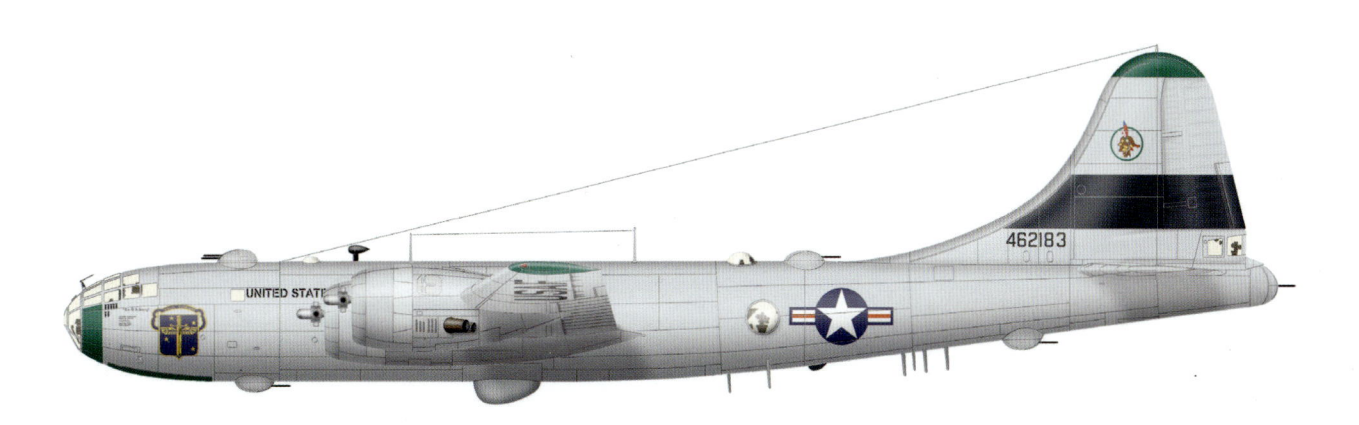

B-29A-60-BW, 44-62183 'Hot to Go', 28th BS/19th BG; Kadena, Okinawa 1951.

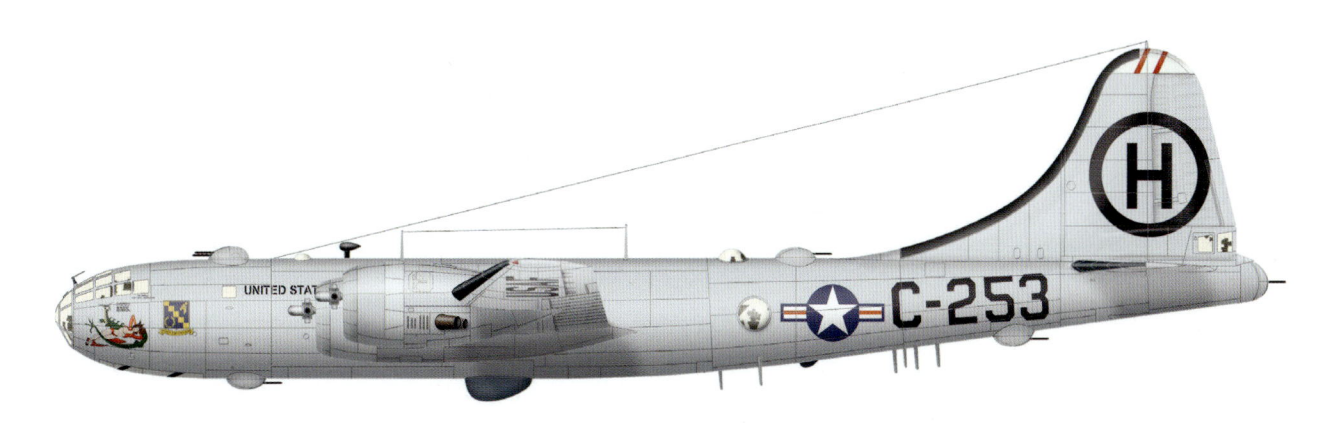

B-29A-70-BN, 44-62253 'Reluctant Drag'on', 345th BS/98th BG; Yokota, Japan 1952.

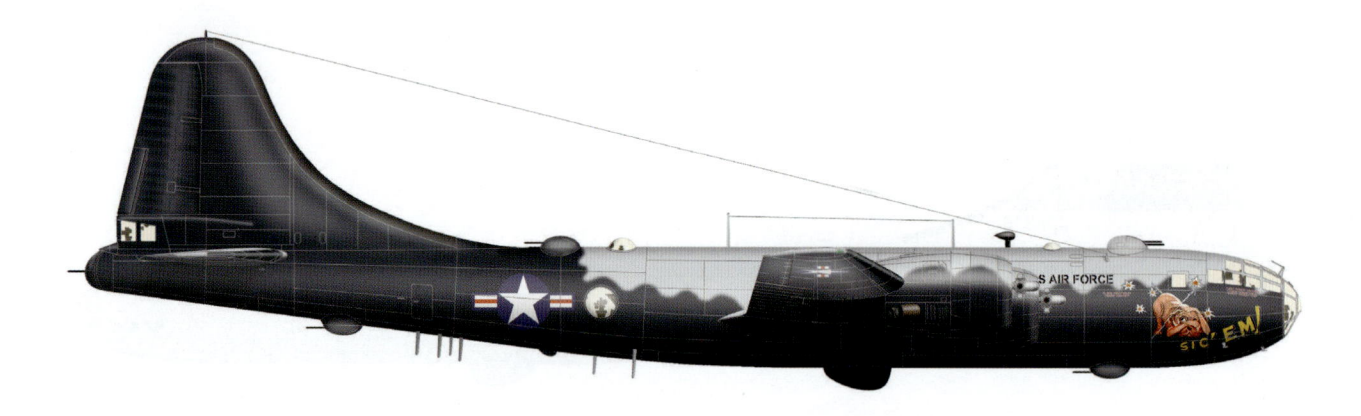

B-29A-50-BN, 44-61809 'Sic 'Em', 343rd BS/98th BG; Yokota, Japan 1952.

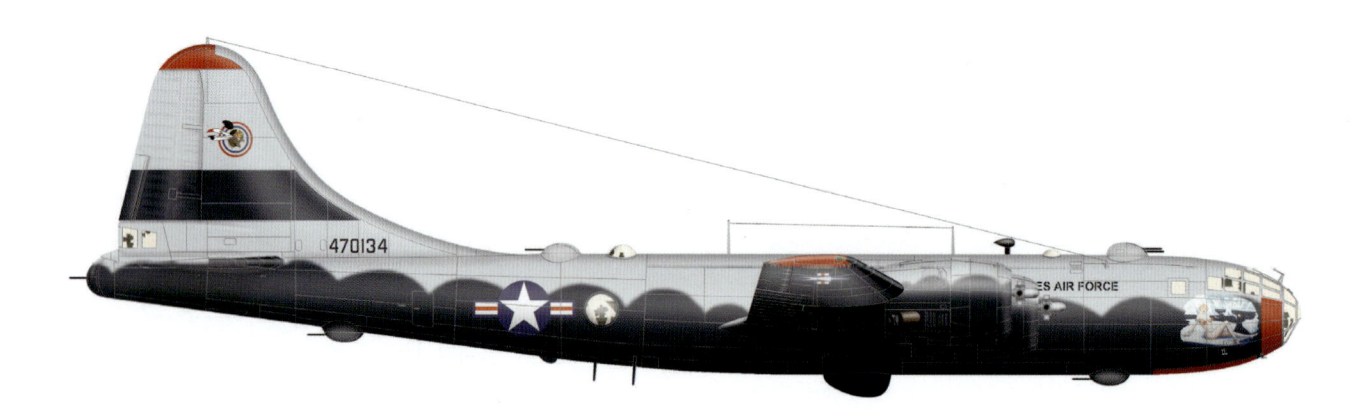

B-29-80-BW, 44-70134 'No Sweat', 93rd BS/19th BG; Kadena, Okinawa 1952.

A map of the theatre of combat operations.

A map of the 64th Fighter Air Corps' combat zone (dated December 1952).

A burst of flak ripped large portions of skin surface from the tail end of a USAF B-29 Superfortress while the 307th Bomb Group was on a daylight bombing attack of targets over North Korea, January 1952. (Courtesy of the US National Archives)

An RB-29 of the 91st Strategic Reconnaissance Group (loaded with aerial cameras) returns from a photo-reconnaissance mission over North Korea. As soon as it lands, any rolls of exposed aerial film will be rushed to the 548th Reconnaissance Technical Squadron, where skilled laboratory technicians and photo interpreters are on alert, February 1952. (Courtesy of the US National Archives)

An important part of the B-29's role remained the bombing raids on North Korea's railway lines, which were carried out with varying degrees of success. In January, reconnaissance identified a section of railway line near the village of Wadong as the most suitable for a bombing raid. At this point, the railway passed along the bottom of a long narrow gorge. The cramped conditions would mean that the North Koreans would not be able to repair the railway quickly. Over the course of 44 days from 26 January, the B-29s flew 77 sorties against this section of line, while a further 125 sorties were flown by Invaders. In total, almost four thousand 227 kg bombs were dropped. However, it was much cry and little wool; only 33 bombs actually hit the railway line. The outcome of this huge effort by Bomber Command was that rail traffic along this section of line was brought to a standstill for a week.

By spring 1952, the Superfortresses had switched to destroying bridges. In March, the Far East Air Force launched 'Operation Strangle', which aimed at reducing supplies getting through to frontline troops – and ideally, stopping them altogether. In contrast to all the other battlefield interdiction operations, 'Strangle' proposed that the entire air forces would be concentrated not on the communications network in North Korea as a whole, but on individual areas – the most vulnerable and least-defended elements of this network. Regular bombing raids on one of these would mean that the enemy's frontline troops would be cut off from their logistics units.

On 25 March, as part of the operation, 46 bombers carried out a bombing raid on the double-track railway bridge at Pyongyang – damaging it in nine places. Three days later, 47 B-29s destroyed the bridge at Chongju – thus two main railway routes leading to Sinuiju were severed once again; 10 bridges sustained 143 direct hits over the course of 66 raids during May. In total, 85 sorties were flown against the bridges in the spring of 1952.

Since the destruction of the airfields was always considered the most important component of the battle for air supremacy, B-29s would visit them regularly. Aerial reconnaissance of the 34 airfields and airstrips in North Korean territory was constant, and information on the course of repair work on these airfields would flow into the Joint Operations Centre. As soon as the photographs showed that repair work was nearing completion, the bombers would hit them again – thus in the spring, more than 400 sorties were flown against the airfields.

At the beginning of June, the bridges and railway stations around Sonchon, Pakchon and Huichon remained the B-29's principal targets. By that time, according to American reconnaissance, more than 200 radar-guided anti-aircraft searchlights – capable of illuminating the bombers for several minutes – were at the disposal of North Korean Air Defence units. The Superfortresses, which were brightly illuminated by searchlights, could fall victim to the fighters. Fortunately, North Korean night-time air defence did not have any aircraft capable of intercepting a B-29. All this changed on the night of 10/11 June when the railway bridge around Kwaksan was the designated target for 11 B-29s from the 19th Bomb Wing. That night recalled for Bomber Command the nightmare of the previous autumn…

※

Up until autumn 1951, resistance to night raids by the US Far East Air Force in Korea had only come from anti-aircraft artillery. Its forces, however, were inadequate to be able to reliably defend all the most important and vulnerable sites. From almost the very beginning of the war, it was decided that the North Korean night-time air defence system would be augmented by Soviet aviation. In order to provide a more robust defence of assets, such as the airfields around Antung

Senior Lieutenant Dushin of the 351st Fighter Air Regiment (who shot down one B-25 in China and two B-26s in Korea) briefs a Chinese pilot before take-off; Jiangwan airfield, summer 1950.

Major Dushin's (Squadron Commander of the 351st Fighter Air Regiment) ground crew prepare his La-11 for a night sortie. Major Dushin scored one victory in China and two victories in Korea.

and Chongsu; the bridges across the Yalu River at Sinuiju and the hydroelectric power station at Suiho during the night, the 351st Fighter Air Regiment – equipped with La-11 aircraft – was incorporated into the 64th Fighter Air Corps under Directive No. 640644, issued by the USSR's Armed Forces Minister.

The 351st Fighter Air Regiment comprised 32 pilots – and 11 Lavochkins were redeployed to Anshan airfield on 23 June. Twenty La-11 aircraft – required to build up forces to a 15/39 state level – arrived from air force units based inside the territory of the USSR. The aircraft that arrived were in an unsatisfactory condition – having component failures, defects, shortcomings and so on – although the regiment's technicians soon turned them into mission-ready aircraft. The regiment began to prepare for combat operations, which was made all the more difficult by the fact that of the 32 pilots, only four of them were trained to fly at night – and even then, they were only able to fly circuits or in a holding pattern. They had to undergo intensive training – and in a short time, every pilot in the regiment had amassed on average 40 'day' and 33 'night' hours, which corresponded to 31 and 77 flights respectively. The regiment was ready for night operations by the beginning of autumn and began to undertake these missions from 9 September. In the order issued by the Commander of the 64th Fighter Air Corps, which was directly responsible for the 351st Fighter Air Regiment, these missions were conceived as follows: '... to destroy individual enemy bomber and reconnaissance aircraft around Anju–Antung operating within the searchlight zone with the potential for ten sorties per night'.[1] This mission was confirmed on 10 October by way of Combat Order No. 19, issued by the Corps Commander.

By November 1951, the regiment's pilots were engaging the light B-26 bombers in combat – and on the basis of the results of two of these battles, the head of the Regimental Air Gunner Service, Captain Simko, was credited with shooting down one Invader and damaging another. The La-11 was able to intercept the B-26 successfully, but was not able to cope with the B-29s that arrived in November. On 28 November, Captains Karelin and Golyshevskiy encountered a Superfortress. Close to Sinuiju, the bomber was caught like a 'moth' in a set of searchlights. After dropping its bombs, it began to head away from the target – entering a descent. The pilots of the 351st Fighter Air Regiment did manage to fire at this aircraft from a great distance, but after evading the glare of the anti-aircraft searchlights, the aircraft disappeared into the darkness. The B-29 was recorded as damaged, but in a private conversation with I. Seidov, however, I.P. Golyshveskiy denied that the bomber had been damaged that night, as the pilots had opened fire from too great a distance.

On 4 December, Captain Dushin – on patrol at an altitude of 7,000 m – noticed a B-29 in the searchlight zone 1,000 m above and in front of him. Dushin went on the attack. To begin with, the closing speed was high and the pilot was able to come within 700–750 m of the aircraft. After the bomber had dropped its bombs, however, the distance between the two aircraft began to increase steadily and Dushin had to open fire, but from a distance of 700 m, this was ineffective and the bomber was not damaged at all. Following Dushin's attempt, this Fortress was again attacked: this time by Senior Lieutenant Khvalenskiy. He was not able to see the outcome of his attack due to muzzle fire coming from his own guns. The B-29 escaped the searchlights and headed out to sea.

At 2330, Dushin encountered a second B-29 and attacked this aircraft twice from a distance 400–200 m at an aspect angle of 1/4–2/4. As he was firing, Dushin watched his shells explode on the engines and the nose section of the fuselage of the Superfortress, but he was not able to shoot this aircraft down, as he ran out of ammunition in the course of his second attack. This bomber was also attacked by Khvalenskiy, but disappeared from the searchlight zone – descending out of sight. Captain Dushin and Senior Lieutenant Khvalenskiy were credited as having damaged this Fortress.

1   Fund of the 64th IAK, inventory 174045ss, file. 102, p.125.

According to Western sources, on the night of 4/5 December, one Superfortress carrying out a raid on Uiju was caught in the glare of the searchlights and was damaged by enemy fighters. Furthermore, on 5 December, one B-29 from the 307th Bomb Wing was written off – and it is possible that this aircraft was damaged by Dushin and Khvalenskiy. Twenty days later, a further two Superfortresses were damaged. On the night of 23/24 December, the bombers took off to hit Uiju. This time, before they even reached the area in which the searchlights were deployed, a lone B-26 from the 3rd Bomb Wing appeared. The pilot of the Invader, Captain Willis Jessup, managed to destroy eight searchlights; those that remained, however, illuminated a group of 'Fortresses' from the 19th Bomb Wing perfectly well. One of the bombers was damaged by cannon fire from a night fighter, while a second was hit by anti-aircraft crews. Both aircraft returned to base successfully; one of them was, however, written off the following day. Our pilots were not credited with shooting down or damaging any aircraft on the night of 23/24 December 1951.

During the air battles at the end of 1951, it was established that the speed, manoeuvrability and rate of climb of the La-11 was insufficient to be able to counter the B-29s successfully at altitudes in excess of 6,000 m – given that the searchlight area had been bounded. If a Superfortress was flying at a speed of 450–460 km/hr before it had dropped its bombs, this would increase to 500–510 km/hr once it had dropped its payload – thus an La-11 fighter that was still at some distance from the enemy would not be able to catch up with a bomber within the illuminated area at the edge of the searchlight field. In their attempts to counter the raids by American bombers, the pilots of the 351st Fighter Air Regiment completed 230 individual sorties on patrols and to intercept enemy aircraft, although our pilots were only able to engage enemy aircraft in combat on 12 of these sorties. Their only encounter with a B-26 on 16 November ended in a victory for Captain Dushin, although we were not able to find any evidence of actual kills to emerge from the remaining air battles with the B-29s. Subsequently, 64th Fighter Air Corps Command concluded that MiG-15 aircraft had to be used during night raids. Out of all the Soviet aircraft available at that time, it was the MiG-15 that was best suited to the challenge of intercepting aircraft such as the B-29. This was demonstrated very clearly in the daylight battles with the 'Fortresses'. Apart from that, the MiG-15bis, which was the 64th Fighter Air Corps' principal fighter, was better suited to night operations than the La-11. The OSP-48 instrument landing equipment that this fighter was fitted with – and which incorporated an ARK-5 'Amur' radio-compass, an RV-2 'Crystal' low-altitude radio-altimeter and an MRP-48 'Chrysanthemum' marker radio-receiver – made flying the MiG at night and in poor weather conditions much easier. The SRO-1 'Barium-M' IFF transponder fitted to the 'Bis' was very highly rated. The way this was tracked on the plan position indicator on a ground-based radar station made the process of controlling the fighters under his command – and guiding them onto their targets – much easier for the guidance officer.

Thanks to this equipment, each MiG in flight had its own unique onboard transponder code – and not only was the guidance officer able to tell his own aircraft from those of the enemy, he could distinguish our fighters from one another. The MiG's armament was also more powerful, but the biggest advantage for the MiGs was in their layout. The cannons in the MiG were located under the nose section of the fuselage – and the face of the muzzle was hidden from the pilot's eyes. In contrast to the 'fifteen', the La-11's armament was located in the upper fuselage section under the engine cowling, right in front of the pilot's cockpit. As a result, the first bursts of muzzle fire, which were particularly bright at night, would temporarily blind the pilot of the Lavochkin and, as a rule, he would lose his aim – therefore repeated night raids using La-11s were only possible against well-illuminated targets; the MiG-15 did not suffer from this drawback.

The MiGs began night operations over Korea from 28 December 1951 when a flight was allocated from the 196th Fighter Air Regiment, 324th Fighter Air Division to protect assets around Antung. One flight from the 303rd Fighter Air Division also began to undergo training for night operations. In the first month of 1952, Lavochkins from the 351st Regiment, MiGs from the 324th Division and the corps' headquarters completed 127 night patrol sorties – spending 233 hours in the air. This was a sufficiently intensive combat regime: every night, each of the corps' patrols would spend around seven-and-a-half hours in the air on average – completing four sorties each. However, for all their efforts, the effectiveness of our fighters remained low. In all of January, the fighters only engaged one B-26 in combat, which was not successful.

One of the reasons behind the lack of effectiveness of our fighters was the insufficient numbers of MiG-15s drafted in for night combat operations. One flight was clearly insufficient, but it was not possible to resolve this situation in January. The combined efforts of the 303rd and 324th Fighter Air Divisions were directed at countering daylight raids by enemy aircraft and on committing the units that had arrived to relieve them. At the beginning of January, the 324th Division began to transfer its materiel to the 97th Fighter Air Division that was replacing it – and for the majority of the month, it operated as a single regiment. On 31 January, the last of the aircraft were handed over to the 97th Division – and the following day, the 324th Fighter Air Division departed back to the Soviet Union.

Since the 97th Air Defence Fighter Air Division had entered the war, the number of pilots trained to fly at night and in adverse weather conditions increased, and the situation began to improve. Of the 16th and 148th Guards Fighter Air Regiments incorporated into this division, four crews from each of them were selected. A night fighter squadron was formed from these crews and introductory flights began on 20 January. The squadron commenced combat operations 10 days later. Apart from that, in February 1952, pilots from one of the squadrons in the 351st Fighter Air Regiment began to assimilate the MiG-15 – completing their first day flights in this jet aircraft in March; night sorties began the following month. By May 1952, the regiment had 12 MiG-15s and 18 La-11s on hand.

On 16 May, the 351st Fighter Air Regiment redeployed in full to Antung. The day before this happened, a squadron from the 147th Guards Fighter Air Regiment – operating from Tatung-kou airfield – commenced combat operations. This regiment was subordinated to the 133rd Air Defence Fighter Air Division, which had arrived in the Korean theatre of operations in mid-April. As soon as the two squadrons of MiGs from the 147th Guards and 351st Air Regiments had come on stream, the 97th Fighter Air Division was withdrawn from night operations – and this unit transferred exclusively to daylight operations. From mid-May, the Commander of the regiment was able to draw up to 17 MiG-15s and up to seven La-11s into battle in the hours of darkness.

June 1952 became a critical month in the night war over the 'land of the morning calm'. Operating from Antung and Tatung-kou airfields, the night fighters of the 64th Fighter Air Corps operated not only in the corps' searchlight zone, but also within the Korean People's Army Air Force's searchlight field around Anju and Huichon. Along with their patrols in the short duration zones close to the searchlight field, the fighters were also sent – using ground guidance – to intercept enemy bombers at inaccessible locations and specially-guarded assets outside this area from the Corps Control Point. That month, the night fighters of the 64th Fighter Air Corps opened their tally of B-29 kills.

On 10 June at 2215, the corps' radar station detected a trace from a B-29 flying in a northerly direction around Chang-Yi. By 2238, the radar screen showed a group of 10 aircraft flying singly at intervals ranging from one to 10 minutes. The corps' fighters began to take to the air at 2226; four MiG-15s were scrambled in the space of 21 minutes.

The pilots – Commander of the 147th Guards Fighter Air Regiment, Lieutenant-Colonel Studilin; his deputy, Major Bykovets; the navigator of the 351st Fighter Air Regiment, Captain Karelin; and his regimental colleague, Senior Lieutenant Ikhsangalyev – were tasked with patrolling at different altitudes to protect assets around Antung from possible strikes by the 'Fortresses':

> ... At 2132 [2232] Lieutenant-Colonel Studilin took off under orders from the Fighter Air Corps' Command Post. The pilot set course for the bombers at an altitude of 5,000 m on the basis of information from the Command Post and navigated using a bearing. At 2145 [2245] Studilin encountered an enemy B-29 illuminated by searchlights above and to the right of him 15 km west of Taesu and at an altitude of 6,500 m. Guards Lieutenant-Colonel Studilin closed on the aircraft in a climb and attacked it from behind, below and to the left at an aspect angle of 1/4 opening fire from a distance of 1,000–800 m. This attack was not successful. The B-29 turned away to the left and increased speed as it began to leave the searchlight zone, firing at our fighter.
>
> The Lieutenant-Colonel made his second attack from behind, to the left and from below the bomber at an aspect angle of 1/4 opening fire from a distance of 600 m. He took aim using a movable gunsight reticle, using all his guns at the same time in a long burst of fire. As a result of this attack the port inboard engine on the B-29 caught fire. After this second attack the aircraft began to head away from the searchlights... as the bomber was heading away from the searchlights Guards Lieutenant-Colonel Studilin used the burning port engine to track the aircraft, making a further two attacks. The first of these was at an altitude of 6,000 m and an aspect angle of 0/4 at a distance of 600–500 m at the same altitude as that of the bomber. His was a concentrated attack with a long burst of fire. He made his second attack from behind and below the bomber at an aspect angle ranging from 1/4–0/4 at an altitude of 5,500 m from a distance of 300 m. The engine on the aircraft's starboard flank caught fire as a result of the second attack and the B-29 departed towards Korea Bay descending sharply in a left turn. Lieutenant-Colonel Studilin did not pursue the bomber any further as he was completely out of ammunition.
>
> The B-29 aircraft continued to descend and crashed into Korea Bay at CHOLSAN some 15 km from the coast. The loss of this bomber aircraft was confirmed by the Chinese volunteer infantry and the local Korean authorities (the Police).
>
> This battle lasted 10 minutes.[2]
>
> Captain Karelin was scrambled at 2154 [2254] along with Snr Lieutenant Iskhangalev at 2157 [2257] to intercept the next batch of bombers that were approaching the Taesu area from the south.
>
> Once over the Taesu area at 2200 [2300] Captain Karelin encountered a B-29 that was illuminated by searchlights and heading towards him at an altitude of 7,800 m. He attacked this aircraft head on at an aspect angle of 1/4. He opened fire from a distance of 300–400 m. As a result of this attack the B-29 exploded in mid-air and the wreckage went down approximately 15-20 km south-east of SONCHON.
>
> As he broke off the attack the left outer wing panel of Captain Karelin's aircraft was damaged by wreckage from the B-29 following its explosion (there was a significant dent and a hole in the left outer wing panel) and the pilot's cockpit was scratched.
>
> As they resumed their patrol of the area around Taesu they received information from the Command Post concerning the approach of a new batch of enemy aircraft and attacked it from a distance of 400–300 m at an aspect angle of 2/4 using a medium burst of fire. As a result of this attack the B-29 caught fire, dropping its bombs haphazardly and losing altitude heading towards the sea on a bearing of 200°. Captain Karelin

---

2   Fund of the 64th IAK, inventory 174045ss, file. 108, pp.66-67.

The best night fighter pilot of the Korean War: Hero of the Soviet Union Major Anatoliy Karelin of the 351st Fighter Air Regiment (he shot down six B-29s).

Fyodor Volodarskiy from the 147th Guards Fighter Air Regiment. (This photograph was provided by I. Seidov)

did not pursue the burning B-29 any further as it had crossed the coast.

On resuming his patrol over this area Captain Karelin encountered a third B-29 caught in the searchlights at 2225 [2325] at an altitude of 7,000 m that he attacked from behind at an aspect angle of 2/4 opening fire from a distance of 400–300 m in one long burst. As a result of this attack the B-29 caught fire and departed out to sea losing altitude rapidly and crashed 35 km from the coast west of SUKCHON. Captain Karelin observed an enemy launch making its way to the crash site to search for survivors.

The Fighter Air Corps' Command Post also observed the aircraft exploding and burning as it went down.

The ammunition expended was as follows: NS-23-71 shells; NS-37-22 shells.[3]

… Snr Lieutenant Iskhangalev who was on patrol over Taesu encountered a B-29 aircraft that was caught in the searchlights, which he attacked from behind at an aspect angle of 2/4 from a distance of 1,000–800 m giving this aircraft one medium burst of fire but without success. Captain Iskhangalev did not attempt to make any further attacks as the B-29 had left the searchlight field.[4]

Western publications state that on the night of 10 June, of the 11 Superfortresses that flew to the complex of railway bridges at Kwaksan, 10 were caught in searchlights. One of the B-29s escaped the glare of the searchlights, and this was the only one to attempt to knock out the radio guidance system for the searchlights (using strips of foil). The MiGs headed for the 12 B-29s illuminated in the searchlights, and two of them were shot down following a hit-and-run air battle, while a third (that was heavily damaged) did not make it back to its home base – making an emergency landing on Kimpo airfield. Five days later, the pilots of the 64th Fighter Air Corps recorded another Fortress in their tally: at 2235 on 15 June, the 147th Guards Fighter Air Regiment's senior pilot – Senior Lieutenant Volodarskiy – intercepted a B-29 that had been caught in searchlights 10 km west of Chungju. According to the archive documents, the Superfortress crashed into Korea Bay 10-15 km west of the Hancheng Peninsula after four attacks; we did not come across any descriptions of the battle itself in Western literature.

⁂

Having encountered active resistance on the part of the MiG-15s, Bomber Command was forced to review tactics. Up until this point in time, the majority of the bomber crews had concentrated their efforts on the Anju–Chongju–Sonchon sector during the raids on the railway bridges. Moreover, since the MiG bases were located on Korea's West Coast, the B-29s started to use the eastern approaches: the 98th Bomb Wing's route was from Yokohama–Hamhung–Huichon, and the 19th and 307th Bomb Wings used a route from Okinawa–Rausu–Huichon. Bombing raids on the Chongju–Sonchon sector would resume only if there was bad weather within range of the MiGs. This being the case, the preference was for night operations, with multiple layers of cloud cover. As the weather improved, the B-29s transferred to reserve targets south of Pyongyang. Bombing on instruments using the radar sight would be very problematic, but in June, the ubiquitous SHORAN navigation system began to be used during these raids.

Installation of the SHORAN system in aircraft from the

---
3 Fund of the 64th IAK, inventory 174045ss, file. 108, pp.69-73.
4 Fund of the 64th IAK, inventory 174045ss, file. 108, pp.73.

19th – and then the 307th and 98th Bomb Wings – began back in June 1951. However, owing to a shortage of the components of this system – as well as a lack of specialists with experience of installing and maintaining SHORAN – it only began to be used effectively a year later. From June 1952 onwards, the vast majority of B-29 sorties were conducted using this system. The first raid after the hiatus – within range of the MiGs – was carried out by 10 B-29s from the 98th Bomb Wing on 29 June on a stretch of railway line from Chongju–Sonchon using SHORAN due to cloud cover. The following evening, this raid was repeated by six 'Fortresses' from the 307th Bomb Wing (also in inclement weather conditions). These changes also affected how the sorties were organised: up until 10 June, the B-29s attacked the target as a group consisting of eight to 12 aircraft – flying at intervals ranging from 1-10 minutes. After 10 June, the Superfortresses appeared over the target in groups of three or four – consisting of two to four aircraft each. The intervals between the aircraft had increased up to 5-20 minutes, with intervals of up to 20-50 minutes between groups of bombers. The groups of B-29s began to be augmented by RB-50G radio-electronic warfare aircraft – making the work of the Soviet radar operators more difficult. In order to reduce the danger of being illuminated by the searchlights, the undersides of the bombers were painted black and the altitude at which they transited to the target was increased.

In July, Bomber Command were given a new target: the Eastern Light Metals Company plant in Yangsi. A total of 63 B-29s participated in a raid on this target – and 70 percent of the structures at the plant were reduced to rubble. Later that same month, the Superfortresses began what were the largest raids on the North Korean capital since the beginning of the war. Whilst not based on any military rationale, these raids were aimed at making representatives of the Korean People's Army and the Chinese People's Volunteers more amenable to negotiating a ceasefire. Incendiary bombs were used more widely than ever, along with possibly the most terrifying conventional weapon of its time: napalm. On the first of these raids, 63 B-29s poured almost 9,000 litres of napalm on the city. Winston Churchill, who had never shown any sympathy towards the communists, announced: 'I really don't like these napalm raids. A horrifying number of people are burnt by the content of these bombs. We could be making a grave error allowing ourselves to wage war in such a terrible way. Napalm was never designed to be used against civilian targets. I shall not bear responsibility for it'.[5] The scale of these raids did worry Britain – and the Archbishop of York, as well as the Methodist and Free Churches of Scotland – called for an end to the indiscriminate use of napalm. Against the backdrop of the Cold War, however, there were no mass protests against the bombing of cities.

This huge B-29 Superfortress takes off from an air base somewhere in Korea. In all kinds of weather – and despite any opposition of flak, searchlights and night fighters – these 'Big Boys' of the Korean War make their trips by night into North Korea, 21 July 1952. (Courtesy of the US National Archives)

For the night fighters of the 64th Fighter Air Corps, June and July were relatively quiet. The fighters maintained their patrols in the short duration zones close to the corps' searchlight zone, were scrambled for interceptions at the furthest reaches and saw action both in the Chinese searchlight field and outside it, but would rarely encounter the enemy. MiG operations were severely hampered by cloud: the presence of cloud, even cirrus clouds, made searching for – and locating the enemy behind the clouds – much more difficult. In this case, the bombers were no longer illuminated by searchlights. Despite all these measures that were adopted – and which were designed to increase the likelihood of locating the enemy, such as the SON-4 fire control radar to guide the fighter aircraft on the target accurately, and calculating and communicating the altimetric flight altitude to pilots (as well as illuminating the bombers using target illumination equipment) – the night fighters in the 64th Fighter Air Corps only engaged B-29s in combat three times in two months. In this case, one Fortress was shot down and another damaged. The only victory was attributed to a navigator in the 351st Fighter Air Regiment, Major Karelin. On the night of 3/4 July, Anatoliy Karelin was on patrol close to Sonchon. At 2234, an order came through from the Command Post to proceed to the Anju area, where enemy aircraft were expected to transit. Two minutes later, Karelin was already over Anju.

The Command Post were constantly relaying information concerning the target's movements:

> ... At 2246 [2346] the pilot sighted an enemy RB-29 aircraft caught in a searchlight at an altitude of 7,200 m, which he attacked from the left at an aspect angle of 4/4 and a distance of 300 m giving a single, short burst... the RB-29 caught fire.
>
> Guided by the flames on the port side of the aircraft's wing centre section and with the searchlights barely illuminating the bomber Major Karelin made

---

5   McDonald, Callum A., *Korea: The War Before Vietnam* (Basingstoke: McMillan Press Ltd, 1986), p.171.

The nose of the Boeing B-29 Superfortress 'Heart's Desire II', which participated in many strikes against Korean targets, 19 August 1952. (Courtesy of the US National Archives)

In the faint light of daybreak, this B-29 Superfortress of the 98th Bomb Wing in Japan taxies up the airstrip at the completion of another bombing mission against military targets above the 38th parallel, August 1952. (Courtesy of the US National Archives)

another attack from behind at an aspect angle of 0/4 and a distance of 200–250 m, firing one medium burst of fire. As a result the flames emanating from the RB-29 grew larger. It was then that the bomber moved away from the searchlights.

As he followed the burning RB-29 the pilot made a further two attacks from behind the bomber at an aspect angle of 0/4 and a distance of 200 m, firing a further two short bursts into the starboard side of the wing centre section... at an altitude of 2,600–1,500 m the RB-29 began to break up and crashed in an area 2 km to the west of Pakchon where it exploded. The crew of nine were taken prisoner.

The ammunition expended was as follows: N-37 – 16 pieces, NR-23 – 60 pieces.[6]

It was subsequently established on the basis of the testimony of the crew that had been captured, together with the wreckage, that the aircraft, which had been shot down, was an RB-50 strategic reconnaissance aircraft. According to information from the opposing side that night, MiGs shot down an RB-29 from the 91st Strategic Reconnaissance Squadron.

The second battle took place on the night of 23/24 August. The weather in the Suiho region that night was favourable for a bombing raid: 10 oktas of cloud cover and a 700 m cloud base that extended to 8,500 m; the drizzle and occasional rain reduced visibility to 4-6 km. Between 0206-0325, 10 B-29s bombed the station at Sukchondong, which was located some 3 km away from the Suiho hydroelectric station – and as such, was hardly the primary target in the 64th Fighter Air Corps' zone of responsibility. The bombers encountered two layers of anti-aircraft artillery and the 64th Fighter Air Corps' MiGs. Among those who were scrambled to counter the bombers was the Deputy Squadron Commander of the 147th Guards Fighter Air Regiment, Captain Poltavets. As he searched for

G.M. Poltavets from the 147th Guards Fighter Air Regiment. (This photograph was provided by I. Seidov)

the bombers in the clouds, Poltavets opened defensive fire outside of visual contact with the target – guided only by information from the Command Post. Our pilot was not visual with the enemy, but the B-29's guns, which pinpointed the MiG's position with their tracer bullets or by the muzzle flashes, damaged Poltavets's aircraft. After the battle was over, Poltavets returned to base – making a standard turn on approach to land and announcing over the radio at 0520 that he was: "Descending towards the outer beacon, heading 80°." These were his last words, as his MiG-15 caught fire and crashed 12 km from Tatung-kuo airfield. The aircraft exploded as it hit the ground and Captain Poltavets was killed. Bullet holes from 12.7 mm ordnance were found in the shattered remains of the MiG; this was the first combat loss that the corps' night fighters endured.

A week after the death of Poltavets (on the night of 30/31

---

6   Fund of the 64th IAK, inventory 174045ss, file. 110, p.61; Fund of the 351st IAP, inventory 655110s, file. 1, p.61.

These B-29 'Superforts' of FEAF Bomber Command's Okinawa-based 19th Bomb Group taxi down the ramp for another mission against the targets in North Korea. The 19th Group's 'Superforts' almost nightly attack troop and supply concentrations, or transportation facilities in enemy-held territory. The group, which has been flying missions for more than two years, recently completed its 500th mission; September 1952. (Courtesy of the US National Archives)

Preparing MiG-15bis No. 546 (serial No. 53210546) from the 351st Fighter Air Regiment for a night sortie.

August), his regimental colleague, Captain Kordyukov, was credited with damaging a B-29.

From the beginning of September onwards, Bomber Command began to pay more attention to the area around the hydroelectric station, which supplied not only North Korea with electricity, but North-Eastern China as well. The first raid was on the city of Suiho (not far from the hydroelectric station) on 3 September. For the first time since the June battles, the Superfortresses carried out a bombing raid in the area protected by the corps' night fighters in cloudless skies on 12 September. This time, the hydroelectric station itself was selected as a target. Tribute should be paid to Bomber Command, as the powerful raid was well planned and executed, and is worthy of a detailed explanation. In this case, we will need to rely on information from our own archives and the free foreign press.

First and foremost, it should be noted that the Americans did not plan for the raid to take place in cloudless skies. The meteorological service forecast a dense layer of cloud over Sukchon on the night of 12/13 September, but then the head of the brigade – General Wiley D. Ganey – decided to strike right under the noses of the MiGs. Furthermore, as he was not relying solely on the weather, Ganey proposed a series of measures aimed at reducing losses among the bombers.

On 12 September between 2032-2045, the Commander's aircraft passed over the hydroelectric station on a sortie, which was a final opportunity to reconnoitre the site prior to the raid. The completely clear skies came as an unpleasant surprise, but the Commander was reliant on his countermeasures, and the raid went ahead without deviating from the plan.

At 2258 – on the Hamhung–Kovon border – the corps' radar detected a target identified as a B-29. The first bomber, which was heading north-east, was followed by a second, a third, a fourth and a fifth… By 0011, the radar operators counted 35 Superfortresses transiting in three echelons consisting of 20, 10 and five aircraft each. According to American information, 31 B-29s participated in the raid.

At 2300, six B-29s were approaching the hydroelectric station from the south-east; these were the electronic warfare aircraft. They operated outside of the firing zone of the anti-aircraft artillery batteries – scattering strips of aluminium foil over the course of 40 minutes, which created passive jamming across metric and centimetric wavebands. These active countermeasures knocked out the electronic warfare equipment's metric waveband in which the corps' P-3, Most-2, LV and SON-ZK radar systems operated. This particularly affected the SON systems, which represented the fire control radar.

At 2330, the first three B-26s emerged at low level to suppress the searchlights. Five minutes later – at 2235 – the first 227 kg high-explosive bombs began to fall from bombers belonging to the 307th Bomb Wing, which comprised the first echelon. By the time midnight had come and gone at 0117, the bombers of the 19th Bomb Wing had arrived over the target – and they also dropped 227 kg high-explosive bombs. Finally, at 0149, the third echelon – comprising B-29s from the 98th Bomb Wing – arrived over the target carrying 908 kg semi-armour-piercing bombs. Despite having attacked the searchlights for two-and-a-half hours, the Invaders only succeeded in destroying eight of the 30 searchlight batteries. They departed at 0200 – and 12 minutes later, the last of the Superfortresses dropped their bombs and headed for home.

Over the course of three-and-a-half hours, the B-29s had dropped up to 500 bombs on Suiho. Three of them hit the upper part of the dam and one hit the ruined section of the turbine hall, while around 50 hit the transformer housing, which had been destroyed previously in a raid by UN forces on 23 July. The rest of the bombs missed the hydroelectric station completely – falling some 1-2 km south-east of the station. The dam, active turbines, generators and transformers were undamaged – thus the raid did not achieve its objective,

Flight Commander of the 2nd Squadron, 147th Guards Fighter Air Regiment, Captain Yuriy Dobrovichan. He shot down three B-29s during night sorties.

The Commander of the Night Fighter Squadron, 147th Guards Fighter Air Regiment, Captain A.S. Trishkin. (This photograph was provided by I. Seidov)

The crash site of B-29A No. 44-86343, which was shot down by Yuriy Dobrovichan on the night of 12/13 September 1952.

Two photographs of the wreckage of B-29A No. 44-86343.

in that the target remained fully operational.[7]

On the other hand, despite the fact that the protection measures that were used did significantly reduce the effectiveness of our fighters and anti-aircraft artillery, the Americans were not able to escape losses: that night, two pilots from the night fighter squadron under the 147th Guards Fighter Air Regiment were scrambled to intercept the bombers. At 2338, when the Superfortresses of the first echelon were dropping their bombs on the hydroelectric station, a MiG-15 – flown by Senior Lieutenant Yuriy Dobrovichan – lifted off from Tatung-kuo airfield. Twenty minutes later, the Commander of the guard's squadron – Captain Trishkin – took to the air in his MiG.

The MiGs commenced their patrol – transiting to the hydroelectric station. Senior Lieutenant Dobrovichan flew at an altitude of 7,000 m, with Captain Trishkin 1,000 m below him. Although skies were clear, a dense mist made it more difficult for the pilots to search for enemy aircraft. Luck, however, was on their side…

At 0011, Dobrovichan noticed a single B-29 south of Suiho – in the glare of the searchlights – at an altitude of 6,500 m. The fighters turned to port and our pilot descended and began to close on the enemy aircraft – opening fire with a single burst from a distance of 1,000–800 m. The MiG opened fire from a great distance and the pilot was not able to see whether his shells hit the target or not. Realising his mistake, Dobrovichan opened fire once again – and he was only really on the tail of the Superfortress at a distance of not less than 300 m. This time, the tracer shells scored a direct hit on the bomber – and one engine on its port side caught fire. Banking

---

7   Fund of the 64th IAK, inventory 174045ss, file. 117, p.12.

A wall newspaper commemorating Yuriy Dobrovichan's victory over a B-29 on the night of 12/13 September 1952.

to starboard away from the Fortress, Dobrovichan turned and prepared to launch a second attack. As it turned out, this was not needed, since the flames had engulfed the bomber and it began to break up in mid-air. At 0015, the burning sections of the bomber crashed into the forest 17 km east of Taegwan. After reporting the loss of the aircraft to the Command Post, Dobrovichan broke off combat.

On patrol at an altitude of 8,000 m, Captain Trishkin followed the bomber as it crashed. Suddenly, he noticed a B-29 below and ahead of him – heading south-east at an altitude of 6,800 m. Strange as it may seem, the bomber's navigation lights were switched on. After closing on the bomber, Trishkin began to pursue it in a descent. After evidently noticing the fighter, the B-29 crew switched off their navigation lights, but they were too late in realising their error; our pilot was able to close on the bomber and could see the lights in the flight deck. Guided by the lights in the cabin, the Squadron Commander approached the bomber from behind – giving a burst of concentrated fire at a narrow aspect angle. The pilot was not able to see the outcome of his attack, as he overshot the bomber – losing it in the darkness; the entire battle lasted for no more than three or four minutes. Some time later, the Command Post gave the order to return to base. At 0028, Senior Lieutenant Dobrovichan landed safely at Tatung-kuo, followed at 0046 by Captain Trishkin.

Senior Lieutenant Yuriy Dobrovichan was credited with shooting down one B-29. Furthermore, according to radio-intercept, a further three B-29s had been damaged that day by anti-aircraft artillery – making emergency landings in South Korea at Suwon and Kunsan airfields. The Superfortress attacked by Captain Trishkin was damaged.

Western researchers note that during the course of the raid, the ground fire, in spite of the countermeasures, ranged from '… moderate to heavy, since the anti-aircraft artillery positions on the Manchurian side of the Yalu River had not come under attack. Several North Korean night fighters, including jet fighters, passed beneath the Superfortresses without opening fire and one unidentified aircraft dropped yellow and white flares in front of the formations of B-29s…'[8] The Americans acknowledge the loss of one B-29 from the 371st Bomb Squadron, 307th Bomb Wing over the hydroelectric station, but there is no consensus of opinion over the reason for the loss of this aircraft. Robert F. Futrell wrote: '… A few bombers were successfully illuminated by searchlights, and sporadic fighter attacks shot down one 307th Wing bomber. Several other bombers were damaged by flak …[9] Others attribute the loss of the B-29 to anti-aircraft artillery. Officially, the reason for the loss of the B-29 from the 371st Bomb Squadron, 307th Bomb Wing over the hydroelectric station on 13 September was due to anti-aircraft artillery. The only survivor from that aircraft's crew, a sergeant, was captured – and under interrogation, he also indicated that his aircraft had been shot down by anti-aircraft artillery and that a further two B-29s from the 98th Bomb Wing had been damaged. It is possible therefore that ground fire from anti-aircraft artillery that night was more likely to have been heavy rather than moderate. One of the pilots who flew in this raid – a veteran of the Second World War, who recalled the thick defensive fire – said that it was 'as good as I ever saw the Germans put up'.[10]

It is true that the two attacks from our fighters were 'sporadic'. In a head-on attack, it is not possible to see the shells fired by the MiG – even if they were tracer – and the transience of Dobrovichan's second attack did not afford the crew of the bomber, which had caught fire immediately, a chance to assess the situation. It is likely therefore that ground fire was a more plausible explanation for the loss of this aircraft. Subsequently, our search team discovered the wreckage of the B-29; specifically, they found maps of the SHORAN radar system. It is likely that the West is unaware of this final fact, as our fighters would later attempt to intercept bombers on the bombing runs indicated on the map, and Bomber Command

---

8 Stewart, *Air Power*, p.151.
9 Futrell, *The United States Air Force in Korea*, p.527.
10 Futrell, *The United States Air Force in Korea*, p. 527.

decided that the enemy had learned from their own experience where the SHORAN beacons are and had positioned searchlights and anti-aircraft artillery batteries in these areas.

※

In the second half of September and October, the B-29s were re-directed to an area inaccessible to the MiGs south of Pyongyang due to predominantly cloudless (or near cloudless) skies. The Korean People's Army and the Chinese People's Volunteers were preparing for an offensive and were drawing their forces up to the front line – presenting Bomber Command with new targets for bombing raids. On 18 September, B-29s bombed North Korean logistics units at Yonpo, Ch'unch'on and Hamhung. This was followed by another raid by 35 aircraft the next day on these same areas. It was this daylight raid – carried out with a heavy fighter escort – that was commanded by General Ganey himself. On 20 September, the B-29s bombed the bridges around Huichon.

On the night of 30 September/1 October, the bombers carried out a successful strike on the chemical factory at Namsanni (not far from the reservoir at Supcheng). Since this target was within range of the night fighters, a night was selected for the raid on which the weather conditions were unfavourable – and the B-29s dropped their bombs using SHORAN. The first aircraft to hit the target were a trio of 'Fortresses' that bombed the anti-aircraft positions with high-explosive bombs, which were fitted with explosives designed to explode in mid-air – and after entering a circuit, they began to 'hammer' enemy radar with their onboard electronic warfare equipment. While the 45 Superfortresses of the main attack force were dropping their load of bombs on the factory one after another, the B-26s were attacking the searchlight positions at low level. On the whole, the countermeasures did their job. Only a few of the 'Fortresses' were caught in the searchlights, but the MiG crews that observed them were not able to attack them at all – and although some of the bombers were damaged by anti-aircraft fire, they all returned to base safely; the factory at Namsanni was destroyed. This chemical factory was the last strategic target in North Korea. After it had been bombed, the Americans analysts remarked that not even the complete destruction of North Korea's industry had made the communist delegation any more amenable to talks concerning a ceasefire in Panmyndzhone. In order to keep up the pressure, the air force needed new targets: those that previously had never been considered targets.

On 6 October – the day that Sino-Korean forces began their new offensive – the intensity of B-29 sorties to the front line increased significantly. For the most part, 227 kg high-explosive bombs were used in sorties against infantry. If the explosives within the bombs were set to explode 15-30 m above the ground, the Korean People's Army and Chinese People's Volunteer Troops' helmets would not protect them from the shower of shrapnel. Furthermore, the accuracy of these bombs using ground guidance could be striking.

These Okinawa-based B-29 'Superforts' run up their engines prior to taking off on another mission against transportation or supply targets in North Korea. Although the planes sometimes take off before dark (as they did here), the bombing attacks are usually made during hours of darkness. A surprise daylight attack was made by the big bombers on 19 September 1952 – the first such attack in 11 months. (Courtesy of the US National Archives)

September 21st is the 10th anniversary of the first flight of a B-29 Superfortress. Here, one of the US Air Force all-weather medium bombers takes off from its Okinawa base into stormy skies for another night strike against military targets in Korea, September 1952. (Courtesy of the US National Archives)

After one of these raids, the Commander of the 2nd US Infantry Division – General Carl L. Raffner – sent a radiogram to Far East Air Force Headquarters, in which he stated:

> The enormous casualties inflicted by your bombers have significantly reduced the pressure that the enemy has been putting on the troops in my care. The accuracy of the bombing raids is simply amazing. These raids undermine the fighting spirit of entire formations of enemy troops that have been massing for an attack some 400 m from the front line. An American soldier

One of the B-29 bombers takes off at sunset into the stormy skies for another mission over Korea, September 1952. (Courtesy of the US National Archives)

In the pale light of early dusk, a B-29 Superfortress of the US Far East Air Force's Bomber Command leaves the runway at Okinawa, headed for North Korea; September 1952. (Courtesy of the US National Archives)

who escaped imprisonment close to midnight during a raid on Suncheon said that a large part of one enemy battalion that had moved up to the front line to attack the 9th Infantry Division had been destroyed, and those that remained had fled in panic.[11]

Superfortresses were also used to drop anti-personnel mines in operational logistics areas behind North Korean lines. The strategic bombers were not just restricted to bombing infantry, but would continue to bomb targets that came within the 64th Fighter Air Corps' zone of responsibility during adverse weather conditions caused by cloud. Encounters with MiGs, though rare, were inevitable.

October 1952 was a relatively quiet month for our night fighters. There were no air battles with the enemy, owing to problems with visual identification in cloud without the aircraft being illuminated by searchlights. The 64th Fighter Air Corps began to search for more efficient ways to intercept the B-29s and turned to the maps giving the locations of SHORAN radar stations that were discovered amongst the wreckage of the B-29 shot down on 12 September. A study of these maps meant that the exact bombing runs the B-29s used to approach their targets could be identified. This gave rise to an idea of using these bombing runs to set up specific search zones, which it was proposed, would increase the effectiveness of our night fighters in poor weather conditions – and when the enemy was making extensive use of radar jamming, would allow our fighters to close on the enemy more quickly and attack them as they entered the searchlight zone. These zones were set up in the immediate approaches to the principal assets under the protection of the corps – namely the Suiho hydroelectric station and the bridges around Andung. Night exercises in protecting the hydroelectric station and the bridges carried out in this area with fighters, anti-aircraft artillery and searchlights proved the potential of guiding fighters using search zones. It was noted that this method provided no less an accurate means of guiding fighters to a target than by using the principal P-3 radar system. There was no opportunity in October to test the effectiveness of this approach in a real battle, since the enemy did not launch any sorties on this region during that month.

The next air battle with the B-29s took place on the night of 18/19 November when a single Superfortress appeared over the Sonchon-Chongju region at midnight. Guards Senior Lieutenant Dobrovichan took off from Tatung-kuo airfield at 0016. At 0040 – at an altitude of 6,500 m – he arrived over Sonchon:

... He noticed a suspicious light ahead and above him, he reported this to the Command Post and requested permission to attack. Since there were a further two MiG-15s in the area permission to attack was not given. Guards Snr Lieutenant Dobrovichan did not take his eyes off the target but made two turns around it and realised that it was a B-29 using photo bombs to take reconnaissance photographs. The pilot obtained permission from the Corps' Command Post to attack the enemy aircraft, which was lit up for a short time by searchlights. The bomber performed a 180° turn and departed, varying altitude and heading.

After closing on the B-29 from behind, Guards Snr Lieutenant Dobrovichan opened fire from behind and below the B-29 at an aspect angle of 1/4 with a single burst of fire, but the tracer passed beneath the aircraft. Without losing sight of the enemy aircraft, the pilot closed to a distance of 300–400 m and made a second attack at an aspect angle of 0/4 using a movable gunsight reticle. After this second attack the bomber caught fire, leaving the searchlight zone at the same time. Guided

---

11 Stewart, *Air Power*, p.104.

by the flames coming from the burning aircraft the pilot gave another two bursts of concentrated fire from a distance of 200–150 m. He broke off combat after he ended up in the B-29's wake, but he continued to follow the burning enemy aircraft as it fell to earth. The B-29 crashed into the sea. Snr Lieutenant Dobrovichan broke off combat under orders from the Command Post and landed safely back at base.

The air battle lasted five minutes. The ordnance expended was as follows: N-37 – 20 pieces, NR-23 – 94 pieces ... [12]

American researchers confirm that on the night in question, a single B-29 from the 345th Bomb Squadron, 98th Bomb Wing did incur serious damage at the hands of a MiG and headed for Cho-do Island, but fell into the sea less than a kilometre short of Cho-do. Furthermore, one crewmember was killed and another eight were lost without a trace. Interestingly, it would appear that MiGs from the 351st Fighter Air Regiment also took part in the battle. Using the 98th Bomb Wing's logbook and the 5th Air Army's intelligence digest No. 201 – dated 23 November – Robert Futrell described the battle thus:

> On the night of 18/19 November 1952 the Reds revealed new tactics when they shot down a 98th Wing B-29 coming off its supply centre target at Sonchon. Riding above the B-29, a Red spotter dropped flares each time the bomber changed direction. The flares allowed searchlights to lock on the bomber, and four Red fighter passes riddled the bomber, forcing its crew to abandon ship over Cho-do.[13]

Therefore both our accounts (and those of the Americans) talk of mysterious bombs – and what Dobrovichan took to be photo bombs, the B-29 crew understood to be flares. Judging by the information that Dobrovichan received from the Command Post, there was another pair of MiG-15s in that area. In our opinion, this pair were from the 351st Regiment. In order to prevent them colliding in the dark, our fighters had adopted their own specific formations. It is likely that in this scenario, a pair of MiGs that climbed intentionally above the B-29 illuminated it using illuminating bombs, which Dobrovichan took to be photo bombs. Moreover (although it is unlikely), this pair would appear to be Combined Air Army fighters.

Despite losing one aircraft, the Superfortresses were sufficiently effective in November; the countermeasures employed by the Americans did their job. Radar jamming and painting the underside of the bombers black reduced the effectiveness of the searchlights considerably, and pilots were only able to identify an aircraft not illuminated by searchlights in very rare and exceptional cases (either as they crossed the

---

12 Fund of the 64th IAK, inventory 174045ss, file. 120, pp.81-82.
13 Futrell, *The United States Air Force in Korea*, p.613.

The Squadron Commander of the 147th Guards Fighter Air Regiment, Captain Nikolai Shkodin (two victories in the Second World War and three victories in Korea).

moon, or when the lights in the flight deck were switched on), as Captain N.I. Shkodin recalled:

> I was the Acting Regimental Commander and completed two or three night sorties to see with my own eyes what it was like. I always went up on very dark nights, even though in the south, the nights were always dark. The 'Fortresses' were dropping their bombs and I wanted to be there amongst them. I ended up in the bomber's wake several times – firing a few provocative bursts of fire – and the shells were tracer, so I thought that they would return fire and I would be able to pinpoint their location, but no, they did not respond.

Searching by the SHORAN beacons did not reap any rewards either, although there were instances when our fighters would get caught in the wake and would enter a spin. These difficulties in locating the bombers meant that the Americans, for example, were able to bomb North Korean airfields at Uiju and Sinuiju – repeating the success of the raid they had made against this target in January of that year. Between 1957 and 2130, up to 32 B-29s bombed the airfields, anti-aircraft artillery positions close to the bridges, apartment blocks and industrial assets in the cities of Uiju and Sinuiju. Four B-29s comprising the electronic warfare aircraft provided cover for the raid. Apart from that, radio-intercept from American crews revealed that up to a dozen fighters provided cover for the bombers.

On that bright moonlit night, the searchlights had a weak signature – losing their profile at an altitude of 4,000–5,000 m. This made tracking the enemy's movements visually much more complicated, and a B-29 was almost invisible against the sky. The photo bombs dropped by the enemy blinded the crews of anti-aircraft batteries, which also made it more difficult to track targets and open fire. Thirty-six B-29s passed through the searchlight zone, but not one of them was illuminated sufficiently to allow our fighters to detect and attack them. There were seven MiG-15s in the air at any one time searching for B-29s – making their bombing runs on the fringe of the searchlight zone – but not one of the pilots saw any enemy aircraft. The consequences of the raid on 28 November were dispiriting: the runway at Sinuiju airfield sustained 80 direct hits; the runway at Uiju airfield sustained 28 direct hits; and a further 21 bombs fell on the taxiways. A paper plant in the Sinuiju area was destroyed by high-explosive bombs, which also set mines and a railway depot on fire. The bombs destroyed a considerable number of residential dwellings, and there were casualties and injuries among the civilian population. A large number of residential dwellings were also destroyed in the area around Uiju; up to 70 people were killed and around 60 were injured. A secondary school was set on fire, and a textile workshop and post office were destroyed; the materiel was damaged.

It has to be said that the raid on 28 November was very successful for the Americans, and that North Korean air defences, which were centred on the 64th Fighter Air Corps, suffered a significant defeat. The situation that command, anti-aircraft artillery crews, searchlight operators and the night crews of the 64th Fighter Air Corps found themselves in was typical, however, of any war in which the opposing forces are more or less evenly matched in terms of strength and experience. After a long search for the optimum tactical procedures and methods with which to counter the MiGs, the United States Far East Air Force Bomber Command had, by November 1952, succeeded in regaining the numbers they had lost that June. The Corps Commander and headquarters – as well as the pilots, anti-aircraft artillery crews, Command Post personnel and those manning the radar stations – carried out a great deal of work to increase the effectiveness of North Korea's nocturnal air defences. At the beginning of December that year, an investigation was carried out along with the commanders of anti-aircraft artillery divisions; the searchlight operator's regiment; the commanders of the 351st Fighter Air Regiment; the 147th Guards Fighter Air Regiment Night Fighter Squadron; and artillery divisions into the actions taken by anti-aircraft, searchlight and fighter crews in countering the raid on 28 November. The following measures were implemented at the earliest opportunity:

- Corps Headquarters drew up a plan for using night fighters, which proposed that 10-12 be launched simultaneously to destroy enemy bombers in the searchlight field and in the outer approaches to assets that are under the protection of the corps, but which lie outside the searchlight field
- Methods were developed for illuminating and tracking targets on the principal bombing runs that used the SHORAN system. Special searchlight stations were allocated to show fighter crews the direction from which the bombers would enter the searchlight zone
- The searchlight field was expanded to include the Chinese People's Liberation Army searchlights
- Pilots, as well as officers from anti-aircraft artillery and anti-aircraft searchlight units, held a joint conference on aerial tactics in which they consolidated their experience of nocturnal combat and developed methods to improve effectiveness
- A conference was held for searchlight units to consolidate their experience and to improve the way they operated while experiencing jamming
- Special training was provided in guidance and control using the plan position indicator on the P-20 radar, as well as two plotting tables for the officer corps responsible for nocturnal combat operations
- A detailed study was carried out, along with flight crews, into ways of searching for aircraft against the moon on a moonlit night and in other weather conditions outside of the searchlight zone
- The flight-performance characteristics of the B-29 and B-26 and their vulnerabilities were researched once again
- The Corps Commander carried out a systematic investigation into the corps' actions in combat – producing a detailed description of the successful and unsuccessful air battles
- A 10-day review containing a summary of the corps' actions in combat was published and was brought to the attention of all personnel

The ECM resistance of our radar systems was improved following the introduction into service of the P-20 'Periscope' radar system, which was rolled out at radar stations close to Andung at the end of November. Up until the introduction of this system, the 64th Fighter Air Corps' radar coverage consisted of the following:

- The P-3, P-3A and P-8 radar detection and guidance systems that protected fighter aviation
- The 'LV' and 'Most-2' anti-aircraft artillery radar detection system, as well as the SON-3K and SON-4 weapons guidance system stations
- The RP-15 and RAP-50 searchlight control radar

The entry into service of the P-20 radar system not only increased the ECM effectiveness of our radar network, but also the accuracy of our fighter guidance systems. The P-20 could detect targets such as a B-29 at a range of up to 250 km, but could detect targets such as fighters at a range of up to 180 km. The P-3A and P-8 radar systems were not capable of detecting a fighter at that sort of range. This meant that it was impossible to guide our interceptors towards enemy aircraft whilst they

The Commander of the Night Fighter Squadron, 535th Fighter Air Regiment, Captain Kirill Syoma. (This photograph was provided by I. Seidov)

were over the furthest reaches; that is to say, at 120–130 km or more away from the assets under the corps' protection. The decisive capability of the P-20 radar system ensured that a MiG-15 could be guided onto the tail of a B-29 at a distance of 600–800 m with altitude error within 80–100 m. The P-3 and P-3A radar systems were much less accurate, which meant that a MiG-15 could only be guided onto an enemy aircraft's tail at a distance of 1,500–2,000 m. Apart from that, the 64th Fighter Air Corps increased the number of pilots trained to operate at night. At the end of November, the 535th Fighter Air Regiment's squadron of night fighters were re-deployed to Andung airfield, which protected North-Eastern China by night, along with the 224th Fighter Air Regiment's Night Fighter Squadron at the highest state of readiness on Mukden airfield.

A new and highly effective system of countering raids by Superfortresses was finally unveiled in December 1952: One squadron would assume the third state of readiness one hour before nightfall, and as dusk fell, the other night fighter squadrons would assume a state of readiness. The number of B-29s participating in a raid would be established by radio intercept 3-3.5 hours before they dropped their bombs. This allowed the Commander of the 64th Fighter Air Corps to assess the situation accurately and to define the number of his forces that would be required to counter the raid effectively, as well as to define the procedure for engaging the enemy in combat. Once the enemy had been detected by our radar systems – usually on the Haeju–Shopko–Wonsan–Kanggye border – some of the pilots would assume the highest state of readiness. When the bombers crossed the Pyongyang–Wonsan border, our fighters would begin to be scrambled. The number of aircraft scrambled would depend on the nature of the raid, the weather conditions and the area in which the air battle would take place. If the bombers were active south-east of the Anju–Huichon border, or if their activity within the corps' zone of responsibility was not significant, only one to three fighters would be scrambled at any one time. If the enemy aircraft were active in the near approaches to the assets under the protection of the corps, the number of fighters would be increased up to four to 10. If the raid was protracted, our forces would be augmented. Once airborne, the MiG-15s would head for the holding pattern within the corps' searchlight zone, or to intercept the bombers over the furthest reaches. In the latter scenario, they would operate within the Chinese Air Force's searchlight zone as well as outside it, and would reach the Huichon–Sukchong border. In this case, the MiGs would search for enemy aircraft at medium and high altitudes, while the La-11s operated at altitudes of 3,000 m or lower. On moonlit nights, the Lavochkins would be able to search for B-26s freely – as well as for ground attack aircraft – outside the searchlight zone up to the Pyongyang–Wonsan border. Pilots were drafted in who were more highly trained in nocturnal operations in favourable and unfavourable weather conditions to intercept bombers at the furthest reaches.

In both the nearest and furthest reaches, the fighters were guided from the Fighter Air Corps' Command Post using the directional method and also by information from the radar system. In the near approaches (at a distance from an asset under the protection of the MiGs of 130–150 km), as well as in the enemy's actual bombing zone, the plan position indicator on the 'Periscope' radar station was used. The fighters were guided using two plotting tables – according to information from the P-3A and P-8 radar stations over the target area – and as the bombers were leaving the target (at a distance of 50–80 km).

The directional method was the principal means of guiding a fighter. The pilot was constantly provided with an altitude and a heading that were calculated so that he would end up on the enemy aircraft's tail within visual range, which on a moonlit night was 800–1,000 m. The fighter would align onto the bomber's heading at a distance of 5-10 km behind. The fighter would then close on the bomber at a speed of 800 km/h. At a distance of 2 km behind the bomber, the pilot would deploy the air brakes and bring the speed down to 550 km/h. As he closed on the bomber, the pilot would be constantly supplied with information concerning the distance to the target and its flight altitude. The P-20 radar made it possible to approach the bomber to a distance of up to 800 m, which meant the enemy could be visually identified. The P-3A and P-8 radar made it possible for a fighter to approach a bomber to a distance of up to 1,500–2,000 m. In any case, the pilot would intensify his observation over the last 2 km to the target. If, for example, he noticed a contrail, he would follow it, but would still not close onto the target until he had established visual contact. Occasionally, the enemy aircraft would be fitted with searchlights, which made searching for and attacking them easier.

The results of all the long, intensive work put in by all the personnel of the 64th Fighter Air Corps were not long in coming: on 9 December at 2031, Guards Captain Dobrovichan – with one of the best night crews in the Guards Corps – took off from Tatung-kuo airfield. The pilot had been tasked with intercepting and destroying bombers in the Sonchon–Chongju area. As he was patrolling the area in which the Superfortresses were active, Captain Dobrovichan was ordered to transit to the Suiho region, where American bombers had also appeared. One of them was identified 20 km south-east of Suiho at an altitude of 7,000 m. The pilot opened fire from a distance of 1,000 m – and as he closed on the B-29, he gave six bursts of fire and saw his shells explode as they hit the fuselage, as well as the bomber's port flank. Dobrovichan broke off the attack at a distance of 150 m. Documents held by the corps indicate that the Superfortress that had been attacked was descending constantly and set off towards Korea Bay – crashing into the sea 10 km west of the Unzenli promontory.

It is known that one of the B-29s was removed from the 98th Bomb Wing and was struck off from the wing's records on 9 December 1952, but nothing is known about the reason for this aircraft being written off. Western authors do not mention the battle on the night of 9/10 December at all. Furthermore, this incident may not have been recorded for several reasons:

- They were not aware of this incident
- It had been forgotten
- The loss of the B-29 was attributed to anti-aircraft artillery (although the anti-aircraft crews did not claim any victories in that period)
- The aircraft was not thought to have been shot down (since it crashed into the sea) and so on

❧

A series of air battles began on the eve of the New Year and lasted for two weeks. During the night battles at the end of December and the first half of January, the MiGs of the 64th Fighter Air Corps dealt the Superfortresses a blow comparable to that dealt to them in 'Black week' during October 1951. On the night of 30/31 December, the Superfortresses attempted to attack an ore-processing plant in the Taegwan area and were protected by four night fighters. The lead aircraft from the group of 12 bombers in the first echelon was detected by our radar 90 km south-west of Huichon at 2032. At 2046, the first of the corps' fighters took off – and a further nine followed this aircraft within the hour. Three of the MiGs headed for the Suiho region and were tasked with destroying the bombers outside of the searchlight zone; they were guided from the Fighter Air Corps' Command Post using data from the P-20 radar system, with five of the fighters allocated to destroy the bombers within the searchlight zone. Of these, two were sent to the Sinuiju region and three were sent to the Cholsan region to intercept the Superfortresses as they headed for Korea Bay. Any B-29s that could have escaped in a south-easterly direction would be met by a further two MiG-15s in the Chongju region. Three guidance officers would be directing six fighters onto a target in the Command Post at any one time using different radio frequencies. This became possible because the MiG-15s in the 64th Fighter Air Corps had their single-channel RSI-6K HF radio sets replaced with RSIU-3M 'Klen' three-channel sets.

Events unfolded as follows:

… At 1950 [2050] Major Karelin was sent to the holding pattern over the Suiho hydroelectric station.

Major Karelin, who was constantly in receipt of information regarding enemy aircraft, was subsequently directed onto a bomber's tail using the directional method – using information from the radio-equipment at the Corps' Command Post. The bomber was heading for Deeguandong [Taegwan] in a south-easterly direction and up to 1,000 m from the MiG. After he had received word that the enemy aircraft was some 800–1,000 m ahead of him the pilot intensified his observation and reduced his engine rpm. On doing so he noticed a contrail above, ahead, and to the left of him with a further two contrails above and to the right. After climbing to an altitude of 8,000 m he identified a B-29 caught in the searchlights on a heading of 190° with a further two B-29s at a higher altitude of 9,000 m on the same heading up to 1,000 m apart and around 3-4 km distant.

After assuming an initial attack position he attacked the B-29 with two short bursts of fire from behind, to the right and beneath the aircraft at an aspect angle of 1/4 and from a distance of 400 m. He launched a second attack from a distance of 400–300 m at an aspect angle of 0/4 firing four medium bursts of fire at the enemy aircraft. As a result of the second attack the inboard port engine on the B-29 caught fire, after which the enemy aircraft began to break up in mid-air.

As he noticed the wreckage of the aircraft that was breaking up in mid-air the pilot broke away sharply to the right and entered a climb, after which he lost sight of the enemy. The port flank and the underside of the aircraft were damaged by the wreckage of the B-29. Strips of duralamin were found in the gun compartments on Major Karelin's MiG-15. He had opened fire using only the N-37 cannons, and had expended 40 rounds.

As a result of these brave and aggressive attacks the B-29, which had broken up in mid-air, crashed into a forested area in flames some 15–20 km west of Kidzyo [Kusong].[14]

… At 1955 [2055] Iskhangalev [a Section Commander in the 351st Fighter Air Regiment and a Senior Lieutenant] was scrambled to intercept enemy bombers that were approaching from a south-easterly direction and heading for Siodzyo [Authors' note: near Suiho] at an altitude of 7,000 m. As he patrolled the area over Siodzyo Snr Lieutenant Iskhangalev was directed onto an enemy aircraft some 800–1,000 m away using the directional method from the Corps' Command Post. As he searched he detected a contrail 500 m above him and to the right against the moon and began to close on the aircraft. He then noticed a B-29 aircraft that had dropped its bombs and was turning away to the left and descending. As he had a considerable

---

14 Fund of the 64th IAK, inventory 174045ss, file. 157, pp.86-88.

advantage in speed Iskhangalev overshot the bomber at an aspect angle of 4/4 without opening fire. Keeping an eye on the bomber he made a second approach and began to close on it from behind. He caught the bomber in the movable reticle in his ASP-3N sight, giving a single short burst of fire from a distance of 600–650 m at an aspect angle of 0/4 and watched the shells explode as they hit the B-29's tail. As he continued to close on the bomber he switched on his movable gunsight reticle and gave another medium burst of fire from behind, and below the bomber at an aspect angle of 1/4 and watched as the shells exploded, hitting the port inboard engine and the centre section. After this second burst of fire the enemy aircraft turned tightly to the right using 90° of bank, descending sharply. The fighter pilot, with a considerable advantage in speed overshot the bomber, losing sight of it.

The pilot had opened fire from all his cannons. The ordnance he had expended was as follows: N-37 – 10 rounds, NR-23 – 26 rounds.

As a result of good judgement as well as the brave and aggressive attacks this B-29 was shot down outside the searchlight zone, crashing in flames south-east of Pyongyang.[15]

... At 1956 [2056] Andreyev [a Flight Commander in the 351st Fighter Air Regiment] took off to intercept enemy bombers approaching from a south-easterly direction and was sent to the Siodzyo area.

... At 2006 [2106] over the Changdanghekou [Authors' note: northward of Suiho] region he was ordered by the Corps' Command Post to turn onto a 90° heading and transit for one minute in a climb, then turn onto a 220° heading. Having carried out this order he was on a 220° heading and one minute later he picked up a contrail 1,000–1,500 m above him. He began to close on to this aircraft, following the contrail on a parallel heading and climbing to 8,000 m.

... At 2025 [2125] he noticed a B-29 at an altitude of 8,000 m in the Kidzyo area and, after closing on this aircraft to a distance of 1,000–800 m he opened fire with two medium bursts at an aspect angle of 0/4. His speed on this occasion was 800 km/h. To avoid a collision he banked away to the right and to adjust his speed the pilot lowered the undercarriage and deployed the flaps. Andreyev made a second attack from behind and to the right of the enemy aircraft, opening fire from a distance of 400–500 m with a single medium burst at a speed of 600 km/h and at an aspect angle of 1/4 at the same altitude as the bomber. As a result of the attack the bomber's starboard engine caught fire. The pilot raised the undercarriage and flaps, after which he made a further three attacks on the B-29 from both left and right of the aircraft at aspect angles ranging from 0/4–

Pilots from the 351st Fighter Air Regiment Captain Karelin (on the steps) and Major Kultyshev (one victory in Korea); Andung, autumn 1952.

1/4 and a distance of 500–400 m. The enemy aircraft made a left-hand turn and descended, heading towards Unzan [Unsan]. Snr Lieutenant Andreyev also made a left-hand turn and closing on the enemy to a distance of 500–300 m and at an aspect angle of 1/4 he opened fire once again. Having used all his ammunition, Andreyev abandoned his pursuit of this aircraft and landed back at base.

The B-29 aircraft was shot down and crashed in flames around 25 km south-west of Sunchon.

... At 2030 [2130] Snr Lieutenant Muravyev [a Deputy Squadron Commander in the 535th Fighter Air Regiment] took off and was sent to the Siodzyo region. Subsequently he was directed towards an enemy bomber nearby using the directional method and by following the contrail he detected a B-29 heading towards him, flying at 220° over the Kidzyo region at an altitude of 8,000 m. He turned away to the right, assuming an initial position from which to attack and began to close on the enemy bomber, which at that time was lit up by searchlights. After closing to a distance of 800–600 m he attacked from behind the bomber and at an aspect angle of 1/4 giving one medium burst of fire. As a result the bomber's port outboard engine caught fire. The enemy aircraft began to descend, turning away to the left. After assuming an initial attack position the pilot attacked once again, giving a single burst of fire from a distance of 600 m at an aspect angle of 1/4.

Snr Lieutenant Muravyev opened fire using his N-37 and NR-23 cannons. He expended 22 N-37 rounds and 28 NR-23 rounds. The B-29 aircraft was shot down and crashed in flames around 60 km south-east of Kaisen [Authors' note: Kunu-ri – Futrell's maps; Kaechon – modern maps].[16]

A pilot from the 147th Guards Fighter Air Regiment, Guards Captain Dobrovichan, also encountered bombers. He subsequently attacked two

---

15 Fund of the 64th IAK, inventory 174045ss, file. 120, pp.88-90.

16 Fund of the 64th IAK, inventory 174045ss, file. 120, pp.92-94.

B-29s, and watched his rounds explode as they hit the American bombers. As he broke off combat turning back towards his home base the pilot saw a large explosion on the ground in the direction in which one of the B-29s he attacked was heading. In his post-flight report the guard's Captain stated that one of the B-29s he had fired upon had crashed. On the basis of the outcome of the battle however Dobrovichan was credited with damaging a single bomber.

The fine weather conditions were conducive to our fighters being guided onto their targets successfully, as well as being able to identify the aircraft; a moonlit night and very clear air made it possible to follow the bombers' contrails. The Superfortresses were identified in good time and were caught in the searchlights. The pilots, who were guided by three radio channels, were able to carry out the orders they received from the Command Post accurately. The use of the plan position indicator on the P-20 'Periscope' radar system assisted crews greatly to guide aircraft onto the fighters efficiently. The coherent and accurate work of the flight crews, radar operators and searchlight crews meant that serious losses could be inflicted on the first echelon of Superfortresses, despite the intensive electronic countermeasures that they deployed. The bomber pilots dropped their bombs in a hurry over Taegwan and to the south – departing to the south-east.

At 2115, Senior Lieutenant Kovalev was ordered by the Command Post to finish off one of the departing Superfortresses. Our pilot caught up with a B-29 that was already on fire and attacked it. The bomber was damaged further, but managed to reach Korea Bay, where Kovalev was not able to pursue it any further, as he was banned from crossing the coast. At 2122, radar picked up a second echelon of Superfortresses on the Ongjin–Haeju border. Thirteen B-29s were heading in a south-westerly direction – and they were protected by three night fighters. The B-29s began to circle as they ventured over Korea Bay some 80 km from the coast. After receiving information concerning fierce opposition from the MiGs – and the losses among the first echelon – the Americans decided to abandon their mission to bomb the ore-processing plant, but to 'finish off' their reserve target: the river crossings close to Anju.

Between 2133-2136, four MiGs were scrambled and were sent to the Anju area, where they commenced their patrols. Our fighters flew 'figure of eights' intersecting the bombing runs and escape routes for the bombers, which set off for the river crossings via Ch'ongch'on at 2140. In order to avoid encounters with the MiGs, the Superfortresses rushed with some haste back to their home bases; the last B-29 left the target zone at 2200.

Fighter cover for this raid was provided by the Skyknights from the 513th Marine Fighter Squadron. As they patrolled the Taechon–Kusong–Cholsan–Chongju area, the pilots would ask their radar guidance stations for the positions of the MiGs and which headings to use to pursue them, but

In the cockpit of MiG-15bis No. 976 (serial No. 2915376) is the Flight Commander of the 351st Fighter Air Regiment, Senior Lieutenant Zhakhman Iskhangaliev (one victory in Korea).

they were not able to offer any resistance. This was the most successful raid for our night fighters. The fighters of the 64th Fighter Air Corps were credited with having shot down four B-29s, while a further two bombers were recorded as damaged. The Americans state that on the night of 30/31 December, one B-29 was shot down from the 28th Bomb Squadron, 19th Bomb Wing and a further two bombers were so badly damaged that following emergency landings on Suwon airfield (near Seoul), they were 'fit only for scrap'.[17]

In the first half of January, the American medium bombers operated predominantly in the Sinanju–Huichon area. The B-29s were forced to adopt brand-new tactical approaches on almost every sortie owing to the high level of activity among fighter aviation. Their principal aim was to reduce the amount of time they spent within reach of the MiGs as much as possible; almost all the approaches and the targets within this area were attacked from over Korea Bay. After they had completed their raid, the B-29s would head straight out to sea. On a number of occasions, they would either approach the target from different directions, or several targets would be struck at once. Intervals between the aircraft on their bombing runs were kept to a minimum, reaching 30 seconds, which reduced the overall amount of time the whole group spent over the target.

The MiGs encountered the Superfortresses again on the night of 10/11 January. During the course of this raid, the Americans used all the protection methods they had available. Our radars were hit with active and passive jamming, and a fighter was patrolling over the Cholsan area. The plan was to attack two targets simultaneously from Korea Bay; these were the river crossings at Anju and the marshalling yards at Chongju.

Ten Superfortresses attacked the first target and four attacked the second. The bombers immediately headed south towards Korea Bay after completing their bombing runs. The Americans thought that this would make intercepting the bombers very difficult, but the MiGs still intercepted them:

---

17 Hallion, *The Naval Air War*, p.181.

Flight Commander of the 1st Squadron, 535th Fighter Air Regiment, Senior Lieutenant A.G. Andreyev. (This photograph was provided by I. Seidov)

Flight Commander of the 1st Squadron 535th Fighter Air Regiment, Senior Lieutenant M.D. Muravyev. (This photograph was provided by I. Seidov)

... At 1914 [2014] the Deputy Commander of the political section of the 351st Fighter Air Regiment Captain Golyshevskiy was scrambled to intercept Superfortresses approaching from Korea Bay via the Ch'ongch'on estuary towards Anju. On his way to Anju Golyshevskiy was directed towards a single B-29 using the directional method based on information from the plan position indicator on the "Periscope" radar. The aircraft was approaching from Korea Bay on a heading of 45°. Our pilot identified the aircraft as it was caught in the searchlights to the right of him and at an aspect angle of 3/4 and a distance of around two kilometres. Golyshevskiy began to close on the bomber but at that moment the Chinese searchlight operators stopped tracking the 'Fortresses' and the enemy melted away into the darkness. Some time later the searchlights came on again behind Golyshevskiy and he made a 180° turn.

He identified a B-29 aircraft flying towards him at an altitude of 8,500 m. After setting the range rheostat on his sight to a distance of 650–700 m and aiming the crosshair of his sight on the enemy aircraft's nose section he closed in on the aircraft until the B-29's flanks filled the sight ranger ring, after which he gave one long burst of fire. He broke off combat underneath the enemy aircraft. After turning 180° for a second attack the pilot noticed that the aircraft he had attacked had caught fire and was descending in a steep bank to starboard. Golyshevskiy did not pursue the aircraft any further since he noticed another aircraft behind him caught in the searchlights. After making a 180° turn the pilot noticed the enemy aircraft caught in the headlights at an altitude of 7,500 m. Using his movable sight reticle to take aim he opened fire with a single medium burst from a distance of 400–500 m and from a head-on position, and watched as the rounds exploded, hitting the middle part of the centre wing section. Passing underneath the enemy aircraft he noticed to the right of him another enemy aircraft spaced 50–100 m apart and flying in a formation, while in front of him and to the right he noticed a third aircraft caught in the searchlights. After making a corrective turn to the right he began to close on this aircraft but at that moment Major Kultyshev fired at this same target. Captain Golyshevskiy watched as Major Kultyshev's rounds hit the B-29's fuselage and centre wing section.

Captain Golyshevskiy opened fire on the enemy aircraft using all his cannons, expending 16 N-37 rounds and 36 NR-23 rounds. A single B-29 was shot down while a second was damaged.[18]

The Squadron Commander of the 351st Fighter Air Regiment, Major Kultyshev, was scrambled directly behind Golyshevskiy at 2015 and was sent to the Chongju area:

> As he arrived over this area at an altitude of 7,500 m, the pilot saw that the searchlights were switched on ahead of him. After increasing speed the pilot noticed an enemy aircraft caught in the searchlights over Anju and began to close on it but at that moment he noticed that Captain Golyshevskiy was firing at this aircraft. After turning away to the right Major Kultyshev noticed the searchlights to the right of him and heading in that direction he saw a B-29 caught in these lights in front of him. He gave a short burst of fire after closing to a distance of 600–800 m at an aspect angle of 1/4 but these rounds passed underneath the target. He continued to close on the target, opening fire for a second time from a distance of 500–400 m and watched as the shells hit the B-29's fuselage and wing. Major Kuybishev gave a third burst of fire from a distance of 100–75 m. He broke off combat turning sharply and climbing away to the right. The pilot noticed that the B-29 had caught fire. After breaking off combat he lost sight of the enemy.
>
> He had opened fire on the enemy using all his cannons in short and medium bursts of fire, and expended 12 N-37 rounds and 30 NR-23s.

---

18 Fund of the 64th IAK, inventory 174045ss, file. 157, pp.104-107.

Bomb-laden and ready to roll, a US Air Force B-29 Superfortress of the 307th Bomb Wing in Okinawa waits on the hardstand for its crew to get aboard and start another nocturnal mission against targets in North Korea, January 1953. (Courtesy of the US National Archives)

The B-29 crashed in flames some 40–50 km north-east of Anju.[19]

At 2023, the 535th Fighter Air Regiment's senior pilot – Senior Lieutenant Khabiev – took off on an interception mission. To begin with, he headed for the short duration zone over Sonchon. As he reached this area at an altitude of 8,000 m:

> ... He received information from the Command Post that the enemy was approaching from Korea Bay on a heading of 50°. As he continued his search for enemy aircraft Snr Lieutenant Khabiev noticed bombs exploding in the Chongju area, and noticed that the searchlights were active. He began to close on this area, noticing an enemy aircraft caught in the searchlights ahead of him. He set his sight to the maximum range, reduced his engine rpm to slow the aircraft down and gave a short burst of fire from an aspect angle of 1/4. He continued to close on the aircraft and gave a second burst of fire, watching as the shells hit the enemy aircraft. He subsequently fired a third burst of fire after which he noticed that the aircraft began to descend sharply in a bank. He broke off combat turning away steeply to the right. As he was completing this manoeuvre the searchlights ceased to track the aircraft and he lost sight of the bomber.
> Snr Lieutenant Khabiev had opened fire using all his cannons, expending 16 N-37 rounds and 45 NR-23 rounds.
> The enemy bomber was shot down ... [20]

According to Western sources, Bomber Command's losses incurred on 10 January consisted of one B-29 from the 307th

19 Fund of the 64th IAK, inventory 174045ss, file. 157, pp.107-109.
20 Fund of the 64th IAK, inventory 174045ss, file. 157, pp.109-111.

Captain Ivan Golyshevskiy of the 351st Fighter Air Regiment (one victory in Korea) in the cockpit of MiG-15bis No. 546 (serial No. 53210546).

Bomb Wing that had been caught like a fly in the searchlights above Sinanju, was damaged by anti-aircraft crews and finally finished off by fighters.

The next B-29 was shot down two days later, on the night of 12/13 January:

> ... At 2119 Snr Lieutenant Gubenko, a pilot in the 351st Fighter Air Regiment, took off to intercept bombers that had been detected over Anju at an altitude of 7,500 m. Five minutes later over Chongju Gubenko, guided by the Command Post, approached a B-29.
> ... After he had begun to close on this aircraft the pilot saw a B-29 in the searchlights and attacked this aircraft on a collision course, giving one medium burst of fire from a distance of 800–1,000 m at an aspect angle of 2/4, he then gave another burst of fire from a distance of 500–400 m. According to the pilot's report the B-29 caught fire as a result of the attack. As he broke off combat in a left-hand turn Snr Lieutenant Gubenko attacked once again from head on and at a distance of 400 m and an aspect angle of 1/4 giving a single medium burst of fire.
> The pilot used all his cannons in the attack, expending 19 N-37 rounds and 63 NR-23 rounds. The enemy aircraft crashed in flames some 5 km north of Sinbi-to [Sinmi-do] Island.[21]

Less than an hour later, Senior Lieutenant Khabiev was to distinguish himself once again: that night, the Commander of the 91st Strategic Reconnaissance Squadron – Major William Baumer – decided to take a look at the situation in North Korea for himself and joined the crew of an RB-29 that was about to set off on a so-called 'paper flight' to drop leaflets. This would appear to be an amusing mission for a strategic reconnaissance aircraft; a great deal of attention, however, was paid to psychological warfare – and the 'flight' that Baumer

21 Fund of the 64th IAK, inventory 174045ss, file. 157, pp.113-115.

chose was a truly dangerous one. The Superfortress would need to 'drop its bombs' along the banks of the Yalu River in 'MiG Alley' itself.

At 2221, the corps' radar system detected an aircraft that, while it was over Yangdok, was heading for Uiju. Half an hour later (at 2251), Senior Lieutenant Khabiev took off to intercept this aircraft. Khabiev was guided onto the tail of the bomber using the remote indicator screen on the 'Periscope' radar:

> ... Two minutes passed in the first impulse to find this bomber, and the pilot saw two intersecting searchlights ahead and to the left of him. He made a left-hand turn and noticed an RB-29 caught in the searchlights. Approaching the enemy aircraft's aft hemisphere at an altitude of 7,000 m at 2210 [2310] Snr Lieutenant Khabiev closed to a distance of 600 m and positioned himself below and to the right of the aircraft, attacking at an aspect angle ranging from 0/4–1/4 and a climb angle of 5–10° with one long burst of fire aimed at the starboard engine, and the enemy aircraft caught fire. Despite the fact that he had reduced the engine rpm, Khabiev turned away to the right to avert a collision owing to the difference in speed, breaking off combat underneath and to the right of the enemy aircraft. He decided to attack the enemy aircraft a second time and began to assume an initial position from which to attack. He turned to the left and as he approached the burning aircraft's tail from behind, he closed to a distance of 500–300 m, attacking once again at an aspect angle ranging from 0/4–1/4 with three long bursts of fire. The enemy aircraft, engulfed in flames, dived steeply towards the ground.
>
> The pilot used all his cannons to fire at the enemy aircraft; using a movable sight reticle he expended all his ammunition in long bursts of fire.
>
> As a result of this attack the B-29 was shot down, crashing in flames in Chinese territory 30 km southwest of Andung in the Ulumbey area.
>
> Out of the crew of 14 on the RB-29, 11 bailed out by parachute and were taken prisoner by our Chinese allies.[22]

Nikolai Nikolayevich Shkodin, a witness to Khabiev's battle, recalls:

> That night we shot an American colonel down in a 'Fortress', he was the head of the entire American reconnaissance effort in Korea. He himself actually flew on a reconnaissance mission; it made for an interesting drama. He entered Chinese airspace and flew along the Yalu River, and we have searchlights there and RP-20 radar stations. The pilot was already airborne... the radar operator told the pilot: "Stay where you are... Increase your speed slightly; I will give the order.... I'm

On the ladder, the Squadron Commander of the 1st Squadron, 351st Fighter Air Regiment, Major Kultyshev (one victory in Korea).

> going to light him up now." A soon as the enemy aircraft reached the searchlights – and the searchlights there have radars – he was lit up. Our pilot gave him a burst and the aircraft caught fire... We came back from our evening meal and we could hear the Chinese shouting "Truman bailed! Truman bailed!" The colonel bailed out and was taken prisoner.

Senior Lieutenant Khabiev's victory became one of the most famous of all the victories attained by the pilots of the 64th Fighter Air Corps. For Major William Baumer, who had been captured, the war was over. Western researchers confirm that the RB-29 shot down by the MiG was the only aircraft to be lost that night.

❧

Following the losses incurred on the night of 10/12 January, Bomber Command restricted B-29 activity north of the Pyongyang–Wonsan border and transferred its principal forces south of this line towards the eastern seaboard. In response, our fighters intensified their activity to Pyongyang in the south and Hamhung in the east – and by the first half of January, they were already engaged in combat with bombers around the North Korean capital. The best pilots were sent to intercept bombers around Pyongyang, with experience of air combat outside the searchlight zone. They were guided to the area where the bombers were active – using radar data from the 'Periscope' radar system – and would begin a visual search for targets independently.

Without a doubt, the best night fighter pilot in the 64th Fighter Air Corps was the Deputy Commander of the 351st Fighter Air Regiment, Anatoliy Karelin. The battles that they fought at the end of January proved that pilots could engage a B-29 in combat on a moonlit night with snow cover even outside the searchlight zone. On 28 January:

---
22 Fund of the 64th IAK, inventory 174045ss, file. 164, pp.111-113.

Senior Lieutenant A.I. Gubenko – a pilot in the 1st Squadron, 351st Fighter Air Regiment. (This photograph was provided by I. Seidov)

Pilots of the 535th Fighter Air Regiment (standing on the far right is Senior Lieutenant Yahkya Khabiev). (This photograph was provided by I. Seidov)

The MiG-15bis No. 759 (serial No. 2715359) of the 236th Fighter Air Regiment, 37th Fighter Air Division; Antung airfield, autumn 1953. This aircraft previously served with the 535th Fighter Air Regiment and was assigned to Senior Lieutenant Ya.Z. Khabiev.

...At 2254 [2354] a single MiG that was permanently on the highest state of readiness was scrambled from Andung airfield following an order from the Command Post... the pilot was Major Karelin who was sent to shoot down an enemy bomber in the SINRI area.

As he headed for the Pyongyang area at an altitude of 7,500 m Major Karelin was constantly receiving updates from the Fighter Air Corps' Command Post concerning the flight of the enemy bomber.

Once over the Pyongyang area the pilot noticed bombs exploding on the ground. As he searched for the enemy at an altitude of 8,000 m he noticed against the moon [Authors' note: means 'in the moonlight'] a glint coming from the flanks of an enemy bomber and as he descended to an altitude of 6,500 m he identified a B-29 bomber flying on a magnetic heading of 180°. As he closed on the enemy aircraft to a distance of 600–500 m Major Karelin attacked from the same altitude at an aspect angle of 1/4 with a single burst of fire, and noticed pockets of fire emanating from the port outboard engine. He broke off combat in front and to the right of the aircraft.

Karelin made the second attack ahead and to the right of the bomber from a distance of 300–200 m at an aspect angle of 3/4 overshooting and passing underneath the bomber without losing sight of it. He assumed an initial attack position behind the bomber, making a third attack at an aspect angle of 0/4 and from a distance of 600–500 m, giving a long, concentrated burst of fire. The enemy aircraft descended in flames and crashed in an area 50 km south-east of Pyongyang. During Major Karelin's attack the enemy fired on him intensively using their own armament but without success.

Major Karelin attacked the enemy bomber using all his cannons, expending 20 N-37 rounds and 80 NR-23 rounds.[23]

A day later – on the night of 30/31 January 1953 – a single MiG-15 was scrambled:

... At 2115 [2215] and was tasked with carrying out a "fighter sweep" in the furthest approaches to the assets under the protection of the Corps. The pilot was Major Karelin and he was sent to the Pyongyang region.

As he transited to the Pyongyang region at an altitude of 7,500 m Major Karelin saw evidence of bombing by enemy aircraft on targets in the Pyongyang area, as he increased his awareness he noticed an enemy bomber in the moonlight at an altitude of 7,000 m,

23　Fund of the 64th IAK, inventory 174045ss, file. 164, pp.114-117.

which turned to the left after dropping its bombs. Major Karelin assumed an initial attack position attacking from behind, above and to the right of the bomber at an aspect angle of 2/4 from a distance of 500–400 m. He was not able to see the results of his attack; without losing sight of the enemy he attacked again from behind the bomber and to the left at an aspect angle of 1/4 from a distance of 300–400 m. He opened fire using all his guns; as a result of this attack the aircraft caught fire. As he was making his second attack Major Karelin was fired upon by the B-29 and twice the rounds entered his cockpit, damaging the instrument panel [Authors' note: the most widespread defensive armament on the Superfortress were the 12.7 mm machine guns, but there were other variants, with 20 mm machine guns mounted in the tail. It is possible that Major Karelin encountered one of these, or the text of the document actually means 'bullets' when it states 'rounds']. In view of the damage his aircraft had sustained Major Karelin attacked the B-29 for a third time from a distance of 500 m at an aspect angle of 0/4 giving two long bursts of fire.

After the third attack Major Karelin stopped firing at the B-29 and watched as some parts fell off the enemy aircraft as it entered a steep descent.

As he pursued the burning bomber in its descent Major Karelin made a fourth attack at an altitude of 3,000 m and an aspect angle of 1/4.

Since his aircraft had been seriously damaged Major Karelin did not pursue the bomber any further and set course back to his home base. On approach to the airfield his engine failed… Karelin demonstrating courage and collectiveness landed normally back at his home base in a damaged aircraft in which the engine had failed.

The enemy aircraft that Major Karelin attacked crashed 70 km south of Pyongyang.

The armament expended was 40 N-37 rounds and 140 NS-23s.[24]

From open Western sources, it is known that on 28 January, a B-29 from the 19th Bomb Wing was lost; but on the night of 30/31 January, a B-29 from the 307th Bomb Wing had been seriously damaged and had not made it back to base, but had made an emergency landing in North Korean territory.

Anatoliy Mikhaylovich Karelin became a truly unique Korean War ace — attaining all six of his bomber victories in the night hours. He was awarded the title of Hero of the Soviet Union — by way of a decree from the Presidium of the Supreme Soviet of the USSR — dated '14 July 1953'. The bomber that Karelin shot down on the night of 30/31 January was to become the last to be shot down by the fighter aircraft of the 64th Fighter Air Corps.

---

24 Fund of the 64th IAK, inventory 174045ss, file. 164, pp.118-120.

✧

In the winter and spring of 1953, the Superfortresses would regularly fly bombing sorties to strike Korean People's Army and Chinese People's Volunteer Army supply bases in North Korean territory – and they did not forget the industrial sites either. On the night of 13/14 March, 12 B-29s bombed the ore-processing plant at Chok Tong – and three nights later, 21 Superfortresses bombed industrial targets around Sinuiju. In May of that year, they participated in an unprecedented operation to destroy the dams at the centre of North Korea's irrigation system. The thinking at Far East Air Force Headquarters was that if 20 dams could be destroyed, more than three-quarters of the rice crop (which was the principal foodstuff in North Korea) would be wiped out. Bomber Command was allocated the Kae-wong dam. On 29 May, they bombed this dam twice using the SHORAN system; seven bombers took part in the first raid on the night of 21/22 May. The dam sustained four direct hits, with 908 kg of bombs, but did not burst. One week later (on the night of 29/30 May), the Superfortresses repeated this raid – scoring five direct hits on the base of the dam. In preparation for the raid, the North Koreans had lowered the water level in the reservoir, which had the effect of reducing pressure on the dam itself and, as such, it did not fail on this occasion either.

Nevertheless, on 28 May Sino-Korean forces launched a trial offensive on the Western Front – on the back of which they launched their final all-out offensive. The B-29s were transferred to bombing infantry on the front line – and in the Kumhva region, where talks were held to negotiate a ceasefire, 970 tonnes of bombs were dropped on the enemy in the course of five days. The B-29s would bomb the bridges and airfields from the end of spring up until the end of the war. According to the terms of the ceasefire, the Korean People's Army could retain the weaponry they had in their possession in North Korean territory up until 2200 on 27 July. The North Koreans desperately tried to redeploy their MiGs from the other side of the Yalu River – and during June and July, the Superfortresses would carry out bombing raids on one or two airfields on a daily basis.

Since February, the B-29s had refused to operate on clear moonlit nights. The preference now was for the darkest time of day: from the end of the evening twilight until the rising of the moon, and from its setting to the first sign of dawn. Moreover, they used inclement weather conditions to their advantage wherever possible (particularly low cloud and mist) – thus of the 13 raids the Superfortresses completed against assets under the protection of the 64th Fighter Air Corps during June, 11 were undertaken in 10 oktas of cloud cover, with a cloud base ranging from 50 to 900 m. In this case, rain, drizzle, fog and mist would often reduce horizontal visibility to just half a kilometre. The B-29s would be protected by intensive radar jamming, as well as night fighters. As before, the 'Fortresses' would avoid entering the searchlight zone and would approach their targets from Korea Bay – heading straight out to sea after completing their bombing runs. There were instances in which the bombing raids would be carried out from two directions: from the south and east. From April onwards, the B-29s began to employ radar evasion tactics; they would suddenly change course a number of times – occasionally using 90° of bank as they transited to the target. All these measures brought their own rewards in that the bombers did not incur any losses from the beginning of January up until the last day of the war.

On 27 July at 1503, an RB-29 from the 91st Strategic Reconnaissance Squadron that had taken off to carry out a reconnaissance mission over North Korean airfields landed on Yokota airfield on the island of Honshu. The crew, led by 1st Lieutenant Denver Cook, brought the aircraft into land from the last combat sortie flown by a Superfortress in the Korean War – and into history. During their combat activities, the Superfortresses of the 19th, 22nd, 92nd and 307th Bomb Wings had completed 21,000 sorties – dropping 167,100 tonnes of bombs on the enemy. During the course of this 37-month-long war – dominated by jet aircraft – these obsolete bombers were only absent from the skies over Korea for 26 days.

※

Apart from anything else, the mission put before the night fighters of the 64th Fighter Air Corps in February 1953 required an expansion of their sphere of operation south to Pyongyang and east to the shores of the South China Sea to force the enemy to abandon organised raids by B-29s in the area (under the protection of the corps in favourable weather conditions). Formally, it could be said that this was successful. The Superfortresses were really only active in the area under the protection of the corps from February 1953 onwards in inclement weather conditions. This, however, had almost no bearing on the effectiveness of their bombing raids. The use of the SHORAN radio-navigation system meant that the American bombers could operate more or less regardless of the weather conditions over the target.

The effectiveness of our fighters was, to a much greater extent, dependent on the weather; the fact that the B-29s transferred to operations in inclement weather conditions meant that our fighters did not shoot down a single B-29 in the last six months of the war, and five 'Fortresses' were damaged. Moreover, the night flights carried out the by corps' MiGs were much higher than in any other period of the war; on average, they amounted to 210 combat sorties a month! The main reason for this dismal situation was that the MiG-15s were not fitted with an onboard search and track radar. In the absence of an onboard radar system, incontrovertible visual contact with the enemy had to be established – and this task was made all the more difficult on a dark moonless night and was, for the most part, impossible. Naturally, this situation did not go unnoticed by the corps' command or the leadership of the air force, air defence forces or the Ministry for Aircraft Production. Moreover, the issue of fitting the MiG-15 with onboard search and tracking systems had been raised long before February 1953.

Bristling guns pointed skyward, these B-29 'Superforts' of the Japan-based US Air Force 98th Bomb Wing line up on the runway bound for another attack on targets in North Korea; March 1953. (Courtesy of the US National Archives)

At the beginning of the year, representatives from one of the Scientific-Research Centres in Moscow visited the 351st Fighter Air Regiment and delivered a new target identification system that used a target's infra-red radiation for testing in combat conditions; this was the SIV-52 infra-red aircraft sight. This consisted of a tube that was 220-250 mm long with a diameter of 100-120 mm, with a small screen at one end and a battery. The tube was installed onto the bracket for the ASP-3N gun sight, and the latter was removed; the battery was located to the right of the pilot's cockpit. As the MiG closed on an enemy aircraft up to a distance of less than 2,000 m, a blip would appear on the infra-red sight. As the distance to the target reduced, the blip would become brighter and more distinct – and from a certain distance, it was possible to determine how many engines the aircraft under attack had.

The first flights using the SIV-52 revealed its significant shortcomings: at night, the bright glow of the screen made it difficult for the pilot to see outside the cockpit, which was particularly acute on take-off and landing. This was resolved by switching the infra-red sight on in-flight. Another serious problem was that the target was shown 'upside-down' on the SIV-52 system. This, of course, made the process of aiming at the target itself significantly more difficult. The SIV-52 was fitted to Senior Lieutenant Iskhangalev's MiG-15 from the 351st Fighter Air Regiment. The pilot flew several combat sorties testing the sight, but he was not able to achieve any positive results.

After the departure of the 351st Fighter Air Regiment back to the Soviet Union during February, the baton for testing this system was passed to the 147th Guards Fighter Air Regiment and then in May to the 298th Fighter Air Regiment. Guards Senior Lieutenant Yu. Dobrovichan tested the SIV-52 sight in the 147th Guards Fighter Air Regiment. Neither Dobrovichan, who was without a doubt an outstanding pilot,

In a twilight take-off line-up – an Armed Forces Day symbol of the big UN air effort in Korea – all-weather US Air Force B-29 warcraft of the 98th Bomb Wing in Japan are ready to begin another night attack against targets in North Korea. In over 34 months of combat operations, B-29s from both Japan and Okinawa have slammed more than 312 million lbs of high-explosives into enemy industrial supply and troop centres, transportation networks and frontline positions. The 11-man 'Superforts' have been the 'heavyweights' of the Korean Air War – flying more than 17,000 combat sorties against the enemy, May 1953. (Courtesy of the US National Archives)

This huge B-29 Superfortress of the US Far East Air Force lands gracefully on the runway after another mission against the enemy. (Courtesy of the US National Archives)

The 'Blue Tail Fly' B-29 Superfortress of the 20th Air Force (having just returned from a bombing mission on North Korean forces) is shown being backed into a hardstand – and preparations for the next mission will start by checking the plane carefully and loading the bomb bays with bombs. (Courtesy of the US National Archives)

nor the pilots of the 298th Fighter Air Regiment were able to achieve significant results using the IR-sight. According to accounts given by the pilots of the 298th Fighter Air Regiment, they only managed to damage one B-29 using this sight. The SIV-52 did not live up to its expectations: all the IR-sights were removed from the aircraft at the beginning of July and were sent to Moscow. The MiG-15s were never fitted with onboard search and tracking equipment, which would have given the aircraft the potential to combat the B-29s successfully.

In this situation, our fighters were reliant on the accuracy of their ground guidance to attack invisible targets – opening fire when they were given the order by the Command Post; there was still the possibility that the Superfortresses would end up within range of our searchlights for a short time. It was not possible, however, to rely on that at all: in the course of the final six months of the war, the corps' MiGs were only engaged in combat within the searchlight zone four times. On 12 April, the Commander of the 298th Fighter Air Regiment – Lieutenant-Colonel V.A. Vasilyev – damaged a single 'Fortress' during one of these battles.

According to our records, a further four B-29s were damaged by cannon fire by the pilots of the 298th Regiment following an order from the Command Post; we did not encounter any mention of spring and summer battles in Western literature. A number of foreign researchers recognise the protestation that several bombers could have been damaged by cannon fire under orders from the ground, since by the end of the war, 'MiG Alley' had once again become a dangerous place to be, as the North Koreans had special MiG night fighters fitted with onboard search and tracking equipment. On 29 May, Captain Vavilov damaged a B-29; on 11 July, Captain Kiberev did the same and on 24 July, it was Major Marayev's turn. The fact that the B-29s had been damaged was confirmed by electronic reconnaissance. The last B-29 was damaged by Captain Vavilov at 0235 on 21 July during a raid on Uiju and Sinuiju airfields.

The weather on the night of 20 July was highly unsuitable for our fighters; the 10 oktas of lingering cloud cover reached a depth of 3-4 km. These weather conditions were, however, almost ideal for the Superfortresses. Between 0000-0038, the corps' radar system detected 12 B-29s tracking in a south-westerly direction from airbases in Japan. The bombers were protected by 10 F-94 and F3D fighters patrolling a triangular area formed of Sonjuri–Phihen–Kusong. After passing over Kunu-ri (Kaechon on modern maps) and Kusong, the B-29s approached Uiju airfield – dropping their bomb load on this

Maintenance crewmen of the US Far East Air Force's 19th Bomb Group's B-29 Superfort, the 'Blue Tail Fly', point with pride to the neat strings of bomb symbols, which add up to 100 – the number of combat assaults this medium bomber has made on targets in Korea. This is the first B-29 in the entire US Far East Air Force to fly 100 missions. Master Sergeant Constantine Profers, maintenance crew chief, points from the cockpit. (Courtesy of the US National Archives)

Major V.M. Kosenko's (Squadron Commander, 1st Squadron, 298th Fighter Air Regiment) ground crew; Andung, 1953. (This photograph was provided by I. Seidov)

Senior Lieutenant Ryabukhin's ground crew (he was a pilot in the 1st Squadron, 298th Fighter Air Regiment); Andung, 1953. (This photograph was provided by I. Seidov)

airbase between 0116-0124. In all, ninety-nine 454 kg high-explosive bombs fell on the airfield. Thirty-seven of these bombs fell on the concrete runway, while a further 33 fell on a spare unmade airstrip. The damage that resulted from the raid was not extensive: there was no damage to materiel and no personnel were lost. The fact that the runway was made of relatively shallow concrete meant that the damage could be put right immediately.

A second group of 13 B-29s was detected between 0101-0245. After making a detour via Huichon, the Superfortresses made a left turn (passing over Pukchin) – bombing Sinuiju airfield between 0253-0306. A total of 173 high-explosive bombs fell on the main runway, while a further 66 fell on the spare runway. Around 100 of these bombs were fitted with delayed-action fuses, and explosions were heard around the airfield the following day; some of the bombs fell on rice fields that surrounded Sinuiju. On this occasion, there were no casualties among the personnel and the raid did not inflict any damage. The sandy soil meant that the airfield could be repaired quickly (a single bulldozer was able to fill in a bomb crater on average in the space of 25-30 minutes). The Superfortresses in the second group were attacked by MiGs. According to the pilots of the 298th Fighter Air Regiment, the corps' Command Post guided Captain Vavilov and Senior Lieutenant Alekseyev directly onto the tail of one of the bombers. Our pilots opened fire on this bomber from a minimal distance and they were almost at flight idle. The next morning, on the basis of electronic reconnaissance, it was announced that the bomber that had been attacked did not make it back to base. Nevertheless, it was recorded on Captain Vavilov's tally simply as having been damaged. Such was the outcome of this battle – the last involving Soviet fighters of the Korean War.

Not satisfied with the outcome of the mission, the Americans repeated the raid on Uiju on the night of 21 July – and this time, the weather suited the Superfortresses. The sky was blanketed with 10 oktas of cloud cover, with patchy rain. Between 0230-0300, the B-29s dropped a large number of low-explosive and incendiary bombs on the airfield. The area that was bombed covered 1,000–2,000 m and included the revetments housing the North Korean MiG-15s. As a result of the raid, 15 MiGs caught fire and a further five were damaged by shrapnel. Three airfield maintenance personnel were killed, along with four civilians; four buildings were destroyed by fire.

The July raids on the Uiju and Sinuiju airfields brought the story of the battle between the B-29 and the MiG-15 to an end. This time, Bomber Command US Far East Air Force had the last word. The search for new tactical solutions, as well as ways

Firefighters stand by – ready for any trouble – as this Boeing B-29 Superfortress comes in for a landing following a mission over North Korea, 10 April 1953. (Courtesy of the US National Archives)

Major-General of Aviation V.A. Vasilyev. In the first half of 1953, he was a Lieutenant-Colonel and the Commander of the 298th Fighter Air Regiment. (This photograph was provided by I. Seidov)

The Deputy Commander of the 3rd Squadron, 298th Fighter Air Regiment, N.M. Vavilov. (This photograph was provided by I. Seidov)

of organising night fighter combat operations within the corps, did nothing to change the situation to any great degree. The only way to recapture the initiative from the Americans would have been to fit fighters with new onboard radar technology. The 64th Fighter Air Corps, however, did not have any such aircraft at their disposal.

The Hidden Roles of the Superfortesses

The old saying that auxiliary aircraft serve alongside frontline types in any war is often overlooked in literature as uninteresting. It is taken as read that in air combat, the decisive role is played by interceptors that intercept; ground attack aircraft that carry out ground attacks; and bombers that (naturally) are engaged in bombing. It is possible though that reconnaissance and transport aircraft also make their own contribution. Furthermore, up to a third of the sorties flown by the US Far East Air Force in Korea encompassed a whole series of 'second line' missions, which had they not been successful, combat effectiveness would have been significantly reduced. Additionally, the Superfortresses, which were initially designed as strategic bombers, proved their worth in other roles – and it is worth mentioning two of them here...

In June 1950, the Far East Air Force had two search and rescue squadrons, and their aircraft were based at Ashiya, Johnson, Yokota and Misawa airbases. It is likely that no other major air force unit had had such a variety of technology at its disposal. The 3rd Search and Rescue Squadron consisted of SC-46, SC-47 and SB-17 search and rescue aircraft that had been converted from transport aircraft and bombers; SA-16 flying boats, S-5 light liaison aircraft, H-5 and H-19 helicopters ... and even coastal launches! SB-29As served in 'B' Detachment, 3rd Search and Rescue Squadron based at Yokota airfield. The SB-29 was a conversion from the standard B-29 that had been adapted to carry a 9.1 m A-3 lifeboat under its fuselage. This aluminium lifeboat had 22 compartments – of which 20 were watertight, while those at the bow and stern carried inflatable life rafts. These life rafts would be tipped overboard and would inflate automatically as they came into contact with water. The lifeboat had a petrol engine and a range of 900 km. Apart from that it had a radio beacon on board, as well as flares, medicines and provisions. The standard procedure for dropping the lifeboat was to release it from an altitude of around 30 m during a low-speed flypast over a stricken crew. To accommodate the lifeboat under the fuselage, the bomber's radio sight was transferred to the lower, forward gun turret housing. To begin with, all the armament on the SB-29 was removed, but was reinstated during the first few months of the war. Rescue crews worked every day for the entire duration of the war – and the following is testament to the pressure they were under: while the three bomb wings flying Superfortresses would fly to North Korea in turn (that is to say every third day), with the exception of the one day on which they were under 'maximum pressure', the SB-17s and SB-29s would accompany the B-29s on *every* sortie over the sea! While the Superfortresses were making their bombing runs, the RB-29s would circle over the sea (close to the Korean Coast) and would return to their home base, along with the bombers.

Pilots from the 3rd Squadron, 298th Fighter Air Regiment. Seated are V.I. Shoytov, Squadron Commander V.G. Borokhta, A.M. Zharkov and N.M. Vavilov. Standing are E.E. Yeremin, P.I. Korotkovskiy, P.I. Fedulichev, V.D. Yershov and M.M. Alekseyev; Andung, 1953. (This photograph was provided by I. Seidov)

Owing to the routine nature of their work – and the lack of outstanding incidents during the course of their service – the work of the RB-29s is rarely mentioned in literature. As such, we are not able to present any detailed information concerning operations by search and rescue Superfortresses during the Korean War. We only know that by the end of the war, every detachment in the 2nd and 3rd Search and Rescue Squadrons – including 'B' Detachment – had grown until they reached squadron proportions.

The other role carried out by Superfortresses in the Korean War is less well known because it was, over the course of the events described, highly classified. This concerns the first instances in history of mid-air refuelling in a combat scenario. It has to be said that the advent of tanker aircraft was not directly linked to the war with Korea, but they did undergo running-in tests in the Korean theatre. The story behind the development of a sustainable in-flight refuelling system is, however, interesting in itself – and we are able to cover this material briefly within the confines of this work… [Authors' note: for anyone interested in the development of a similar system in the USSR, we would certainly recommend the wonderful book *From Wing to Wing*, written by Test Pilot Igor Shelest.]

The idea behind tanker aircraft came about after the war at one of the meetings between representatives of the United States Air Force, Great Britain and the Commonwealth countries. During one of the lectures, the British shared the results of their work on refuelling and briefed their allies on mid-air refuelling equipment developed by Sir Alan Cobham. He was famous for his pre-war long-range flights around the Commonwealth countries – and it is possible that the idea for mid-air refuelling came to him during those long flights. This was the 'probe and drogue' refuelling method: not the most practical, but the easiest system to use. The tanker aircraft would be fitted with a hose, with a drogue at one end, which also acted as a stabiliser; the aircraft receiving the fuel would be fitted with a refuelling probe. During the course of refuelling, the tanker would trail the hose in the slipstream and maintain level flight in a straight line at a constant speed. The pilot of the aircraft that was to receive the fuel would need to position his aircraft in such a way as to place the probe inside the drogue on the end of the hose. To test the system, the British used Meteors and a Lancaster that had been converted into a bomber.

The Second World War ace Colonel David C. Schilling became interested in mid-air refuelling, which was particularly important for the United States, given its position far from Europe. He turned to the Commander of the United States Air Force, Holt Vandenberg – and a short time later, a pair of F-84Es were sent to England to have the equipment fitted. On 22 September 1950, Schilling and his wingman took off from Manston airfield and set course for Bangor airfield (in the State of Maine) across the Atlantic Ocean. It was proposed that they would be refuelled three times on this long-range flight. A head wind made the flight more difficult; they lost more than an hour looking for the tanker to refuel over Iceland. They had to take fuel for the final time over Labrador – and when Schilling engaged with the refuelling hose, he only had three minutes of fuel left in his tanks. His wingman, Lieutenant-Colonel William D. Ritchie, was not able to take on any fuel at all because the probe in his aircraft had broken off. He headed for the coast after his engine failed and ejected before he was able to reach the large airfield at Goose Bay. Schilling flew on alone – and 10 hours two minutes after he took off, he landed at Bangor.

The air force became interested in the idea of mid-air refuelling and Boeing converted 92 B-29s and B-29As into tanker aircraft. A tank holding 8,700 litres of additional fuel was installed in each of the bomb bays, and a winch was fitted in the aircraft's tail section to deploy and retract the hose, as well as the fuel transfer equipment. This aircraft was designated the 'KB-29M'. In the summer of 1951, the tanker aircraft had already undergone testing in a real-life combat situation. To achieve this, 12 KB-29M aircraft from the 43rd Refuelling Squadron were incorporated into the 91st Strategic Reconnaissance Squadron as the so-called '4th Detachment'. They commenced regular refuelling operations with RB-45C Tornado jets from 'A' Detachment in the same 91st Strategic Reconnaissance Squadron on 14 July. On a typical sortie, the RB-45s – which would have taken off from Yokota airfield – would have refuelled either over the Sea of Japan or over South Korea. If the aircraft's fuel tanks were full, it would allow them to open up to full throttle long before they reached the target. They would then pass over the target at high speed and set course for their home base without throttling back. Time spent over the high-risk MiG areas was kept to a minimum, but the increased fuel consumption – with the engines at a high rpm – meant that they had to refuel again on their return leg. The successful combination of the KB-29 with the RB-45 continued right up until the end of the war. Refuelling the fighters, however, turned out to be much more complicated...

The first fighter 'recipients' were three RF-80s from the 67th Reconnaissance Wing, which had refuelling probes fitted onto the tip tanks. The reconnaissance aircraft would rendezvous with the tanker over Wonsan Bay – 150 km from the coast – and would set course for the Yalu River estuary following completion of a successful refuelling, where they would photograph the airfields and then return to base; a unique flight was flown in September of that year that involved refuelling an F-80C. Lieutenant-Colonel Harry W. Dorris Jr took off from Yokota airfield with two 227 kg bombs and four HVAR rockets – and after hitting his designated target, he returned to base. During the sortie (which lasted 14 hours and five minutes!), Dorris refuelled from a tanker six times. Incidentally, this sortie was considered equivalent to five combat sorties in the pilots' logbook.

Refuelling with a group of fighters still had to be tested. The refuelling probes were fitted onto the tip tanks of the F-84Es operating under the 116th Air Wing, United States Air Force, which were temporarily assigned to Japan's self-defence forces (and which were performing an air defence role for the Japanese islands). The second F-84 air wing in the Korean theatre was the 136th Fighter Wing, which was based on the South Korean airbase of Taegu and which did not require in-flight refuelling. Development of in-flight refuelling began in February 1952 – and pilots encountered serious problems during the first few flights.

First and foremost, it has to be said that the equipment with which the Thunderjets of the 116th Air Wing were fitted was fundamentally different to that fitted to Schilling and Ritchie's F-84s in their long-range flight across the Atlantic; the latter aircraft used a single in-flight refuelling probe that fed fuel to all the tanks simultaneously. This design made refuelling easier, but meant that the whole fuel system had to be modified. The F-84s in the 116th Air Wing underwent a different modification – and each of the tip tanks were fitted with a refuelling probe. This being the case, the fuel tanks in the wings and fuselage were not filled at all in flight. This made modification of the materiel easier, but increased pilot workload.

Pilots needed to make three approaches to refuel the aircraft: first, one of the tip tanks would be filled half full; then a second would be filled up – and only after this would the first tip tank be topped up. It was thought that this would make it easier for the pilot to control the aircraft with fuel tanks that had not been filled evenly. The pilot, however, had to perform the delicate task of ensuring contact with the probe three times to refuel fully! What if the sortie required a pilot to refuel several times? The flight crew therefore decided that it would be better to put up with the difficulties of flying with one empty and one full fuel tank and reduce the contacts with the refuelling probe to two, and to fill the tanks 'up to the filler cap' in one go. Moreover, even a single contact was fraught with difficulty using the 'probe and drogue' refuelling method.

The primary point to consider is that the Thunderjets and the slower, piston engine and heavily-laden KB-29s flew at different speeds – thus contact at a higher speed often led to the probe breaking off; what's more, ensuring that the probe engaged with the drogue was very complicated. The end of the flexible hose would move around in the tanker's slipstream – and in some cases, it would fly up over the wing just prior to contact with the probe. As it came down, it would damage the trailing edge of the ailerons or the wing. Apart from that, the probes on the tip tanks were almost six metres away from the pilot, which made orientation much more difficult. To begin with, a technique was developed for refuelling four aircraft simultaneously; then as the right skills were acquired, this grew steadily before it reached 36 aircraft. In May, 36 F-84s and 12 KB-29s took off on a demonstration flight around the Japanese islands. This sortie, however, did not go as planned: many of the Thunderjets were not able to take on fuel for one reason or another and landed at the nearest available airfields.

Combat sorties proper commenced in the final days of spring 1952. On the first of these, which took place on 29 May, 12 F-84Es took off from Itadzuke airbase and bombed targets close to Sariwon – refuelling over Taego on the return journey from a KB-29. Three Thunderjets were forced to land on this same South Korean airbase – and two of them didn't even have enough fuel to undertake the refuelling; the equipment on the third aircraft failed. In all, the F-84s completed four sorties with in-flight refuelling over the course of the summer. Due to the imperfect nature of the 'probe and drogue' refuelling method and the lack of a centralised refuelling probe on the F-84E, each of these sorties turned out to be extremely complex – and of course, they had no military significance. At the behest of the air force, the Boeing Company developed a new in-flight refuelling system using a refuelling probe with a telescopic tip. This was fitted into the tanker's tail section and featured stabilisers, which the operator sitting in the bomber's rear gunner position used to control deviations. The 116 B-29 aircraft that were converted to use the telescopic boom were designated 'KB-29P' – and their first regular 'clients' were the F-84Gs. The in-flight refuelling receptacle on this modification was located in its own housing in the port wing root, and was centralised. The fixed telescopic probe was not subject to deviations in the slipstream, which made the process of engaging with the probe much easier. An F-84G pilot would position his aircraft in such a way that the inlet valve was beneath and a little aft of the probe and that his speed matched that of the tanker. The boom operator on the KB-29R would then make final adjustments to the boom's heading and altitude, extend the telescopic tip and make contact with the inlet valve.

This system was not tested in a combat environment in Korea. To begin with, the 5th Air Army did not have any KB-29Ps or F-84Gs at their disposal – and when they did arrive, they no longer felt the need for them. On 10 July 1952, the 116th Air Wing was renamed 'the 474th' and was withdrawn from the Japanese self-defence forces and transferred to come under the control of the 5th Air Army. They were then immediately re-deployed to the South Korean airfield at Kunsan, which was close enough to the target area to allow the aircraft to reach the targets without refuelling. The first F-84Gs arrived at the Korean theatre at the end of July when the 31st Escort Air Wing, led by Colonel Schilling, arrived at Misawa airbase in Japan. It has to be said that the air wing arrived 'under their own steam' – crossing the Pacific Ocean in a flight covering approximately 11,600 km with two refuellings. On arrival at Misawa, they did not participate in any of the fighting, but replaced the 116th Air Wing providing air defence for Japan.

Conclusion

During the course of the war in Korea, the pilots of the 64th Fighter Air Corps completed 64,300 sorties between 1 November 1950 and 27 July 1953 – in the course of which, they were engaged in 1,872 dogfights. In all that time, the battles involving B-29s amounted to less than 50 (that is to say, less than three percent). However, when the history of the encounters between the Superfortresses and the MiG-15s are taken into consideration, one inevitably arrives at the notion that this three percent made more of a lasting impression on military aviation than the remaining 97.

In the air battles over Korea, the opposing forces made widespread use of jet technology for the first time, and jets were engaged in the lion's share of air battles – therefore, if it is to be judged superficially, the Korean War became the first 'modern' war (if it were not completely modern, then at least it was modern in terms of that 97 percent). This judgement, however, is not correct: the jet fighter's onboard armament remained the same as that used during the Second World War – cannons and machine guns. In order to defeat an enemy, the MiG and Sabre pilots had to get into an aircraft's aft hemisphere and close to a distance from which firing the guns would prove effective in exactly the same way their predecessors in the Yaks, Messerschmitts and Spitfires had done (and even further back than that, in Sopwiths and Nieuports). Owing to the fighters' much higher speeds, the scale of the air battles naturally increased, but in essence, they remained the same as they had been 10, 20, or even 40 years ago. On the other hand, the fighters in service at the end of the 20th century with their onboard radars, which are comparable to (or exceed the power of) the Korean P-20 ground radars and their all-aspect missiles, unimaginable aerodynamics and thrust-to-weight ratios, are not fighting the same battles as the 'early jets'. Naturally, they retain in their arsenal manoeuvres that proved their worth in Korea, but which (and we come back to this again) were around prior to the Korean War. It was probably whilst fighting air battles at high altitude that the fighters really acquired any truly invaluable experience, but this same value turned out to be ambiguous. Prior to the Korean War, there were no air battles in the tropopause, but there were none after Korea either. Even in the contemporary Gulf War, aircraft did not climb above 8,000 m. On the other hand, it was in these same battles between MiGs and Superfortresses that approaches to waging war, which today form the basis of armed combat for aviation of all kinds, were devised and developed. These include interception beyond visual range of a target, searching for an enemy using infra-red, precision bombing of an unseen target, using 'smart weapons', widespread use of electronic warfare aircraft and much more. The B-29 was also directly involved with the development of in-flight refuelling – without which a military operation of any kind (in the West at least) is unthinkable.

❧

We now come to a long-awaited subject, which according to Mark Twain, is nothing but a bare-faced lie, but which we all love: statistics. The gunners on the B/RB-29s were officially credited with shooting down 27 enemy aircraft – of which 26 were MiG-15s and one was an unidentified piston-engine aircraft – thus the Superfortress took second place in the hierarchy of MiG killers after the Sabre. (By way of a comparison, pilots who flew F-80, F-84, F-94, F-3D and Meteor fighters were credited with having downed a total of 27 MiGs.) The gunners of the 19th Bomb Wing attained the greatest success: their tally numbered 16 MiG-15s. Superfortress aces even emerged in the two squadrons that made up the wing – the 28th and 30th Squadrons – with the crews reporting five MiG kills each. The 98th and 307th Bomb Wings each attained five kills, while the 91st Strategic Reconnaissance Bomb Wing recorded one kill.

The majority of the gunners recorded one kill each, with the exception of Sergeant Billy Beach and Staff-Sergeant Michael Martocci from the 28th Bomb Squadron, who were credited with two MiG-15s each. In reality, neither the 64th Fighter Air Corps – nor the Combined Air Army – sustained any *incontrovertible* losses as a result of defensive fire from the B-29s. In both cases (on 6 December 1950 and 23 August 1952), there were suggestions that MiGs had been shot down by the B-29s gunners, but the Americans do not have any recorded victories for either of those days. In a further three cases, nobody witnessed the circumstances surrounding the losses (this refers to 7 April, 1 June and 9 July 1951); the MiGs could just as easily have been shot down either by defensive fire from a B-29, or by escort fighters. On the other hand, the pilots of the 64th Fighter Air Corps recorded 69 victories in their tally during the course of the Korean War.

It is now possible to reveal the exact number of actual Superfortresses lost in these air battles: we consider this to be just 40 aircraft. This includes those recognised as losses by Bomber Command; those that were shot down over the target and crashed into the sea; those that broke up over North Korea and those written off as a result of damage – as well as those that were either not recognised, or were not mentioned but, in the opinion of the authors, sustained sufficient damage at the hands of our own forces. The pilots of the 303rd Fighter Air Division recorded the greatest number of victories in the day battles. Their tally stood at 18 B-29s shot down, and the Americans confirmed 13 of these losses. The Deputy Commander of the 18th Guards Fighter Air Regiment, 303rd Fighter Air Division Guards Lieutenant-Colonel A.P. Smorchkov, who had shot down three bombers, became the most successful 'Fortress killer' in the day battles. The highest number of victories (two B-29s) attained in a single battle was achieved by the Commander of the 523rd Fighter Air Regiment, Guards Major D.P. Oskin – and we wish to draw your attention to the fact that the enemy acknowledged each of these victories.

The 351st Fighter Air Regiment became a nightmare for Bomber Command. Of the 10 B-29 kills recorded by its pilots, seven were either acknowledged by the Americans, or other irrefutable proof exists of these losses. Moreover, of these seven victories, six were attained by the best night hunter in the 64th Fighter Air Corps: Major A.M. Karelin. Naturally, this figure of 40 B-29 aircraft shot down in air combat is approximate – and in our opinion, may only reflect the minimum number of actual losses; the maximum number remains a matter for debate. Larry Davies, whom we have previously cited, thinks that: ' ... Although there were only 17 B-29s lost over North Korea, there were dozens more that never flew again after making it to their home field. Even with proper escort, the B-29s were meat on the table for the MiGs ...'[25]

❦

The fact that the pilots of the 64th Fighter Air Corps inflicted appreciable losses on Bomber Command's forces is undeniable, and this galvanised American military leadership into reviewing the concept behind the development of its air forces. In an analysis of the situation, the *Washington Post* newspaper wrote:

> The MiG-15 really is a deadly weapon against our existing strategic bombers. It is obvious that the Air Force has made a serious error of judgement in making the B-36 and B-50 the principal bomber types to the detriment of short range jet bombers.
>
> Increasing the number of escort fighters accompanying the bombers did not solve the problem posed by the MiG-15. The Korean experience has shown that an escort of jet fighters is in fact useless when accompanying slow bombers: interceptors permeate the escort fighter formation in a dive before the latter are able to accelerate, and they then go after the bombers.
>
> The most important lesson of Korea is that long-range strategic raids using slow bombers are no longer able to produce results.[26]

From 1950 onwards, the Far East Air Force had been using the newest jet bomber – the B-45C Tornado – in the photo-reconnaissance variant. In the first batch of three aircraft serving with the 84th Light Bomber Squadron, which were undergoing service testing as part of the 91st Strategic Reconnaissance Squadron, two were shot down by MiGs. Moreover, on 8 April 1951, Senior Lieutenant N.K. Shelamonov from the 196th Fighter Air Corps shot down an RB-45C which was escorted by an F-86. In a further incident, a Tornado that was also escorted by Sabres escaped a similar fate by virtue of a mistake that one of our pilots made when he forgot to switch on the cannons and 'fired' at the reconnaissance aircraft using the gun camera. It would, therefore, probably be no mistake to say that the 'short-range jet bombers' would not have solved the 'problem posed by the MiG-15'. Naturally, three skirmishes with Tornadoes are not sufficient for such a far-reaching conclusion.

There are, however, very comprehensive statistics concerning encounters between MiG-15s and F-80 and F-84 fighter-bombers: although they possessed (aside from speed) excellent horizontal manoeuvrability, they had by 1953 been effectively displaced from the 64th Fighter Air Corps' zones of responsibility. They were replaced by the F-86/F-30 ground-attack Sabres, which conceded little to the MiGs after they had dropped their bombs – therefore during the course of the Korean War, the United States Air Force was never able to completely solve the issue of a reliable escort for its strike aircraft. Moreover, no air arm in any country has ever been able to solve this issue in any conflict.

As far as the bombers were concerned, United States Strategic Air Command, which had rejected the B-36 and B-50 after the Korean War, put their faith in the jet-powered B-47 and B-52. The B-47 Stratojet, which saw service in the reconnaissance role, was (in the second half of the 1950s) involved in a series of incidents on the Soviet border: on 18 April 1955, one of these aircraft was shot down by a MiG-15 over

---

25 Davis, *Mig Alley*, p.70.

26 *Washington Post*, 16 February 1952.

'Command Decision': A B-29 Superfortress of the 19th Bomb Group has the distinction of being highly decorated for the high score of shooting down MiG-15 jet fighters during the Korean War, 10 August 1953. (Courtesy of the US National Archives)

Kamchatka. The B-52, which represents the new generation of 'Fortresses' – and which have now become stratospheric – was destined to encounter the supersonic, missile-carrying descendants of the MiG-15 some 20 years after the end of the Korean War. This occurred in 1972 in a place called Vietnam, but that is an altogether different story …

Appendix I

Deployment of formations and units from United States Air Force Bomber Command in the Far Eastern Zone

25 June 1950 – the first day of the war

Anderson Air Force Base on the island of Guam
19TH BOMBARDMENT GROUP:
    28th Bombardment Squadron, Medium   B-29
    30th Bombardment Squadron, Medium   B-29
    93rd Bombardment Squadron, Medium   B-29
KADENA AIR FORCE BASE, ON THE ISLAND OF OKINAWA
    31st Strategic Reconnaissance Squadron   RB-29

27 June 1950
This remained unchanged until the beginning of July 1950:

Kadena Air Force Base, on the island of Okinawa
19TH BOMBARDMENT GROUP:
    28th Bombardment Squadron, Medium   B-29
    30th Bombardment Squadron, Medium   B-29
    93rd Bombardment Squadron, Medium   B-29
YOKOTA AIR FORCE BASE, ON THE ISLAND OF HONSHU
    31st Strategic Reconnaissance Squadron   RB-29

8 July 1950 – formation of United States Air Force Bomber Command in the Far East
The 22nd and 92nd Bombardment Groups were ordered to redeploy from the continental United States to the Korean theatre of operations on 3 July. The exact date of the beginning of this deployment is not known. Officially, these groups became part of the United States Air Force Bomber Air Corps in the Far East on 8 July.

This remained unchanged until the beginning of August 1950:

Yokota Air Force Base, on the island of Honshu
92ND BOMBARDMENT GROUP:
    325th Bombardment Squadron, Medium   B-29
    326th Bombardment Squadron, Medium   B-29
    327th Bombardment Squadron, Medium   B-29
    31st Strategic Reconnaissance Squadron   RB-29

Kadena Air Force Base, on the island of Okinawa
19TH BOMBARDMENT GROUP:
    28th Bombardment Squadron, Medium   B-29
    30th Bombardment Squadron, Medium   B-29
    93rd Bombardment Squadron, Medium   B-29

22ND BOMBARDMENT GROUP:
    2nd Bombardment Squadron, Medium   B-29
    19th Bombardment Squadron, Medium   B-29
    33rd Bombardment Squadron, Medium   B-29

6 August 1950
The 98th and 307th Bombardment Groups were ordered to redeploy from the continental United States to the Korean theatre of operations on 1 August. The exact date of the beginning of this deployment is not known. Officially, these groups became part of the United States Air Force Bomber Air Corps on 6 August.

This remained unchanged until the end of September 1950:

Yokota Air Force Base, on the island of Honshu
92ND BOMBARDMENT GROUP:
    325th Bombardment Squadron, Medium   B-29
    326th Bombardment Squadron, Medium   B-29
    327th Bombardment Squadron, Medium   B-29
98TH MEDIUM RANGE BOMBER AIR GROUP:
    343rd Bombardment Squadron, Medium   B-29
    344th Bombardment Squadron, Medium   B-29
    345th Bombardment Squadron, Medium   B-29
    31st Strategic Reconnaissance Squadron   RB-29

Kadena Air Force Base, on the island of Okinawa
19TH BOMBARDMENT GROUP:
    28th Bombardment Squadron, Medium   B-29
    30th Bombardment Squadron, Medium   B-29
    93rd Bombardment Squadron, Medium   B-29
22ND BOMBARDMENT GROUP, MEDIUM:
    2nd Bombardment Squadron, Medium   B-29
    19th Bombardment Squadron, Medium   B-29
    33rd Bombardment Squadron, Medium   B-29
307TH BOMBARDMENT GROUP, MEDIUM:
    370th Bombardment Squadron, Medium   B-29
    371st Bombardment Squadron, Medium   B-29
    372nd Bombardment Squadron, Medium   B-29

16 November 1950
The 91st Strategic Reconnaissance Squadron began to replace the 31st Strategic Reconnaissance Squadron at the beginning of November (the exact date is not known) – and this was completed on 16 November.
This remained unchanged from 16 November until the end of the war:

Yokota Air Force Base, on the island of Honshu
98TH MEDIUM RANGE BOMBER AIR GROUP:
    343rd Bombardment Squadron, Medium   B-29
    344th Bombardment Squadron, Medium   B-29
    345th Bombardment Squadron, Medium   B-29
    91st Strategic Reconnaissance Squadron   RB-29, KB-29, RB-36, RB-45, RB-50, WB-26

Kadena Air Force Base, on the island of Okinawa
19TH BOMBARDMENT GROUP:
    28th Bombardment Squadron, Medium   B-29
    30th Bombardment Squadron, Medium   B-29
    93rd Bombardment Squadron, Medium   B-29

307TH BOMBARDMENT GROUP:
    370th Bombardment Squadron, Medium   B-29
    371st Bombardment Squadron, Medium   B-29
    372nd Bombardment Squadron, Medium   B-29

Note: The average numerical strength for Bomber Command – not counting the reconnaissance squadrons – was (according to *Air Force Magazine*, April 1996):
    July 1950 – 87 B-29s and 81 crews
    July 1951 – 104 B-29s and 86 crews
    July 1952 – 118 B-29s and 112 crews
    July 1953 – 117 B-29s and 109 crews

Appendix II

Deployment of formations and units from the 64th Fighter Air Corps of the Soviet Air Force engaged in active combat with the B-29

The operative group of the 64th Fighter Air Corps (IAC) was established in Mukden in the period of 15-24 November 1950 in accordance with Coded Telegram of the Head of Soviet Army General Staff #5564 of 15 November 1950.

The division had in its strength 30 airplanes in each regiment, plus two combat aircraft for the division staff (i.e. 62 fighters for two-regiment divisions and 92 machines for three-regiment).

IAC – Fighter Air Corps
GvIAD – Guards Fighter Air Division
IAD – Fighter Air Division
GvIAP – Guards Fighter Air Regiment
IAP – Fighter Air Regiment

Division/Regiment	Combat period	Base airfields	Aircraft
151st GvIAD	01.11.50 – 30.11.50 and 06.02.51 – 02.04.51	Became a part of 64th IAC under the Directive of Military Minister # 395/498/635018 of 23.01.51	
28th GvIAP		11.1950 – Mukden, from 06.02.51 – Andung	MiG-15
72nd GvIAP		11.1950 – Anshan, from 02.03.51 2nd Air Squadron and from 14.03.51 1st Air Squadron – Andung	MiG-15
28th IAD	01.11.50 – 30.11.50	Became a part of 64th IAC under Coded Telegram of the Air Force Chief Commander #43/1449 of 21.11.50	
67th IAP		Liaoyang	MiG-15
139th GvIAP		Liaoyang	MiG-15
50th IAD	25.11.50 – 06.02.51	Became a part of 64th IAC under Coded Telegram of the Air Force Chief Commander #43/1449 of 21.11.50	
29th GvIAP		25.11.50 – Anshan, from 03.12.50 – Andung	MiG-15bis
177th IAP		25.11.50 – Anshan, from 15.12.50 single air squadron and since 25.12.50 the whole regiment – Andung	MiG-15bis
324th IAD	03.04.51 – 30.01.52	Became a part of 64th IAC under the Directive of Military Minister # 395/498/635018 of 23.01.51	
176th GvIAP		From 02.04.51 – Andung	MiG-15, MiG-15bis
196th IAP		From 03.04.51 – Andung	MiG-15, MiG-15bis
303rd IAD	08.05.51 – 20.02.52	Became a part of 64th IAC under the Directive of Military Minister # 395/498/635018 of 23.01.51	
17th IAP		From 11.06.51 – Tatung-kao	MiG-15bis
18th GvIAP		From 08.05.51 – Andung, from 05.07.51 – Tatung-kao	MiG-15bis

APPENDIX II

Division/Regiment	Combat period	Base airfields	Aircraft
523rd IAP		From 28.05.51 – Tatung-kao	MiG-15bis
97th IAD	25.01.52 – 28.08.52	Became a part of 64th IAC under the Directive of Military Minister #641649 of 15.12.51	
16th IAP		From 25.01.52 – Andung, from 13.05.52 – Mukden-Western	MiG-15bis
148th GvIAP		From 25.01.52 – Andung, from 30.03.51 – Tatung-kao, from 05.05.52 – Andung, from 05.07.52 – Mukden-Western	MiG-15bis
190th IAD	14.02.52 – 10.08.52	Became a part of 64th IAC under the Directive of Military Minister #641649 of 15.12.51	
256th IAP		From 14.02.52 – Tatung-kao, from 25.05 – Anshan, from 31.06.52 – Dapu	MiG-15bis
494th IAP		From 14.02.52 – Tatung-kao, from 30.03.52 – Andung, from 05.05.52 – Anshan, from 25.05.52 – Tatung-kao	MiG-15bis
821st IAP		From 14.02.52 – Tatung-kao	MiG-15bis
133rd IAD	15.05.52 – 27.07.53	Became a part of 64th IAC under the Directive of Military Minister #45047 of 19.03.51, Order of Head of the Air Force General Headquarters #774154 of 20.03.52*	
147th GvIAP		Night fighter squadron from 15.05.52 – Tatung-kao, from 29.04.53 – Mukden-Western; day fighter squadrons from 05.07.52 – Andung, from 13.01.53 – Mukden-Western	MiG-15bis
415th IAP		09.07.52 – Andung, from 16.08.52 – Dapu, from 20.01.53 – Mukden-Western	MiG-15bis
726th IAP		From 12.07.52 – Dapu, from 16.08.52 – Andung, from 20.01.53 – Anshan	MiG-15bis
578th IAP**	26.09.52 – 16.02.53	From 26.09.52 – Andung, from 23.01.53 – Mukden-Western	
216th IAD	30.07.52 – 27.07.53		
518th IAP		Tatung-kao	MiG-15bis
676th IAP		Dapu	MiG-15bis
878th IAP		Tatung-kao	MiG-15bis
781st IAP**	21.02.53 – 27.07.53	Tatung-kao, Dapu	
32nd IAD	27.08.52 – 27.07.53		
224th IAP		From 27.08.52 – Mukden-Western, from 20.01.53 – Dapu, from 10.04.53 -Andung	MiG-15bis
535th IAP		From 27.08.52 – Mukden- Western, from 20.01.53 – Andung, from 10.04.53 – Dapu	MiG-15bis
913rd IAP		From 27.08.52 – Anshan, from 24.01.53 – Andung	MiG-15bis
351st IAP (night-fighter)	09.09.51 – 16.02.53	Anshan, Andung	La-11, MiG-15bis
		Directive of Military Minister #640644 of 21.5.51	
298th IAP (night-fighter)	20.02.53 – 27.07.53	Tatung-kao, from 05.1953 2nd Air Squadron – Andung, 1st Air Squadron – Tatung-kao	MiG-15bis

* – Among other subjects, the Order of Head of the Air Force General Headquarters stated that the 133rd IAD should be taken to air force strength from the strength of air defence forces by 26.03.52.

** – Regiment of the Pacific Fleet Air Force, which arrived to the 64th IAC without airplanes and ground support crews. The regiment flew the airplanes of the corresponding division – replacing its pilots.

Appendix III

Results of air combat

Date of the Air Battle*	Number of Victories**	Type	Pilot (Gunner)	Rank	Unit	Actual Enemy Losses (according to date from the Opposing Side)***
9 November 1950	64th IAC - 1	1 B-29	A.Z. Bordun L.M. Dymchenko	Major Snr Lieutenant	72nd GvIAP	One RB-29 from the 91st Medium Reconnaissance Squadron was seriously damaged during an emergency landing at Kimpo; five crewmembers were killed. According to other data, this aircraft made an emergency landing at Johnson air base in Japan.
	Far Eastern Air Force - 1	1 MiG-15	Harry J. Lavene	Sergeant	91st Medium Air Reconnaissance Squadron	No losses.
10 November 1950	64th IAC - 2	1 B-29 1 B-29	Yu.I. Akimov G.I. Kharkovskiy	Lieutenant Major	139th GvIAP 139th GvIAP	One B-29 was shot down (serial No. 45-21814) from the 371st Bombardment Squadron of the 307th Bombardment Group.
	Far Eastern Air Force - none					No losses.
12 November 1950	64th IAC - none					One B-29 from the 98th Bombardment Group was seriously damaged and made an emergency landing in South Korea.
	Far Eastern Air Force - none					No losses.
14 November 1950	64th IAC - 5	1 B-29 3 B-29 1 F-80	Podgorniy G.I. Kharkovskiy Sokolov	Captain Major Captain	67th IAP 139th GvIAP 67th IAP	One B-29 from the 19th Bombardment Group and 1 from the 307th Bombardment Group were heavily damaged. It is possible that the 19th Bombardment Group aircraft carried the serial No. 44-62152 and was written off the following day.
	Far Eastern Air Force - none	1 MiG-15	Richard W. Fisher	Staff-Sergeant	371st Bombardment Squadron	Captain Podgorniy's MiG-15 from the 67th IAP was damaged after being fired upon by a B-29.
1 December 1950	64th IAC - 2	1 B-29 1 B-29	G.M. Grebenki P.I. Orlov	Snr Lieutenant Snr Lieutenant	29th GvIAP 29th GvIAP	No losses.
	Far Eastern Air Force - none					A B-29 fired on Lieutenant Grebenkin's MiG-15 from the 29th GvIAP; holes were found in the cockpit canopy, the port side of the stabiliser and the port wing plane.
6 December 1950	64th IAC - 3	1 B-29 1 B-29 1 B-29	I. Bogatyrev A.S. Minin S.I. Naumenko	Captain Lieutenant Captain	29th GvIAP 29th GvIAP 29th GvIAP	No losses.
	Far Eastern Air Force - none					Lieutenant N.N. Serikov failed to return from the sortie; it is assumed he was shot down by a B-29.
10 January 1951	64th IAC - 1	1 B-29	P.M. Mikhaylov	Major	177th IAP	No losses.
	Far Eastern Air Force - none					No losses.

APPENDIX III 103

Date of the Air Battle*	Number of Victories**	Type	Pilot (Gunner)	Rank	Unit	Actual Enemy Losses (according to date from the Opposing Side)***
14 February 1951	64th IAC - 1	1 B-29	V.I. Kolyadin	Lieutenant-Colonel	28th GvIAP	This battle is not mentioned in the resources researched.
	Far Eastern Air Force - none					No losses.
25 Febuary 1951	64th IAC - 4	1 B-29	V.G. Monakhov	Snr Lieutenant	28th GvIAP	No losses.
		1 B-29	P.B. Ovsyannikov	Major	28th GvIAP	
		1 B-29	A.I. Parfenov	Captain	28th GvIAP	
		1 B-29	N.G. Pronin	Captain	28th GvIAP	
	Far Eastern Air Force - none					Captain Pronin's MiG-15 from the 28th GvIAP was damaged – the starboard wing was holed and the aileron rods were damaged.
1 March 1951	64 IAC - 2	1 B-29	V.I. Kolyadin	Lieutenant-Colonel	28 GvIAP	Ten B-29s from the 98th Bombardment Group were seriously damaged; three of these (serial Nos. 44-27341, 44-61830 and 44-69977) made emergency landings and were written off. According to other sources, only three B-29s were damaged.
		1 B-29	P.B. Ovsyannikov	Major	28 GvIAP	
	Far Eastern Air Force - 1	1 MiG-15	William H. Finnegan	Staff-Sergeant	343rd Bombardment Squadron	No losses.
30 March 1951	64th IAC - none					One B-29 from the 19th Bombardment Group was seriously damaged.
	Far Eastern Air Force - 2	1 MiG-15	Norman S. Greene	Staff-Sergeant	28th Bombardment Squadron	No losses.
		1 MiG-15	Charles W. Summers	Technical Sergeant	28th Bombardment Squadron	
7 April 1951	64th IAC - 3	1 B-29	S.P. Subbotin	Captain	176th GvIAP	One B-29 (serial No. 44-86268) from the 371st Bombardment Squadron of the 307th Bombardment Group was shot down. The fighter escort did not incur any losses.
		1 B-29	I.A. Suchkov	Captain	176th GvIAP	
		1 F-84	B.A. Obraztsov	Snr Lieutenant	176th GvIAP	
	Far Eastern Air Force - none					One MiG-15 from the 196th IAP was shot down; the pilot, Lieutenant Andrushko, ejected.

Date of the Air Battle*	Number of Victories**	Type	Pilot (Gunner)	Rank	Unit	Actual Enemy Losses (according to date from the Opposing Side)***
12 April 1951	64th IAC - 14	1 B-29 1 B-29 1 B-29 1 B-29 1 B-29 1 B-29 1 B-29 1 B-29 1 B-29 1 F-80 1 F-80 1 F-84 1 F-80	G.I. Ges A.M. Kochegarov P.S. Milaushkin V.A. Nazarkin B.A. Obraztsov A.A. Plitktin S.P. Subbotin I.A. Suchkov F.A. Shebanov K.Ya. Sheberstov S.M. Kramarenko I.V. Lazutin S.P. Subbotin V.N. Fukin	Captain Captain Snr Lieutenant Captain Snr Lieutenant Snr Lieutenant Captain Captain Snr Lieutenant Captain Captain Snr Lieutenant Captain Snr Lieutenant	176th GvIAP 196th IAP 176th GvIAP 196th IAP 176th GvIAP 176th GvIAP 176th GvIAP 176th GvIAP 196th IAP 176th GvIAP 176th GvIAP 176th GvIAP 176th GvIAP 196th IAP	One B-29 each from the 19th Bombardment Group and the 307th Bombardment Group were shot down. Five B-29s from the 19th Bombardment Group and one B-29 from the 307th Bombardment Group were seriously damaged. The last one made an emergency landing at Suwon and was written off. According to the authors' assessment, Bomber Command losses amounted to no more than six B-29s - of which four were lost over the target or over the sea, and a further two were written off following emergency landings.
	Far Eastern Air Force - 11	2 MiG-15 1 MiG-15 1 MiG-15 1 MiG-15 1 MiG-15 1 MiG-15 1 MiG-15 1 MiG-15 1 MiG-15 1 MiG-15	Billy G. Beach Royal A. Veatch Ercel S. Dye Lyle R. Patterson David R. Stime Robert A. Winslow James Jabara Howard M. Lane John C. Meyer Bruce H. Hinton	Sergeant Sergeant Staff-Sergeant Sergeant Sergeant Sergeant Captain Captain Colonel Lieutenant-Colonel	28th Bombardment Squadron 30th Bombardment Squadron 371st Bombardment Squadron 30th Bombardment Squadron 371st Bombardment Squadron 30th Bombardment Squadron 334th Fighter Squadron 336th Fighter Squadron 4th Fighter Wing 336rd Fighter Squadron	Five MiG-15s from the 196th IAP were damaged: - Snr Lieutenant B.S. Abakumov's aircraft - eight holes; the pilot landed back at base - Snr Lieutenant Vermina's aircraft - one hole; the pilot landed back at base - Snr Lieutenant A.V. Dostoyevski's aircraft – four holes; the pilot landed back at base - Snr Lieutenant Zykov's aircraft - two holes; the pilot landed back at base - Snr Lieutenant Yakovlev - made an emergency landing in a damaged aircraft 15 km away from the airfield
31 May 1951	64th IAC - none					No losses.
	Far Eastern Air Force - 3	1 MiG-15 1 MiG-15 1 MiG-15	Michael R. Martocchia Otis Gordon Jr Bobbie L. Smith	Staff-Sergeant Junior Lieutenant Junior Lieutenant	28th Bombardment Squadron 335th Bombardment Squadron 335th Bombardment Squadron	Sabres from the B-29 close support group shot down Major Perevozchikov (from the Air Force Scientific-Research Institute Group). Two MiG-15s from the 196th IAP were damaged: - Snr Lieutenant Alekhnovich's aircraft (from the Air Force Scientific-Research Institute's Group) - seven holes - Snr Lieutenant Boboin's aircraft (from the Air Force Scientific-Research Institute's Group) - the tail section of the fuselage was crumpled slightly by the jettisonable external fuel tanks

APPENDIX III

Date of the Air Battle*	Number of Victories**	Type	Pilot (Gunner)	Rank	Unit	Actual Enemy Losses (according to date from the Opposing Side)***
1 June 1951	64th IAC - 2	2 B-29	Ye.M. Stelmakh	Snr Lieutenant	18th Guards Fighter Air Division	One B-29 from the 98th Bombardment Group was shot down; a further two were seriously damaged.
	Far Eastern Air Force - 4	1 MiG-15	James C. Davis	Staff-Sergeant	343rd Bombardment Squadron	Snr Lieutenant Stelmak's MiG-15 from the 8th GvIAP was shot down. The pilot ejected, but was killed in a skirmish with the Chinese People's Volunteer Army. A MiG-15 from the 8th Guards Fighter Air Division was damaged; the pilot, Snr Lieutenant Ageyev, landed back at base.
		1 MiG-15	Earl A. Kanop	Sergeant	343rd Bombardment Squadron	
		1 MiG-15	Simpson Evans Jr	Lieutenant US Navy	336th Fighter Squadron	
		1 MiG-15	Richard O. Ransbottom	Captain	336th Fighter Squadron	
26 June 1951	64th IAC - none		There was a suggestion that one B-29 had been destroyed by Snr Lieutenant Fokin (from the 17th IAP). This suggestion though was not confirmed at a later stage.			One B-29 damaged, but returned to base.
	Far Eastern Air Force - 1	1 MiG-15	Harry L. Underwood	Cptain	182nd Tactical Fighter Squadron	Snr Lieutenant Agranovich's MiG-15 from the 17th IAP was shot down; the pilot was killed.
			Arthur E. Oligher	Junior Lieutenant	182nd Tactical Fighter Squadron	
9 July 1951	64th IAC - none					No losses.
	Far Eastern Air Force - 2	2 MiG-15	Gus C. Opfer	Sergeant	30th Bombardment Squadron	One MiG-15 from the People's Liberation Army Air Force was shot down; the pilot was killed.
		1 MiG-15	Milton E. Nelson	Captain	335th Bombardment Squadron	
22 October 1951	64th IAC - 6	1 B-29	A.P. Smorchkov	Lieutenant-Colonel	18th GvIAP	One B-29 (serial No. 44-61656) from the 19th Bombardment Group was shot down. The escorting fighters did not incur any losses.
		1 B-29	Stepanov	Snr Lieutenant	18th GvIAP	
		1 B-29	V.S. Shabanov	Snr Lieutenant	18th GvIAP	
		1 F-84	Konev	Snr Lieutenant	18th GvIAP	
		1 F-84	A.P. Smorchkov	Lieutenant-Colonel	18th GvIAP	
		1 F-84	L.K. Shchukin	Snr Lieutenant	18th GvIAP	
	Far Eastern Air Force - none					Two MiG-15s from the 18th GvIAP were damaged - supposedly by an F-84.
23 October 1951	64th IAC - 13	1 B-29	S.A. Bakhayev	Captain	523rd IAP	Between eight and 10 B-29s from the 307th Bombardment Group were lost:
		1 B-29	Bykov	Snr Lieutenant	17th IAP	- Three shot down over the target - serial Nos. 44-70151 (370th Bombardment Squadron), 42-94045 (371st Bombardment Squadron) and 44-61940 (372nd Bombardment Group)
		1 B-29	Bychkov	Captain	17th IAP	- Between five and seven B-29s were damaged or destroyed during emergency landings in South Korea, or were written off on their return to base
		1 B-29	G.K. Dyachenko	Snr Lieutenant	523rd IAP	One F-84E (serial No. 50-1220) from the 111th Tactical Fighter Squadron was shot down; the pilot, Junior Lieutenant John W. Shewmaker, vanished without trace.
		1 B-29	Kornienko	Captain	18th GvIAP	
		1 B-29	A.N. Nikolayev	Snr Lieutenant	17th IAP	
		2 B-29	D.P. Oskin	Major	523rd IAP	
		1 B-29	A.P. Smorchkov	Lieutenant-Colonel	18th GvIAP	
		1 F-84	A.M. Shevarev	Snr Lieutenant	523rd IAP	
		1 F-84	I.A. Rybalko	Snr Lieutenant	523rd IAP	
		1 F-84	V.F. Shulev	Snr Lieutenant	17th IAP	
		1 F-84	L.K. Shchukin	Snr Lieutenant	18th GvIAP	

Date of the Air Battle*	Number of Victories**	Type	Pilot (Gunner)	Rank	Unit	Actual Enemy Losses (according to date from the Opposing Side)***
	Far Eastern Air Force - 5	1 MiG-15 1 MiG-15 1 MiG-15 1 MiG-15 1 MiG-15	Fred R. Spivey Jerry M. Webb Ralph E. Banks Richard D. Creighton Farrie D. Fortner	Sergeant Sergeant Captain Major Junior Lieutenant	371st Bombardment Squadron 371st Bombardment Squadron 336th Fighter Squadron 336th Fighter Squadron 154th Tactical Fighter Squadron	The aircraft was shot down by Sabres on its return to base over the People's Republic of China and Snr Lieutenant Khrutin (from the 523rd IAP) was killed. Three MiG-15s were damaged: - Snr Lieutenant A.N. Nikolayev's aircraft (from the 17th IAP) - one hole in the tail fin after being fired upon by a B-29 - Lieutenant A.P. Smirnov's aircraft (from the 18th GvIAP) - four holes in the nose section of the fuselage close to the cockpit - Snr Lieutenant Ustyuzhaninov's aircraft (from the 18th GvIAP) – supposedly hit by an F-86 whilst breaking away from an attack on a B-29
24 October 1951	64th IAC - 1	1 B-29	A.P. Smorchkov	Lieutenant-Colonel	18th GvIAP	One B-29 (serial No. 44-61932) from the 98th Bombardment Group was seriously damaged; it made an emergency landing on water in Wanson Bay.
	Far Eastern Air Force - 1	1 MiG-15	Harold M. Setters	Technical Sergeant	344th Bombardment Squadron	Lieutenant-Colonel Smorchkov's MiG-15 was damaged.
27 October 1951	64th IAC - 4	1 B-29 1 B-29 1 F-84 1 F-84	A.N. Karasev D.A. Samoylov D.A. Samoylov A.P. Treflov	Lieutenant-Colonel Snr Lieutenant Snr Lieutenant Major	523rd IAP 523rd IAP 523rd IAP 523rd IAP	Four B-29s from the 19th Bombardment Group were damaged (one seriously).
	Far Eastern Air Force - 5	1 MiG-15 1 MiG-15 1 MiG-15 1 MiG-15 1 MiG-15	Merle A. Goff Michael R. Martocchia Harry E. Ruch Leeman M. Tankersley Leonard B. Eversole	Sergeant Staff Sergeant Private 1st Class Sergeant Corporal	28th Bombardment Squadron 28th Bombardment Squadron 28th Bombardment Squadron 93th Bombardment Squadron 30th Bombardment Squadron	Three MiG-15s from the 523rd IAP confirmed: - Snr Lieutenant M.A. Zykov's aircraft - one hole in the fuselage
10 June 1952	64th IAC - 3	2 B-29 1 B-29	A.M. Karelin M.I. Studilin	Captain Lieutenant-Colonel	351st IAP 147th GvIAP	Two B-29s from the 19th Bombardment Group were shot down - serial Nos. 44-62183 (from the 28th Bombardment Squadron) and 44-61967 (from the 30th Bombardment Squadron) One further B-29 (serial No. 44-87775) from the 28th Bombardment Squadron was seriously damaged and made an emergency landing near Gimpo.
	Far Eastern Air Force - None					Captain Korelin's MiG-15 was damaged by wreckage from a B-29.
14 June 1952	64th IAC - 1	1 B-29	F.S. Volodarskiy.	Captain	147th GvIAP	This battle is not mentioned in the Western publications researched.
	Far Eastern Air Force - None					No losses.

APPENDIX III 107

Date of the Air Battle*	Number of Victories**	Type	Pilot (Gunner)	Rank	Unit	Actual Enemy Losses (according to date from the Opposing Side)***
3 July 1952	64th IAC - 1	1 RB-29	A.M. Karelin	Major	351st IAP	One RB-29 (serial No. 44-61727) from the 91st Strategic Reconnaissance Squadron was shot down; 11 crewmembers were taken prisoner (they were handed back at the end of the war) and two were missing.
	Far Eastern Air Force - None					No losses.
23 August 1952	64th IAC - None					No losses.
	Far Eastern Air Force - None					1 MiG-15 flown by Captain Poltavets (from the 147th GvIAP) was destroyed whilst returning home following a battle 12 km from its base. The aircraft was damaged by fire from 12.7 mm machine guns; this was supposedly from a B-29.
9 September 1952	64th IAC - None					No losses.
	Far Eastern Air Force - 1	1 piston-powered aircraft	Robert L. Davis Robert W. Smith	Private Private	343rd Bombardment Squadron 343rd Bombardment Squadron	No losses.
12 September 1952	64th IAC - 1	1 B-29	Yu.N. Dobrovichan	Snr Lieutenant	147th GvIAP	64th IAC documents indicate that that this B-29 crashed 17 km east of the city of Tegvan. Specifically, maps of SHORAN radar sites were found in the wreckage of the bomber. According to American statistics, one B-29 (serial No. 44-86343) from the 371st Bombardment Squadron of the 307th Bombardment Group failed to return from a sortie; this is attributed to anti-aircraft artillery fire.
	Far Eastern Air Force - None					No losses.
18 November 1952	64th IAC - 1	1 B-29	Yu.N. Dobrovichan	Snr Lieutenant	147th GvIAP	1 B-29 (s/n 44-86392) from the 345th Bombardment Squadron of the 98th Bombardment Group was shot down.
	Far Eastern Air Force - None					No losses.
9 December 1952	64th IAC - 1	1 B-29	Yu.N. Dobrovichan	Snr Lieutenant	147th GvIAP	One B-29 (serial No. 45-21822) from the 98th Bombardment Group was lost; the reason for this loss is not specified.
	Far Eastern Air Force - None					No losses.
30 December 1952	64th IAC - 4	1 B-29 1 B-29 1 B-29 1 B-29	A.G. Andreyev Z. Iskhangaliev A.M. Karelin M.D. Muravyev	Snr Lieutenant Snr Lieutenant Major Snr Lieutenant	535th IAP 351st IAP 351st IAP 535th IAP	One B-29 (serial No. 44-62011) from the 28th Bombardment Squadron of the 19th Bombardment Group was shot down. A further two were written off on the basis of the damage they incurred.
	Far Eastern Air Force - None					Major Karelin's MiG-15 was damaged by wreckage from the B-29.

Date of the Air Battle*	Number of Victories**	Type	Pilot (Gunner)	Rank	Unit	Actual Enemy Losses (according to date from the Opposing Side)***
10 January 1953	64th IAC - 3	1 B-29 1 B-29 1 B-29	I.P. Golyshevskiy Kultyshev Ya.Z. Khabiev	Captain Major Snr Lieutenant	351st IAP 351st IAP 535th IAP	One B-29 (serial No. 44-61802) from the 307th Bombardment Group was damaged by fire from a MiG-15; it was destroyed on its return to Okinawa.
	Far Eastern Air Force - None					No losses.
12 January 1953	64th IAC - 2	1 B-29 1 RB-29	A.I. Gubenko Ya.Z. Khabiev	Snr Lieutenant Snr Lieutenant	351st IAP 535th IAP	One RB-29 (serial No. 44-62217) from the 91st Strategic Reconnaissance Squadron was shot down.
	Far Eastern Air Force - None					No losses.
28 January 1953	64th IAC - 1	1 B-29	A.M. Karelin	Major	351st IAP	One B-29 (serial No. 42-62357) from the 28th Bombardment Squadron of the 19th Bombardment Group was shot down.
	Far Eastern Air Force - None					No losses.
30 January 1953	64th IAC - 1	1 B-29	A.M. Karelin	Major	351st IAP	One B-29 (serial No. 44-27262 or 44-61920) from the 307th Bombardment Group was seriously damaged and made an emergency landing in South Korea.
	Far Eastern Air Force - None					Major Karelin's MiG-15 was seriously damaged by defensive fire from a gunner on board a B-29. The pilot landed back at base after an engine failure.

* For night battles, the previous day's date is used. For example, for a battle that took place on the night of 10/11 July, the date is given as '10 July'.

** The number of victories officially recorded in sorties against B-29s. The data in this section does not include information concerning damaged enemy aircraft, and may not reflect the total number of victories per day, but does include:
- 64th IAC - victories over B-29s or close escort aircraft only
- Far Eastern Air Force - victories attained by B-29 gunners or pilots in close escort fighter groups only

*** The data in this section may not coincide with the total number of losses on both sides per day, and only include:
- 64th IAC - B-29 and escort fighter losses (recorded in the available Western publications used in our research; see Bibliography)
- Far Eastern Air Force - actual MiG-15 losses as a result of enemy fire from a B-29 or from escort fighters (according to material from the Central Archive of the Ministry of Defence, Russian Federation)

Appendix IV

Contemporary geographical names for sites mentioned in quotes from 64th Fighter Air Corps documents

In documents	Contemporary
Ansiu p.c.	Anju City
Antung p.c.	Antung, Dandong
Gisiu p.c.	Uiju
Dzyunsen	Suncheon
Deeguandong p.c.	Tegvan
Yiotok	Yandok
Kaisen p.c.	Gochon
Kaisyu p.c.	Haeju
Kidzio p.c.	Goseong
Mukden	Henang
Nansi p.c.	Namsi
Seisen-ko r.	Ch'ongch'on
Sensen p.c.	Sonchon
Sindi-to Is.	Sinmi-do Island
Singisiu p.c.	Sinuiju
Siodzio	Chongsu
Sup'ung HPP	Sui ho
Shukusen p.c.	Sukchon
Taishen p.c.	Taechon
Tetsuzan p.c.	Cholsan
Tetsu p.c.	Chongju
Yunshan p.c	Unsan
Hakusen p.c.	Pakchon
Aitszu p.c.	Wonju

p.c population centre
Is   island
r   river

Bibliography

Documents from the Central Archive of the Ministry of Defence of the Russian Federation

f. 16, op. 3139, d. 15

f. 64th Fighter Air Corps, op. 174045ss, d. d. 51, 56, 75, 98, 101, 102, 108, 110, 116, 117, 120, 157, 164; op. 565835s, d. 1

f. 50th Fighter Air Division, op. 539809s, d. 4

f. 133rd Fighter Air Division, op. 152681ss, d. 1

f. 151st Guards Fighter Air Division, op. 152688ss, d. 7; op. 152691s, d. 8

f. 303rd Fighter Air Division, op. 152694s, d. 1; op. 174133ss, d. 1

f. 324th Fighter Air Division, op. 152706ss, d. 7; op. 152839s, d. 2; op. 539839s, d. 1

f. 17th Fighter Air Regiment, op. 539850s, d. 11; op. 683351s, d. 5

f. 147th Guards Fighter Air Regiment, op. 152757ss, d. 3; op. 152760ss, d. d. 1,3

f. 351st Fighter Air Regiment, op. 655110s, d. 1

f. 523rd Fighter Air Regiment, op. 539914s, d. 3

Literature

Davis, Larry, *Air War over Korea* (Carrollton: Squadron/Signal Publ.Inc., 1982).
- *MiG Alley* (Carrollton: Squadron/Signal Publ.Inc., 1978).

Detzer, David, *Thunder of the captains* (New York: Thomas Y. Crowell Co., 1977).

Dorr, Robert. F.; Lake, Jon; Thompson, Warren, *Korean War Aces* (London etc.: Osprey Publishing, 1995).

Futrell, Robert F., *The United States Air Force in Korea 1950-1953* (New York: Duell, 1961).

Hallion, Richard P., *The Naval Air War in Korea* (The Nautical & Aviation Publ.Co. of America, 1986).

Jackson, R., *Air War over Korea* (London: Ian Allan, 1973).

Johnson, James E., *Full circle. The Story of Air Fighting* (London: Chatto & Windus, 1964).

McDonald, Callum A., *Korea: The War Before Vietnam* (Basingstoke: McMillan Press Ltd, 1986).

O'Neill, Robert, *Australia in the Korean War 1950-53,* Vol. 2 (Canberra: The Australian War Memorial and the Australian Goverment Publ. Serv., 1985).

Simpson, Albert F., *Historical study No. 81: USAF Credits for the Destruction of Enemy Aircraft, Korean War* (HQ USAF: Office of Air Force History, 1975).

Stewart, James T., *Air Power the Decisive Force in Korea* (Toronto, London, New York: Van Nostrand, 1957).

Periodical publications

Air Enthusiast
Air Force Magazine
Air International
Aviation Week
Flight International
Herald Tribune

International Defence Review
Newsweek
U.S. Naval Institute Proceedings
U.S. News
Washington Post